# Islamic
## ART & CULTURE

Nicola Barber

**www.raintreepublishers.co.uk**
Visit our website to find out more information about **Raintree** books.

To order:
 Phone 44 (0)1865 888113
Send a fax to 44 (0)1865 314091
  Visit the Raintree bookshop at **www.raintreepublishers.co.uk** to browse our catalogue and order online.

 Produced for Raintree by
White-Thomson Publishing Ltd
Bridgewater Business Centre, 210 High Street,
Lewes, East Sussex BN7 2NH.

First published in Great Britain by Raintree, Halley Court, Jordan Hill, Oxford OX2 8EJ, part of Harcourt Education.
Raintree is a registered trademark of Harcourt Education Ltd.

© Harcourt Education Ltd 2005
First published in paperback in 2006
The moral right of the proprietor has been asserted.

Editorial: Kay Barnham, Nicole Irving, and Louise Galpine
Design: Simon Borrough and Ron Kamen
Illustrations: Tinstar Design
Picture Research: Elaine Fuoco-Lang
Production: Amanda Meaden

Originated by Ambassador Litho Ltd
Printed and bound in China by South China Printing Company

ISBN 1 844 21053 7 (hardback)
09 08 07 06 05
10 9 8 7 6 5 4 3 2 1

ISBN 1 844 21058 8  (paperback)
10 09 08 07 06
10 9 8 7 6 5 4 3 2 1

**British Library Cataloguing in Publication Data**
Barber, Nicola
World Art and Culture: Islamic
709.1'767
A full catalogue record for this book is available from the British Library.

**Acknowledgements**
The publishers would like to thank the following for permission to reproduce photographs: Art Archive pp. 19 (British Library), 30 (Museum of Islamic Art Cairo / Dagli Orti), 16 (National Museum Damascus Syria / Dagli Orti), 12 (Private Collection / Eileen Tweed), 31, 42, 48 (Victoria and Albert Museum London / Sally Chappell); Bridgeman Art Library pp. 21 (Dost Yayinlari), 17 (Bibliothèque Nationale, Paris, France), 18 (Detroit Institute of Arts, USA, Gift of Robert H. Tannahill in memory of Dr. W.R. Valentiner), 33, 37; Corbis pp. 28 (Angelo Hornak), 14 (Archivo Iconografico, S.A.), 43 (Arthur Thévenart), 22 (Carmen Redondo/CORBIS), 50 (Charles & Josette Lenars), 23, 47 (Chris Hellier), 44 (Chris Lisle), 13 (David H. Wells), 11 (Gérard Degeorge), 39 (John and Lisa Merrill), 15 (Lindsay Hebberd), 40 (Nevada Wier), 24 (Nik Wheeler), 25 (Origlia Franco / Corbis Sygma), 37 (Owen Franken), 27 (Roger Wood), 45 (Ruggero Vanni), 9 (Werner Forman), 26 (Yann Arthus-Bertrand); Harcourt p. 7; Popperfoto.com p. 5; Topfoto p. 51; Werner Forman Archive pp. 35 (Museum of Islamic Art, Cairo), 1, 8, 10, 20, 29, 34, 41.

Cover photograph of tile with hares reproduced with kind permission of Scala Archives, and of background tiles, reproduced with kind permission of Werner Forman.

The publishers would like to thank Dr Tim Insoll for his assistance in the preparation of this book.

Every effort has been made to contact copyright holders of any material reproduced in this book. Any omissions will be rectified in subsequent printings if notice is given to the publishers.

The paper used to print this book comes from sustainable resources.

# Contents

Introduction 4

Calligraphy 12

Book illustration 16

Architecture 22

Carving 28

Rock crystal and glass 32

Metalwork 36

Pottery 40

Tiles 44

Textiles and carpets 46

Cross-currents 50

Further resources 52

Glossary 54

Index 56

Words printed in the text in bold, **like this**, are explained in the Glossary.

# Introduction

The Islamic faith began almost 1400 years ago in Arabia, when the Prophet Muhammad received messages from God (**Allah**). Muhammad began to preach the central message of Islam: there is no God but God, and Muhammad is the messenger of God. The meaning of the Arabic word 'Islam' is 'submission', and those who converted to Islam agreed to submit to the will of God. They became known as Muslims. Islam quickly spread from the Arabian peninsula, extending its influence to Spain in the west and, eventually, to South-east Asia in the east.

## Islamic art

The term 'Islamic art' covers a broad range of traditions – from metalwork to carpet weaving, **calligraphy** to architecture. It includes religious art, as well as art made by and for Muslims, objects made by Muslims for **patrons** of other faiths, and objects made for Muslim patrons by workers of other faiths. Islamic art is found across a wide range of cultures from Spain and northern Africa, to Central Asia, and Anatolia (Turkey), to South-east Asia. The Islamic religion provides a common link between these cultures.

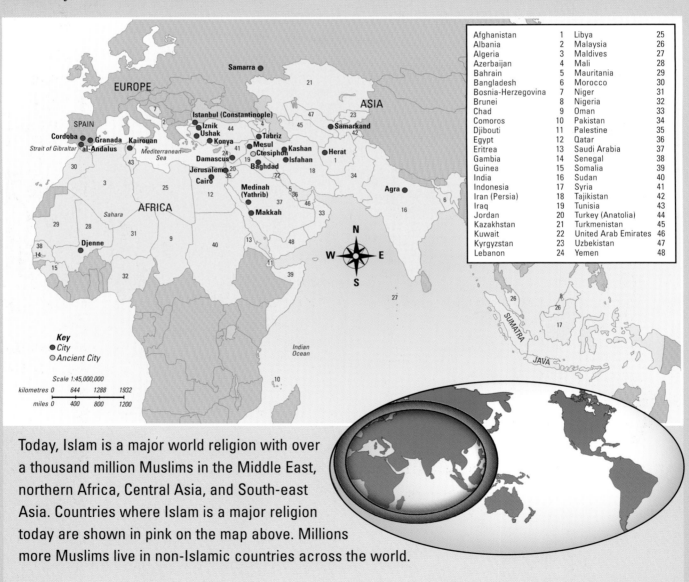

| | | | |
|---|---|---|---|
| Afghanistan | 1 | Libya | 25 |
| Albania | 2 | Malaysia | 26 |
| Algeria | 3 | Maldives | 27 |
| Azerbaijan | 4 | Mali | 28 |
| Bahrain | 5 | Mauritania | 29 |
| Bangladesh | 6 | Morocco | 30 |
| Bosnia-Herzegovina | 7 | Niger | 31 |
| Brunei | 8 | Nigeria | 32 |
| Chad | 9 | Oman | 33 |
| Comoros | 10 | Pakistan | 34 |
| Djibouti | 11 | Palestine | 35 |
| Egypt | 12 | Qatar | 36 |
| Eritrea | 13 | Saudi Arabia | 37 |
| Gambia | 14 | Senegal | 38 |
| Guinea | 15 | Somalia | 39 |
| India | 16 | Sudan | 40 |
| Indonesia | 17 | Syria | 41 |
| Iran (Persia) | 18 | Tajikistan | 42 |
| Iraq | 19 | Tunisia | 43 |
| Jordan | 20 | Turkey (Anatolia) | 44 |
| Kazakhstan | 21 | Turkmenistan | 45 |
| Kuwait | 22 | United Arab Emirates | 46 |
| Kyrgyzstan | 23 | Uzbekistan | 47 |
| Lebanon | 24 | Yemen | 48 |

**Key**
● City
○ Ancient City

Scale 1:45,000,000

Today, Islam is a major world religion with over a thousand million Muslims in the Middle East, northern Africa, Central Asia, and South-east Asia. Countries where Islam is a major religion today are shown in pink on the map above. Millions more Muslims live in non-Islamic countries across the world.

Muslim pilgrims crowd around the **Ka'bah** shrine in the Grand **Mosque** at Makkah. Arabs believed that this shrine had been set up by **Ibrahim** (Abraham), and the shrine was full of idols of many gods and goddesses. When Muhammad destroyed the idols, the shrine became one of the holiest places of Islam.

## Arabia

The traditional heartland of Islam is centred around Arabia and the Middle East. Islam began in the 7th century CE in the Arabian town of Makkah (in present-day Saudi Arabia). As now, much of Arabia was harsh, arid desert. In the south-west was a mountainous area, now part of Yemen, where there was enough rainfall for farming. The Romans called this area *Arabia Felix* (fruitful Arabia) because of its reputation as a land of great wealth and prosperity.

When the Prophet Muhammad was born, the majority of the inhabitants of Arabia, known as Arabs, lived in settlements built near a water source such as an **oasis**. However, large numbers of Arabs, called Bedouin, lived semi-**nomadic** or nomadic lives. They moved from place to place with their flocks of camels, sheep, and goats, looking for grazing. Most Arabs worshipped many different gods and goddesses.

## Beyond Arabia

The northern edge of the Arabian peninsula was bordered by two great empires. To the west lay the **Byzantine Empire,** with its capital city of Constantinople, now Istanbul. To the east was the **Sasanian Empire,** which covered Persia (modern-day Iran). Its capital city was Ctesiphon.

The Byzantines and Sasanians were frequently at war with each other, but the Muslim Arabs achieved victory over both their powerful neighbours. As Islam began to spread and establish itself the first Islamic works of art were produced.

## The Prophet Muhammad

Muhammad was born in about 570 CE in Makkah. He became a merchant and led an ordinary life until the age of 40. It was then that he received the first of the messages from God, brought to him by the Angel Jibril (Gabriel). When Muhammad began to preach the messages of God, some people converted to Islam, but others treated Muslims with great suspicion and hostility. In 622 the Prophet Muhammad and his followers decided to leave Makkah. They went to Yathrib, a city about 400 kilometres (250 miles) to the north. This was to be Muhammad's home for the rest of his life, and was renamed Madinah, meaning 'City of the Prophet'. Muhammad died in 632.

## The succession

After Muhammad's death there was disagreement about who should succeed him. Muhammad's father-in-law and closest friend, Abu Bakr, was chosen as the first **Khalifah** (successor). He died two years later, and three more Khalifahs followed before the Umayyad family seized power in 661. The Umayyads founded the first Islamic dynasty, meaning that the title of Khalifah was passed from father to son.

## The spread of Islam

In the years following the death of the Prophet Muhammad, Islam spread rapidly. The Arabian peninsula was quickly conquered and Muslim rule extended across Palestine and Syria (formerly controlled by the Byzantines), and Iraq and Iran (formerly controlled by the Sasanians). The Muslim armies took control of another Byzantine province, Egypt, in 641, and extended their power along the Mediterranean coast. The inhabitants of this area of northern Africa were called Berbers and many converted to Islam. By 750, Muslim lands extended from north-western Africa and Spain in the west to Afghanistan in the east.

 **Shi'a and Sunni**

The disagreement over Muhammad's successor caused a rift in the Islamic world that continues to this day. Most Muslims believed that the Khalifah should be the person best able to uphold the customs and traditions (the *sunnah*) of Islam. These Muslims became known as **Sunni**. Others, known as **Shi'a**, believed that only someone from the same family as Muhammad should succeed the Prophet.

c.570: birth of the Prophet Muhammad

622: Hijrah (migration) from Makkah to Madinah

632: death of the Prophet Muhammad

661–750: Umayyad dynasty: the Dome of the Rock and the Great Mosque in Damascus are built

711: Muslim invasion of Spain

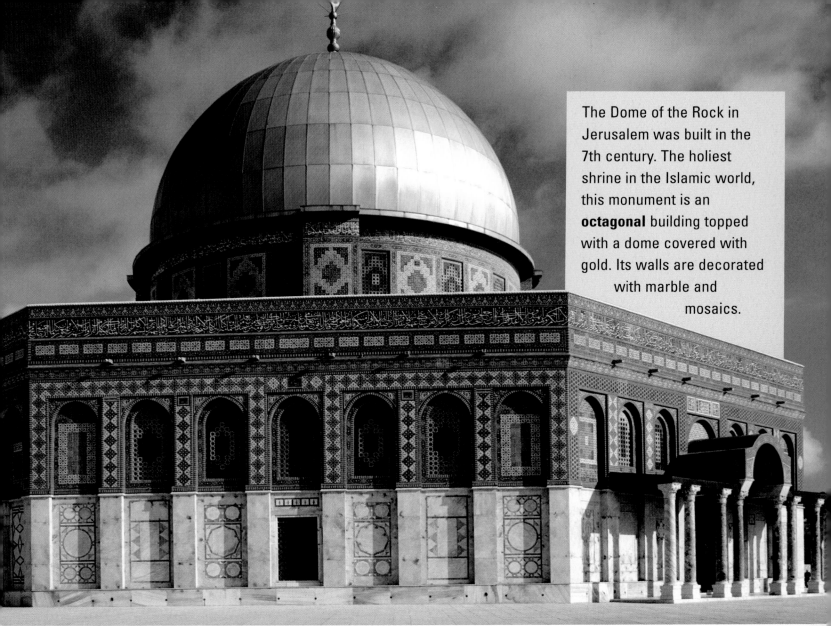

The Dome of the Rock in Jerusalem was built in the 7th century. The holiest shrine in the Islamic world, this monument is an **octagonal** building topped with a dome covered with gold. Its walls are decorated with marble and mosaics.

## The Umayyads

The Umayyads established their capital at Damascus in Syria, and it was under their rule that the first major Islamic monuments were built, including the Dome of the Rock in Jerusalem. They were removed from power by the Abbasids in 750.

During the 8th and 9th centuries, the Abbasids built a new capital at Baghdad in Iraq, which became a centre of the arts and of learning. They held the title of Khalifah until the Mongol invasions of 1258.

**750–1258:** Abbasid dynasty: new capital is founded at Baghdad, which becomes a centre of learning and the arts

**756:** Abd al-Rahman takes control of al-Andalus: construction of Great Mosque at Cordoba, in Spain, begins

**c.960:** Seljuks convert to Islam

**969:** Fatimids conquer Egypt: period of great **opulence** in the arts

## Islam in Spain

In 711 Islamic troops – mostly Berbers from northern Africa – crossed the Strait of Gibraltar and began the Muslim invasion of Spain. They soon established the Muslim province of al-Andalus. In 756, an Umayyad prince called Abd al-Rahman took control of al-Andalus. Abd al-Rahman had made a dramatic escape from Syria after the overthrow of his dynasty by the Abbasids and the slaughter of the whole Umayyad clan. He made his capital at Cordoba, which became a centre of the arts and learning during the 9th century.

## The Fatimids and the Seljuks

The power of the Abbasid Khalifah was attacked by peoples such as the Seljuks and the Fatimids.

This is the stunning interior of the Great Mosque at Cordoba. Work on the mosque began in the 8th century. The roof of the great prayer hall is supported by double arches, shown here, built from contrasting brick and stone. In the early 16th century, a Gothic chapel was built in the middle of the original mosque.

The Seljuks were Turkish **nomads** from Central Asia who converted to Islam in about 960 and went on to create an empire that extended from Anatolia across the Middle East. Under Seljuk rule, art and architecture flourished, particularly pottery at centres such as Kashan in Persia.

The Fatimids came from Tunisia in northern Africa. They took Egypt from the Abbasids in 969 and established their capital at Cairo. The Fatimid court was hugely wealthy and ostentatious and, under Fatimid rule, Cairo became a very important cultural centre.

**1055:** Seljuks enter Baghdad: under their rule art and architecture flourish, particularly pottery

**1206:** Mongol tribes unite under leader Genghis Khan

**1221:** Genghis Khan sacks Samarkand

**1227:** Death of Genghis Khan

**1250–1517:** Mamluks rule Egypt: beautiful **Qur'ans** commissioned for mosques and **madrasahs**, and glassmaking skills developed

## The Mongols and Timurids

The year 1258 is a significant date in the Islamic world. This was when the Mongols sacked Baghdad, finally ending the Abbasid dynasty. The Mongols were tribes of nomads from the grasslands of Central Asia, who united under their leader, Genghis Khan, in 1206. Genghis Khan conquered parts of China before starting his attacks on the Islamic lands, destroying towns and cities as he went. His sons continued this work after the death of Genghis in 1227. The Mongols were not Muslims, but many converted to Islam during the 13th century. At its height, the Mongol Empire stretched across the Islamic lands, and many Muslim artists and craftworkers were influenced by new ideas from the Far East.

Mongol power was quite short-lived, but at the end of the 14th century another Mongol leader – Timur the Lame (Tamerlane) – tried to re-establish the Mongol Empire. Timur spent much of his life taking part in military campaigns, but he also built many fine buildings at his capital in Samarkand, bringing artists and craftworkers from all over his empire to enrich the city.

## The Safavids

The Safavids established their empire in 1501, when Ismail I captured Tabriz and made it the Safavid capital. The greatest of all the Safavid rulers was **Shah** Abbas I (1571–1629), known as Abbas the Great. He moved the Safavid capital to Isfahan (now in Iran), and built an impressive new city there. Abbas encouraged crafts such as carpet-weaving, and set up royal workshops where carpets were made for export. After his death, the empire began to decline, and in the 18th century different groups competed for power in the region.

This bowl, decorated with a horse, dates from Fatimid times in Egypt.

1258: Mongols sack Baghdad: centre of book production moves to Iran (Persia)

1369–1405: Timur revives Mongol power: many mosques built in Samarkand

1453: Ottomans capture Constantinople and rename it Istanbul: royal **patronage** ensures production of fine, luxurious goods

1501: Safavids found their empire with the capital at Tabriz

1514: Ottomans defeat Safavids: many Iranian artists taken to work in royal studios in Istanbul

## The Ottomans

The Safavids were Shi'a Muslims, and were constantly at war with the Ottomans – their Sunni neighbours to the west. The Ottomans had been establishing themselves in Anatolia since the 14th century, but their breakthrough came in 1453 when they captured the city of Constantinople from the Byzantines. The Ottomans made the city their capital and renamed it Istanbul. The Ottoman court and government was based at the Topkapi Palace in Istanbul, which also became a centre for the arts, with court studios and workshops producing luxury goods such as jewellery, metalwork, and fine textiles.

The Ottoman Empire was under attack throughout the 18th and 19th centuries, finally collapsing in 1918, when its provinces were occupied by European powers at the end of World War I.

## The Mughals

In India, a Muslim empire was founded in 1526 by Babur (1483–1530), who claimed to be directly descended from both Genghis Khan and Timur. At its height the Mughal Empire covered the whole of India except for the southern tip.

The six great Mughal emperors – Babur, Humayan, Akbar, Jahangir, Shah Jahan, and Aurangzeb – were all patrons of the arts, each with their own particular interests. Book illustration flourished, and many fine monuments were built, including the 17th-century **mausoleum**, the Taj Mahal.

The Mughal Empire declined after the death of Aurangzeb in 1707 as Hindu power reasserted itself, and as the British extended their colonial claims. The Mughal Empire came to an end in 1858, when India was declared a British Crown **Colony**.

This beautiful dagger dates back to Mughal times. Its hilt (handle) is decorated with gold and enamel lotus leaf and flower motifs, and set with rubies.

1526: Babur founds Mughal Empire: great lover of books who establishes Mughal tradition of book illustration

1627–58: reign of Mughal ruler Shah Jahan: Taj Mahal is built as a memorial to his wife Mumtaz Mahal

1858: fall of Mughal Empire; declaration of India as a British Crown Colony

1918: collapse of Ottoman Empire: end of the last great Islamic empire

Calligraphic tiles like these are found on buildings throughout the Islamic world. Muslims avoid representations of living beings on religious buildings.

## Modern times

In 1798, French troops under Napoleon occupied Egypt. This marked the beginning of increasing European domination of Islamic countries. After the collapse of the Ottoman Empire, the republic of Turkey was founded in 1923. This was a **secular** state, with laws that did not explicitly refer to sacred texts. Iran also became a secular state under Riza Shah, who made himself **shah** in 1925.

After World War II, many former European colonies became independent, and in the Middle East states such as the United Arab Emirates, Qatar, and Bahrain were formed. Pakistan was founded in 1947 as a home for Muslims of the Indian subcontinent. In many of these states, people began to reject Western influences and to reassert the importance of Islam and its laws. In Iran, the Shah was overthrown in 1979 and replaced with Islamic clerics under the leadership of Ayatollah Khomeini.

During the 1990s, terrorism perpetrated by Islamic extremists became an increasing worldwide threat, often targeting the USA. As part of the 'war on terror', a coalition led by the USA invaded Iraq in 2003.

The impact of these and many other events on Islamic arts and crafts has been dramatic. With no royal patronage, cheap manufactured goods such as glass and pottery began to be imported from Europe, while Western styles also influenced many Islamic artists. However, many traditions have survived, most notably the art of calligraphy.

1925: Riza Shah founds Pahlawi dynasty in Iran

1947: founding of Pakistan

1948: state of Israel founded, followed by first Arab-Israeli war

1979: revolution in Iran and overthrow of shah

1980–8: Iran-Iraq War

1991: Gulf War in response to Iraqi invasion of Kuwait

2003: coalition led by USA and Britain invade Iraq: threat to artefacts and archaeological monuments

# Calligraphy

When the Prophet Muhammad received messages from God through the Angel Jibril, he memorized them. Later he dictated them, word for word, to scribes who wrote them on various materials – pieces of bone and papyrus, and bits of leather. After the death of Muhammad, a complete version of the messages from God was collected together to form the sacred book of Islam – the **Qur'an**. The scribes wrote out the words in beautiful **calligraphy**. Muslims believe that not one word of the revelations was changed, and that the Qur'an is the literal word of God. Calligraphy is therefore the means by which the word of God is recorded and transmitted and, as a result, it is the most precious and noble of all the Islamic arts.

## Arabic

The Qur'an was revealed in Arabic, the language of the first Muslims. The Arabs delighted in the spoken and written word, and poetry was a very important part of everyday life. Writing the words of the Qur'an was an act of worship on the part of the scribe, and great skill and care was, and is, taken in the creation of beautiful calligraphy worthy of the word of God.

These pages from an early Qur'an show the beautiful, flowing style of naskhi script.

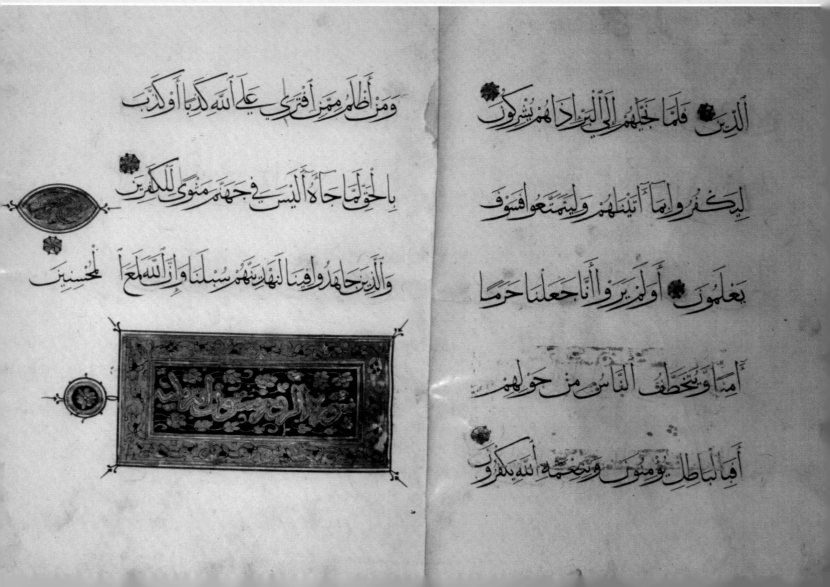

## ◈ Calligraphy tools

The tools of the calligrapher's trade have changed little over the centuries. They include reed and brush pens, scissors, a knife for cutting the pens, ink, and a sharpening tool. The reed pen, called a *qalam*, is used by many Islamic calligraphers. In the past, reed pens were valuable items traded across the Islamic world.

Calligraphers have a variety of pens of different thicknesses, and learn to shape and sharpen them with a knife.

There are many recipes for inks, some coloured, others perfumed. Traditionally, most were based on a mixture of soot or **lamp-black**, water, and **gum arabic**, which is still used.

A girl practises her Arabic calligraphy at the annual Arab Festival of Arts, Mahrajan al-Fan, held in New York City, USA. A woman in Islamic dress watches her.

Different types of Arabic script have developed over the centuries. The earliest styles are often grouped together under the name kufic, which comes from an early centre of calligraphy, Kufa, in Iraq. Kufic was an angular style, while naskhi was a more flowing, **cursive** style. Naskhi was often used for **secular** writing, while kufic script was suited for ornamental use on buildings or pottery. In the 10th and 11th centuries, the famous calligraphers Ibn Muqlah and Ibn al-Bawwab established six different classical types of Arabic script: naskhi, thuluth, muhaqqaq, rayhani, riqa, and tauqi. These styles are still used by Islamic calligraphers today.

## Calligraphy as decoration

Throughout the history of Islamic art, calligraphy has been used for surface decoration in **mosques** and **madrasahs**, as well as on smaller objects such as tiles, plates, or mosque lamps. Often the text for the calligraphy is taken from the Qur'an. Calligraphy is used partly because of the importance that Muslims attach to the power of the word of God. But it is also a result of the Muslim tradition of avoiding the representation of living things on religious buildings and objects. There is no specific wording in the Qur'an that forbids the practice, but from the earliest times Muslims did not use any such images to decorate their mosques.

## The Dome of the Rock

This tradition, and the power of calligraphy, can be seen in the earliest surviving Islamic monument and one of the holiest Islamic shrines – the Dome of the Rock in Jerusalem. The exterior is decorated with marble panels, beautiful mosaics in geometric patterns, and a panel of kufic script that runs around the entire building. The calligraphy is not only a beautiful surface decoration – its text, taken from the Qur'an, sends out a powerful message about the beliefs of Islam.

## Calligrams

Another development in the calligrapher's art was the calligram – a picture made from words that also have a symbolic meaning. The letters of the Arabic language have been shaped into boats, mosques, and even people and animals. The words for calligrams are often those of the Shahadah (the Muslim declaration of faith): 'There is no god but God'; 'Muhammad is the messenger of God', or of the Bismillah: 'In the name of God'.

## Modern calligraphy

Calligraphy continues to be an important part of Islamic culture today. Schools of calligraphy flourish in many Islamic countries, particularly Iran, Pakistan, and Turkey, with international competitions held annually. Some Islamic artists have pushed beyond the traditional boundaries to use calligraphy in new and individual ways. Examples include the work of the Iraqi calligrapher Hassan Massoudy and Algerian artist Rachid Koraichi, who uses Islamic calligraphy together with Chinese and Japanese characters and other symbols to create **abstract** works of art.

## Tugras

A feature of calligraphy in the Ottoman Empire was the tugra (imperial seal) of the **sultan**. This was a kind of ornamental signature, made up of the name of the sultan and of his father, together with the words 'ever victorious'. The tugra was used on documents, on coins, and in inscriptions on buildings. Tugras were copied and lavishly decorated for important documents. There is also evidence that stencils or stamps were used to reproduce tugras on the thousands of official documents that needed to carry the sultan's seal.

This tugra was created in 1575 for the Ottoman sultan, Murad III.

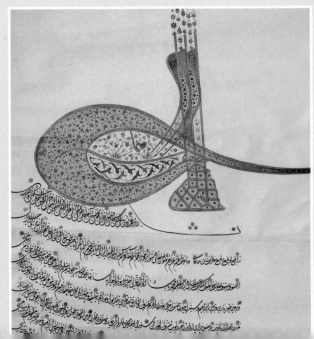

The outside of the **mausoleum** at the Taj Mahal in India is decorated with an inscription of verses from the Qur'an in beautiful ornamental calligraphy and accompanied by panels of floral motifs. The inscription dates back to the 1630s.

# Book illustration

The Muslim tradition of avoiding the depiction of living things applies to the **Qur'an** – the sacred book of Islam – and other religious texts. A tradition of illustrating **secular** texts with paintings of exquisite beauty developed in the Islamic world, although representations of the Prophet Muhammad and other holy men were nearly always avoided.

## Qur'an illumination

The earliest types of **illumination** to appear in copies of the Qur'an were decorative bands filled with geometrical or floral patterns. These were used to separate verses and chapters in the text. This kind of illumination may have been used as early as the Umayyad period (661–750), but the oldest examples that survive date from the time of the Abbasids (750–1258).

## The paper revolution

In the 8th century, papermaking was introduced into the Islamic world. It is said that Chinese papermakers were among the prisoners captured during a battle in 751 between the Muslims and the Chinese. Before paper, vellum (fine parchment made from animal skin) was the most common material used for copies of the Qur'an. Paper was made from cotton, flax, or silk, and was polished with a smooth stone to give a fine surface before the **calligrapher** began to write. Today, the best quality paper is usually used for printing Qur'ans.

These highly decorated pages are taken from a 14th-century Qur'an found in Damascus, Syria.

## Early books

While no pictures were ever used in copies of the Qur'an, other manuscripts were illustrated. The earliest illustrated books were often scientific works such as medical, botanical, and astronomical books, where pictures were used to help explain the text. One of the oldest surviving examples is the *Book of the Fixed Stars,* which dates from the early 11th century. It shows the **constellations** as human and animal forms, and was based on the work of the ancient Greek astronomer, Ptolemy. In time, other types of books began to be illustrated. One of the most popular was the *maqamah* (assemblies) of al-Hariri (1054–1122), which related the adventures of a hero called Abu Zayd.

This village scene is taken from a copy of the *maqamah* of al-Hariri, illustrated in Baghdad in 1237. On the left is a mosque with a blue-tiled dome and a **minaret**. On the right a figure is spinning yarn. In the foreground, the hero Abu Zayd talks to a man from the village.

As time went on, the decorative bands became wider and more elaborate, often containing the chapter titles. Decorations in the margins were also used to indicate different points in the text. From these early beginnings, Qur'an illumination became increasingly **opulent**. Whole pages of intricate patterns, often using a wide range of coloured inks as well as gold, were placed at the beginning and end of the text.

In all the great Islamic empires, Muslim rulers commissioned beautiful Qur'ans as an indication not only of their piety but also of their wealth. For example, the Mamluks, who ruled Egypt from 1250 to 1517, were well known for buying large, exquisitely decorated Qur'ans, which were often given to religious foundations such as **mosques** and **madrasahs**. Today, the need for handwritten and illuminated Qur'ans has been overtaken by the technology of printing. Qur'ans are printed at special printing houses such as the King Fahd Complex for Printing the Holy Qur'an in Saudi Arabia. Great care continues to be taken over the production of this sacred text.

## History books

Many early illustrated manuscripts were produced at the Abbasid capital, Baghdad. After the sack of Baghdad in 1258, however, the centre of book illustration moved to Iran (Persia), which was under Mongol control. The Mongol rulers commissioned historical works such as Rashid al-Din's *Universal History* (1306–7), and the *Shahnama* ('History of the **Shahs**', c.1336). Rashid al-Din's book recounts the history of the Islamic peoples, as well as the Mongols, Turks, Jews, Chinese, and Indians. The illustrations show a wide variety of influences, from Chinese scroll paintings to European Christian paintings. The *Shahnama* was a history of Persia before the arrival of the Muslims. It originally contained 200 large pictures, but only a quarter of this number survives.

## Portraits

During the reign of Shah Abbas I, artists began to produce works of art on single pages that could be sold separately. This practice continued over subsequent centuries in the Mughal and Ottoman empires, as wealthy patrons collected single sheets in albums. These paintings were often portraits of people, as well as pictures of animals, plants, and flowers. They were often signed by individual artists, unlike the paintings done for books at the Safavid court, which were usually unsigned. The most famous artist who worked for Shah Abbas was Riza Abbasi. He painted many portraits, often of ordinary people.

This painting comes from the *Shahnama*, a book created for Shah Tahmasp.

## Shah Tahmasp

Beautifully illustrated books were prized possessions at the courts of Islamic rulers, and during the 15th century Herat (in modern-day north-western Afghanistan) became a centre of book production. Certain texts became favourites for illustration, among them the *Shahnama* and the *Khamseh* 'Five Books' by Nizami, a 12th-century poet.

During the Safavid dynasty, Persian book production reached new heights, particularly under the **patronage** of Shah Tahmasp I. The *Shahnama* made for Shah Tahmasp was one of the most luxurious Islamic books ever created. It had over 740 pages, more than 250 illustrations and took ten years to make. It was completed in about 1535.

This beautiful illustration, showing Rudaba letting her hair down to assist Zal to climb up to her balcony, is taken from the *Shahnama*.

### ◈ Creating a book

A huge project, such as the *Shahnama* commissioned by Shah Tahmasp, required the talents of a wide range of people in the royal studio. Calligraphers, designers, painters, and bookbinders all worked together on such projects. The layout of the manuscript was decided first, before the calligrapher began to copy the text. When the text was in position, the painters started work. The artist first sketched in the outlines of the painting with thin black ink. Then colours were added, starting with gold and silver, followed by landscape and body colours, and ending with the fine details. For the final stage, the bookbinders gathered the pages together and sewed them into a leather binding.

## Painting at the Mughal court

The tradition of book production was continued by the Mughals. Under Akbar's rule, the royal studios employed more than a hundred artists and had a huge output of illustrated books. Akbar's wide-ranging interests are reflected in the great variety of books produced during his reign. Persian translations of **Hindu epics** such as the *Mahabharata* and the *Ramayana* were produced, while popular classics of Persian literature such as the *Khamseh* of Nizami were also illustrated. Like the Mongols, Akbar also commissioned works of history, such as the *Akbarnama*, which chronicled the events of his own life. The illustrations are often finely detailed and patterned, with brilliant, jewel-like colours. Mughal artists were also influenced by prints that came from Europe, and began to use elements of shading and **perspective** that were new to Islamic painting.

This 17th-century hunting scene is taken from the *Akbarnama*, the 'History of Akbar'. It shows Akbar surrounded by his followers and kneeling by his prey.

### ◈ Modern Islamic painting

During the 20th century, schools of painting were established in many Islamic countries, often as a result of contact with European styles and techniques. In Iran, Muhammad Ghaffari set up an art school after studying in Europe. He introduced painting on easels, and used Western styles of perspective and light and shade in his work. Not all painters embraced European values, however. Some Iranian painters looked back to traditional Islamic styles, such as those seen in Timurid and Safavid miniatures. After the revolution in Iran in 1979, when the shah was overthrown, poster art became important as a way of showing support for the new revolutionary spirit in the country. It used a mixture of traditional and nationalistic styles.

## Maps and portraits

As the Ottoman world expanded in the 16th century, artists were brought back from all corners of the empire to work in Istanbul. These artists brought their own traditions, which were combined with the styles and interests of the Ottomans.

Like the Mughal emperors, the greatest Ottoman **sultan**, Sulaiman, commissioned a history of his own life – the *Sulaimannama*. Some illustrations showed maps – bird's-eye views of cities besieged or captured by the Ottomans on their campaigns. Another aspect of Ottoman painting was an interest in accurate portraits of individuals. This could also seen in the *Sulaimannama*, with careful representations of the sultan and his courtiers.

### The Thousand and One Nights

Book illustration continued into the 19th century. The most notable example from this time was a massive project commissioned by Nasir al-Din, ruler of Iran, in the 1850s to illustrate the tales of *The Thousand and One Nights*. The court painter, Abu'l-Hasan Ghaffari, led a team of 34 painters and the book ran into six volumes, with a total of 1134 pages – each with several illustrations. Ghaffari had studied in Italy and the paintings show this Western influence in their startling and direct realism. Traditions of book illustration died out, however, as printing and the technique of **lithography** replaced the labour-intensive work of illustration.

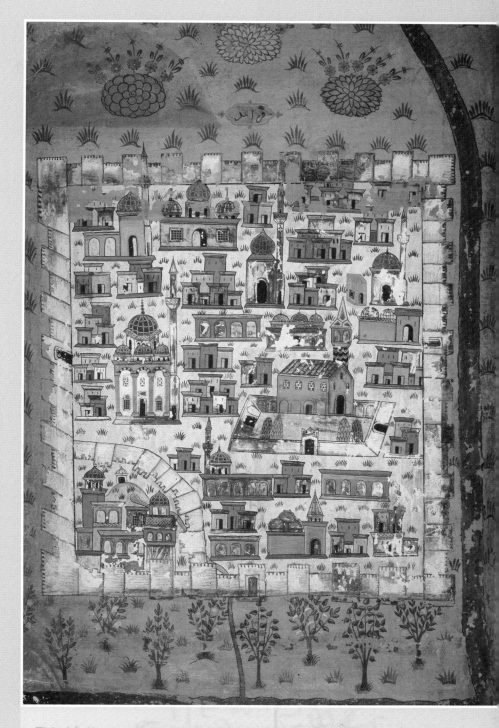

This bird's-eye view of the Turkish town of Diyarbakir was created by the Ottoman artist Nasuh al-Silahi in the 16th century. Diyarbakir was the scene of a revolt against Ottoman rule in the late 16th and early 17th centuries.

# Architecture

In the 7th century, Muslim armies invaded and conquered a huge expanse of land. Once the Muslims had taken control of a region, their first need was for somewhere to worship – a **mosque**.

## Early mosques

Mosques were built from the earliest days of Islam, and the first ones were based on the layout of the Prophet's own house in Madinah. The house of the Prophet Muhammad had a large central courtyard with deep porches to the north and the south. The north porch provided shelter from the sun for the homeless, while the south porch was for worshippers. The south wall indicated the **qiblah** – the direction of prayer towards Jerusalem. Later, the *qiblah* faced Makkah. This simple layout provided the main elements that were to be incorporated into all mosques: an open space for prayer with some shelter from the weather, and indication of the *qiblah*.

At first, Muslims put up simple buildings based on the model of the Prophet's house or adapted existing buildings, such as churches, for their own worship. Then, under the Umayyads, the first great monuments of Islam were built.

The wall of the huge prayer hall in the courtyard of the Great Mosque of Damascus is decorated with mosaics.

22

## Jerusalem and Damascus

As the Muslims conquered the lands of the Sasanians and the Byzantines in the 7th century, they came across some well-established styles and methods of building. The Dome of the Rock in Jerusalem shows the influence of Byzantine buildings in its use of beautiful marble and mosaics on the walls, both inside and out. The Great Mosque of Damascus was built on the site of a Byzantine Christian church. Its layout is a large courtyard with a huge prayer hall along the south, or *qiblah*, wall. A new innovation was a semicircular **mihrab**, set into the *qiblah* wall. This quickly became popular throughout the Islamic lands.

## Cordoba

The Great Mosque in Cordoba, Spain is a reminder of the splendours of Muslim al-Andalus. Now a tourist attraction, it was begun during the reign of Abd al-Rahman (756–788). It shows the influence of Umayyad architecture in Syria, from where Abd al-Rahman had fled. For example, the beautiful mosaics in the Great Mosque, which date from the 10th century, were probably intended to equal the splendours of the mosaics on the Dome of the Rock in Jerusalem and the Great Mosque in Damascus. The workmen who made the mosaics came not from al-Andalus itself, nor from the Abbasid Empire, but from Constantinople, capital of the **Byzantine Empire**.

## The features of a mosque

Over time, extra features were added to the basic design of the mosque. The **minbar**, a type of stepped pulpit, was based on the high seat with three steps from which Muhammad talked to his followers. The *mihrab* is a niche set into the *qiblah* wall to indicate the direction of prayer. During the time of the Prophet Muhammad, the call to prayer, or *adhan*, was given from the roof of the house. Later, the **minaret** – a tall tower from which the **adhan** is called – was introduced.

This photograph was taken inside the Sokullu Mehmet Pasha Mosque in Istanbul, Turkey. You can see the highly decorated *mihrab* in the centre, and the *minbar* on the right.

The impressive mud walls of the Great Mosque in Djenne tower above the weekly open-air market.

## African styles

In the dry lands south of the Sahara Desert, a distinctive style of mosque has developed, incorporating traditional aspects of mosque architecture with local building materials and styles. These mosques are made from sun-dried mud bricks, built around a wooden framework. The bricks are held together with mud and plastered over with more mud to give a smooth surface. One of the best known examples is in Djenne in Mali. Every year, a festival is held during which thousands of people help to re-plaster the mosque walls with fresh mud.

## Types of mosque

Mosques are not only places of worship but also community centres where food and shelter are available to those who need it. Many mosques also have areas for teaching and administration. Over the centuries, different types of mosque have developed, too. Everyday prayers can be performed anywhere, although many choose to do them in small mosques. The main prayer of the week, held on Friday, must be performed by all Muslim men in a mosque. At this meeting, an *imam* (a Muslim leader) addresses the worshippers from the *minbar*. Large 'Friday' mosques are usually at the centre of Islamic towns and cities.

## Madrasahs

Over time, the different functions of the mosque separated, and new types of building emerged. **Madrasahs** are Islamic schools where students come to study the Islamic sacred texts and Islamic law. The first madrasahs were founded in the 10th century, and a large number were built by the Seljuks in Central Asia in the 11th century.

Traditionally, the layout of many madrasahs was, like many mosques, based around a courtyard. In many central Asian madrasahs there was a large **vaulted** open-air hall, called an *iwan*, on each of the four sides of the courtyard. Teachers and students lived in small rooms around the courtyard.

Today the tradition of building madrasahs continues, for example, as part of the large complex of the Great Mosque of Hassan II in Morocco, completed in 1993.

## Tombs

Before his death, the Prophet Muhammad insisted that he should be buried very simply and that his grave should not be marked. But as Islam spread, it inherited the burial traditions of other cultures in which the graves of the dead were often marked with lavish structures. The desire to commemorate the dead meant that tombs were built throughout the Islamic world, although they were regarded with mixed feelings by some Muslims.

Tombs were often cube-shaped, topped by a dome. Another style was the tomb tower, topped with a cone-shaped roof. Tombs of this design were built in northern Iran.

Tombs gradually became bigger and more ornate, culminating in examples such as the Gur-i Amir, Timur's **mausoleum** in Samarkand, and the Taj Mahal built by the Mughal emperor **Shah** Jahan for his wife Mumtaz Mahal.

## Modern mosques

In the modern era, architecture in most Islamic cities has become international in style. The exception is mosque architecture, which often retains traditional layout and features. However, these elements have also been combined with new materials and building techniques.

This mosque in Rome opened in 1992. Designed by the Italian architect Paolo Portoghesi, it combines traditional features such as the dome (shown right) with modern technology and materials.

The Topkapi Sarayi in Istanbul housed about 5000 people, and the huge complex included parks, a parade ground, gardens, living quarters, and offices for government administration, as well as the sultan's quarters and a harem.

## Palaces

From the Umayyad dynasty onwards, Islamic rulers built lavish palaces for themselves. The Umayyads built palaces in the Syrian Desert. The design of these palaces was a square enclosure surrounded by walls and containing living areas, baths, a small mosque, and a throne room. The palaces were decorated with carved **stucco** and mosaics.

The finest surviving example of palace architecture in the western Islamic lands is the Alhambra in Granada, Spain. Granada was the last Muslim stronghold in Spain after the Christian kings began to reconquer the land in the 11th century. When Granada fell to the Christians in 1492, the Alhambra was preserved as a symbol of victory. The Alhambra is a group of palaces arranged around courtyards, and lavishly decorated with wood, tiles, and carved plaster. The same rambling style of architecture is found in the Topkapi Sarayi – the palace of the Ottoman **sultans** in Istanbul.

## Everyday structures

Other types of structure found across the Islamic world include the caravanserais, the bazaar, and the homes of ordinary people. Caravanserais were a type of medieval motel, situated at regular intervals along trade routes. Many had the same layout as was used for madrasahs – a large courtyard with an *iwan* on each side.

The bazaar is the centre of trade in many Muslim towns and cities. Most are roofed to provide some shelter from the hot sun. One of the largest is in the Safavid capital of Isfahan, where the alleyways of the bazaar stretch for many kilometres.

The traditional Islamic home is based around a courtyard. The outside walls are either blank, or with small windows. A single door leads into the men's rooms, where visitors are received, while the women's quarters, or **harem**, are separate. Many people still live in such houses, although Western-style houses and apartment blocks are also common in many Islamic cities.

## ◈ Gardens

In many parts of the Islamic world, gardens are highly prized. In places where the climate is hot and the landscape arid, a lush, green garden with the sound of flowing water is seen as a kind of paradise. Indeed, references in the **Qur'an** to Paradise describe it as a garden, with rivers and fountains as a dominant feature. Many Persian and Mughal book illustrations show beautiful gardens, and gardens are important areas in palaces such as the Alhambra and the Topkapi Sarayi.

In the centre of Isfahan, behind the Shah Mosque, is a huge open space called the Maydan. The Maydan was a space for markets, games of polo, military parades, and other state ceremonies.

# Carving

From the earliest times, Islamic buildings have been decorated with intricate carving. Sometimes the carving is into the stone of the building itself, at other times it is into a type of plaster called **stucco**. Some of the earliest surviving examples come from the Umayyad palaces built in the Syrian Desert. For example, at Mshatta the outside stone walls were decorated with elaborate carving. This carving includes intricate loops of leaves, stems, and bunches of grapes arranged in large geometric shapes.

The carving at Mshatta and at Khirbat al-Mafjar – another desert palace – shows the influence of the great empires that went before the Islamic conquests – the ancient Greek and Roman worlds, the **Byzantine Empire**, and a Persian flavour from the **Sasanian Empire**. Byzantine and Sasanian artists had long used plant and geometric ornaments for decoration, while the animals and figures that decorate Khirbat al-Mafjar were based on Sasanian models.

## Abbasid carving

Nothing remains of the Abbasid capital at Baghdad. However, in the middle of the 9th century, when the Abbasids were forced to abandon Baghdad for a time, they built a new capital at Samarra. Evidence from excavations at Samarra shows that the Abbasids used panels of stucco to decorate the inside walls of their palaces. Three different styles of stucco carving have been identified at Samarra. The first followed in the tradition of the Umayyad designs, the second used little dots across the surface of the stucco, and the third style used slanted cuts in the plaster to create large, **abstract symmetrical** designs. This last style quickly became popular across the Islamic world, and was used not only for stucco decoration, but also for carving in wood, glass, and rock crystal.

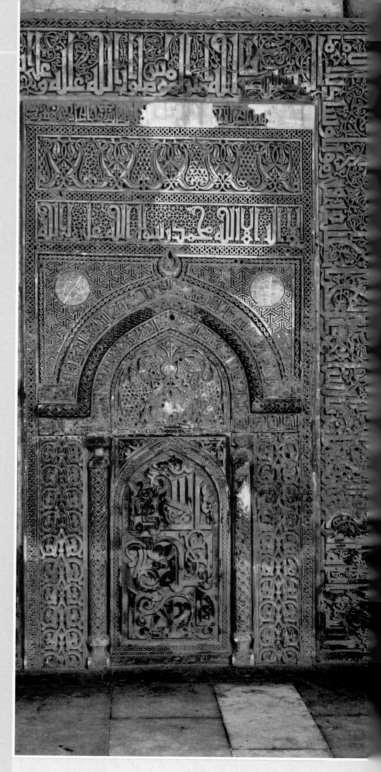

This beautifully carved stucco *mihrab* was added to the 9th-century **Mosque** of Ibn Tulun, in Cairo, in 1094. The **calligraphy** inscriptions are carved using the angular kufic style (see page 13).

## The Alhambra

Some of the finest stucco carving in the Islamic world has been preserved at the Alhambra Palace in Granada, Spain. The fine carving in the Court of the Lions gives a sense of weightlessness and light. In the Palace of the Lions there are two plaster ceilings featuring **muqarnas** – a style of ornament that hangs down, rather like a stalactite. This became a popular feature in Islamic architecture from the late 10th century onwards.

This picture shows the exquisite stucco carving in the Court of the Lions, part of the Alhambra Palace in Granada, Spain.

### ◈ The arabesque

The designs used as surface decoration in much Islamic art are often based on motifs such as leaves, tendrils, and flowers. The abstract geometrical patterns made from these motifs are known as 'arabesque', meaning 'in the Arab style'. Geometric patterns are a feature of art in the Islamic world, largely because of the tradition of avoiding the representation of living beings in religious settings. Some patterns use arabesque styles, while others draw on simple forms such as the circle and the square.

## Woodwork

Carving in wood is closely related to carving for architectural decoration. Wood is used for **mosque** furniture, as well as for doors, shutters, beams, screens, and other everyday furniture. The work is often extremely fine, as it can be viewed and appreciated from close up. Woodcarving is still practised as a local craft in many parts of the Islamic world.

The oldest surviving example of a wooden **minbar** is in the Great Mosque at Kairouan in Tunisia. Made in 862–3, from **teak**, it is thought that the carved panels may have been brought from Iraq. The panels have delicately carved designs, which have their origins in Umayyad and Abbasid ornament.

## Ivory

Carving in ivory often uses similar styles to carving in wood, but the work is usually of higher quality and more detailed. This is because ivory has always been an expensive material, treated with care and refinement. During the early Islamic period, ivory came from African elephant and hippopotamus tusks and was brought across the Sahara to Egypt and north Africa. Some was exported to Cordoba in Spain (al-Andalus), which became particularly noted as a centre for ivory carving. The ivory was used to make highly decorated containers. Only very wealthy **patrons** could afford such objects, and many containers have calligraphic inscriptions stating the owners' names. Ivory was also used in the Ottoman Empire to make small objects such as buckles and belts.

30

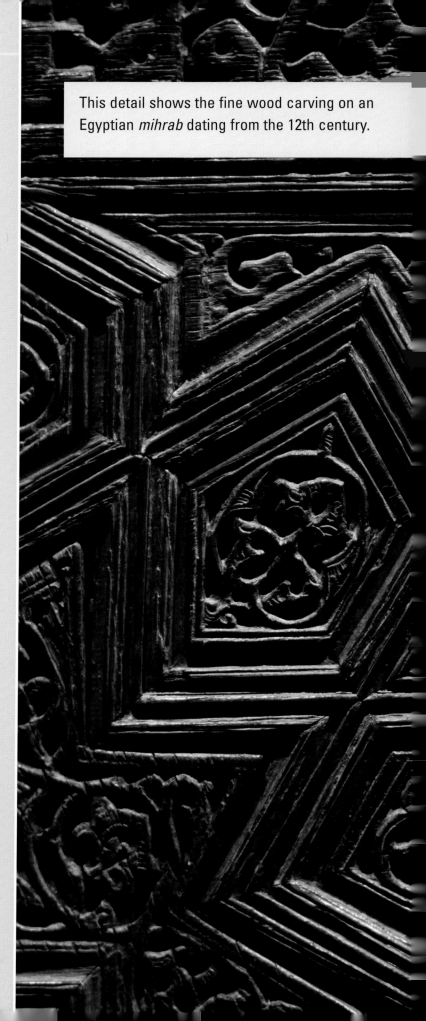

This detail shows the fine wood carving on an Egyptian *mihrab* dating from the 12th century.

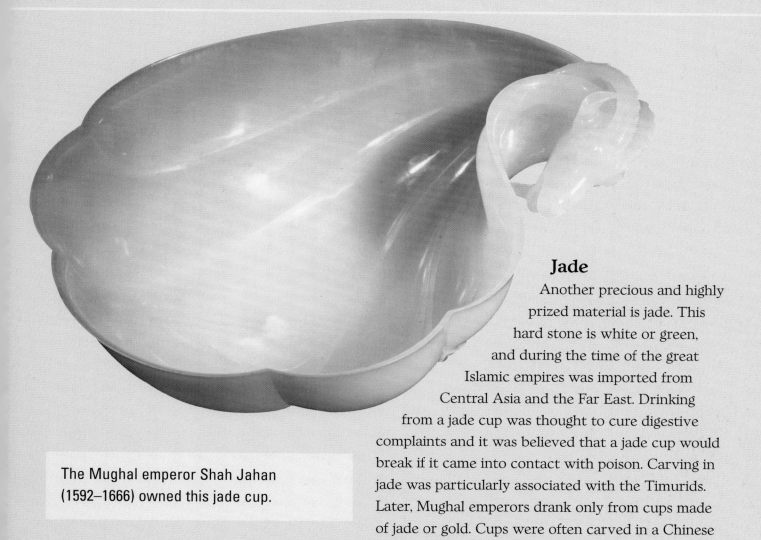

The Mughal emperor Shah Jahan (1592–1666) owned this jade cup.

## Jade

Another precious and highly prized material is jade. This hard stone is white or green, and during the time of the great Islamic empires was imported from Central Asia and the Far East. Drinking from a jade cup was thought to cure digestive complaints and it was believed that a jade cup would break if it came into contact with poison. Carving in jade was particularly associated with the Timurids. Later, Mughal emperors drank only from cups made of jade or gold. Cups were often carved in a Chinese style, with handles shaped like small dragons.

 ## Papier mâché

Papier mâché is a material made from a mixture of paper and glue. It can be moulded or built up on a frame. When it hardens it is both light and surprisingly strong. This unusual material was used to decorate the inside of the Gir-i Amir (Lord's Tomb) in Samarkand, built by Timur and the site of his burial in 1405. The papier mâché was moulded and sculpted, and then painted to decorate the vaults inside the tomb – one of the first known uses of this material in a building. Today, papier mâché is used for traditional crafts, such as trays, boxes, and other items made in Kashmir, in the far north of India. The surfaces of these objects are painted with floral designs in jewel-like colours, usually on a dark background.

# Rock crystal and glass

Rock crystal is a type of quartz – a transparent, colourless stone – used in the Islamic world to make beautiful bowls, **ewers** and cups. Rock crystal was highly prized by the Fatimids – thousands of rock crystal objects were made for the **opulent** Fatimid court. The Fatimids imported rock crystal from Arabia and Iraq, as well as East Africa. Rock crystal was also a favourite of the Ottoman **sultans**, who commissioned lavish pieces that were often encrusted with precious stones such as emeralds and rubies.

## Magic properties

One reason that rock crystal was popular in the Islamic world was that crystal cups are mentioned in the **Qur'an** in association with Paradise. But rock crystal was also thought to have other, magical properties. Drinking from a rock crystal cup was believed to prevent nightmares and to protect against some illnesses. It was also thought that rock crystal, like jade, would shatter if it came into contact with poison. Although most of the surviving pieces of rock crystal are objects such as bowls or cups, other items were made from the material. A crescent-shaped piece of rock crystal, inscribed with the name of the Fatimid ruler al-Zahir, was probably mounted on the harness of the **Khalifah's** horse. It would have flashed and sparkled beautifully in the sunlight.

## Making glass

The tradition of making objects from glass was well established in Egypt, Syria, Iraq, and Iran by the 7th century. Islamic glassmakers refined and developed new glass technologies. Glass was made from sand and lime, which was heated to a high temperature. It was shaped by pouring into moulds, or by blowing. This involved placing a lump of molten glass on the end of a long tube. The glassmaker then blew down the tube, creating a hollow shape in the glass. In some modern workshops, glass is still made in this traditional manner. However, glass production in the Islamic world declined after the 19th century with the introduction of mass-produced European glass. European factories even made special designs for the Middle Eastern markets, based on traditional Islamic wares. In the 20th century, glassmaking techniques were revived in Egypt. Today, factories in Cairo produce blown glass made from recycled bottles.

 ## Carving rock crystal

Rock crystal is a very hard and brittle substance – great skill was required to hollow it out without shattering or blemishing it. The outside surface was decorated by cutting away at the crystal with a rough material mounted on a turning wheel.

This ewer was carved out of a solid piece of rock crystal in the 10th century. Made for the Fatimid court, it is decorated with birds.

## Decorating glass

The Islamic glassmakers continued the traditions of decorating glass that had been practised in the **Byzantine** and **Sasanian Empires**. Glass could be decorated before it had cooled and hardened, by pushing moulds into the soft glass to leave an impression, or by pinching and manipulating the glass with tools. Glass could also be blown into a decorative mould. Sometimes, threads of hot glass were poured on to the outside of the object to create spiral effects. Hard glass was scratched with an even harder point such as a diamond, or cut and ground with a wheel. Glass could also be coloured by adding metallic oxides.

This 7th-century glass bottle from Syria is decorated with spiral patterns and covered with a lustre glaze.

Many glass objects were simple undecorated objects, designed for everyday use. These were usually made by the blown-glass method. Other pieces were beautifully decorated and were obviously made for wealthy **patrons**. Several cut-glass beakers survive from Fatimid Egypt. Some have decorations very similar to those seen on the **stucco** wall of Samarra, while others are engraved with pictures of lions, eagles, and **griffins.**

## Lustre glazes

The technique of decorating glass with **glazes** containing metallic **pigments** was probably developed in Egypt in the 7th century. These glazes are known as **lustre** glazes because they give off a metallic shine. The use of lustre glazes quickly spread to pottery and became an important method of **ceramic** decoration.

Richly decorated glass was a speciality in Egypt and Syria during the 13th and 14th centuries. Ayyubid and Mamluk glassmakers used both lustre and enamel – a type of coloured glass – to ornament their wares. Red enamel was used to outline the shapes of the decorations, which were then filled in with lustre and with white, yellow, green, blue, purple, or pink enamels. Decorated bottles, goblets, bowls, and vases were made not only for wealthy patrons, but also for sale and export, and influenced the famous glassmakers in Venice, Italy. However, the object most commonly associated with Mamluk glassmakers was the **mosque** lamp.

In the 20th century, glass-making techniques were revived in Egypt. Today, factories in Cairo produce blown glass made from recycled bottles.

# Mosque lamps

Thousands of richly decorated lamps were made for the mosques of the Mamluk capital in Cairo, and for Damascus in Syria. Typically, such lamps were decorated with **calligraphy** inscriptions. Often these inscriptions gave the name of the sultan who had commissioned them, as well as a verse from the Qur'an. These 14th-century mosque lamps are made of enamelled glass.

# Metalwork

Over the centuries, different traditions of metalworking developed in various parts of the Islamic world. Wealthy **patrons** paid for elaborate items to display their importance and power, and beautiful objects such as plates were often given as gifts. Less luxurious metals, most commonly brass, were used to make objects such as **ewers**, buckets, incense burners, bottles, candlesticks, and lamps. However, in the 19th century, manufactured items from the industrialized countries of Europe began to be imported into the Islamic world, and craft industries such as metalworking suffered as a result. Nevertheless, local traditions of metalworking continue in many Islamic countries, supplying both locals and the tourist industry.

## Early metalwork

Metalworking was well known throughout the Middle East from ancient times. Gold, silver, copper, iron, zinc, and lead were all mined in areas of the Islamic world. Iron and steel (iron and carbon) were used to make weapons and armour. But brass (usually copper and zinc) was the most common **alloy,** used for everyday items and as the base material for more luxurious objects. It is still the most widely used metal today.

Gold and silver were more costly and therefore used to make precious objects, such as luxury tableware, fine jewellery, and coins. However, few objects made from gold and silver survive from early Islamic times because the metal was so valuable that the objects were often melted down. Those items that have survived are mostly from hoards of treasure buried by their owners and never reclaimed.

## Working metal

Many examples of early Islamic metalwork were made using moulds. However, the more common method of working metal was by beating or hammering a sheet of metal into shape – a technique that is still widely used today. Hollow metal objects were also made by spinning on a lathe. A disc of metal was attached to a lathe and spun rapidly. It was then shaped by pressing a piece of shaped wood against the metal. The earliest known examples of this technique date from the 13th century.

### ◈ Forbidden metals

Although gold and silver have been highly prized throughout the Islamic world, the sacred texts of Islam warn against these precious metals. The **Qur'an** condemns the hoarding of gold and silver. The *Hadith* (the collected sayings of the Prophet Muhammad, which are a source of Islamic law and tradition) says: 'He who drinks from a silver vessel will have hellfire gurgling in his belly.' This prohibition may explain the popularity through the centuries of inlaid brass, which has the luxurious appearance associated with gold and silver while remaining within Islamic religious law.

These metalworkers in Indonesia are making stars and crescents – symbols of Islam – for **mosques**.

## Herat and Mosul

The 10th century saw the beginning of an age of fine metalwork in the Islamic world. One of the main centres of production was Herat (in modern-day north-west Afghanistan). Brass was still used as the main metal for most metal objects, but it was transformed by the technique of inlaying more precious metals, such as silver, red copper, or gold. The effect was one of great **opulence** and luxury, with metal objects covered in arabesque and geometric designs.

One of the best-known examples of this work is the 'Bobrinsky' bucket (its name comes from the Russian collector who bought it). It is made from brass and inlaid with silver and copper in horizontal bands that alternate Arabic inscriptions and scenes from everyday life. Other objects from the workshops in Herat include intricate candlesticks, also inlaid with silver and copper. They have designs which were made by hammering the brass from the inside, so that the ornament stands out from the outside surface.

After the Mongol invasions of the 13th century, Mosul (in northern Iraq) emerged as an important centre of metalworking. Designs and techniques mastered in Mosul spread to other parts of the Islamic world, for example to Syria. A flask from Syria shows that Islamic craftworkers were making goods not only for Muslim customers, but also for Christian **patrons** too. The flask is decorated in Mosul style but with Christian images, including the Virgin and Child, and the Nativity.

This 13th-century Persian **ewer** is made from brass. Its surface is finely decorated with inlaid silver in intricate patterns.

## Ottomans and Mughals

In the Ottoman Empire, interest in fine metalworking grew during the 16th century. This probably reflected the fact that it was the practice for **sultans** to be trained in a craft, and both Selim I and Suleiman I learned goldsmithing.

A feature of Ottoman metalwork was the use of jewels such as ruby, emerald, and turquoise set into the metal body of an object. Jewels were used to ornament a wide range of items, from weapons to mirrors. The Mughals also loved richly decorated metalwork, particularly weapons such as daggers, to display their wealth.

The manufacture of metal goods continues today in countries such as Iran and Pakistan. Metalworkers still use many of the traditional decorative techniques, including inlaying and **embossing**, which are centuries old. Some fine pieces are made entirely by hand, while others are die-cast, a process in which the melted metal is poured into a mould that is removed once the metal has cooled. Brass is still widely used to make objects for everyday use, as well as decorative items. In Iran, there are local traditions of making certain metalwork items, for example buckles, jewellery and weapons.

## ◈ Jewellery

Metal has been used throughout the Islamic world to make jewellery, most often silver and gold. In North Africa, a common feature of Islamic jewellery is the 'khamsa' or 'hand of Fatima'. This is a hand-shaped charm, often with an eye on the back of the hand, named after the daughter of the Prophet Muhammad. It is meant to ward off the evil eye. The most common type of jewellery in Morocco is the *tizara*, a necklace made from gold coins, pearls, and jewels.

Doorknockers are still made in the traditional shape of the 'hand of Fatima', a good-luck symbol that is meant to ward off evil spirits.

# Pottery

The use of clay to make **ceramics** was well established by the time of the Muslim conquests in the 7th century. Clay is a type of very fine earth found along riverbanks. Together with sand and water, it was formed into simple earthenware pots which were used to carry and store water and food. Various methods of making pottery have developed since those early days. The clay can be shaped with the hands as it turns rapidly on a wheel, it can be pressed or poured into a mould, or built up in coils and slabs. Whatever method is used, it is then left to dry before being fired in a special furnace called a kiln.

## ◇ William De Morgan

Techniques of applying lustre glazes were revived during the Safavid period in the late 17th and early 18th centuries, but then fell into disuse. In the 19th century, a British artist called William De Morgan was inspired by the beauty of Persian lustre pottery from Kashan, which he saw in new collections in London museums. He began experiments to try to recreate the effects of lustre, and soon produced copper-red, gold, and silver lustres.

This Turkish potter is using a wheel to make a fine vase.

Earthenware is porous – it can absorb water and air. Potters discovered that by painting a thin, glassy substance, called a **glaze**, on to the surface of pots, they could make them waterproof. The glaze could also be coloured, allowing for simple decoration of the pot.

## Early developments

The earliest pottery of the Islamic lands was simple and practical, but potters soon began to experiment with new techniques and designs. Great developments in pottery were made under the Abbasids. Different coloured glazes were combined to make patterns, and **lustre** glazes were developed. The use of **calligraphy** to decorate pottery was also introduced. But in particular, Abbasid potters were influenced by the designs of Chinese ceramics, which began to be imported to the Abbasid court during the 8th century. China was to remain a major influence on Islamic pottery for many centuries to come.

## Lustreware

Lustre glazes had been used to decorate glass since the 7th century, but the technique was adapted for ceramics by Abbasid potters. At first, the lustre glaze was painted across the whole vessel to give a uniform metallic sheen. But from about 850, Abbasid potters began to experiment with increasingly complex designs in different-coloured lustres. These designs featured animals or humans, often surrounded by **abstract** patterns.

Lustreware was popular with the Fatimids, who ruled Egypt from the 10th to the 12th centuries. This gold lustreware plate shows a seated figure holding two cups.

## Kashan

In the late 12th century, a new pottery technique developed, possibly at Kashan in western Iran. A type of body material was made from quartz, which was ground and mixed with white clay and a ground glaze called frit. 'Fritware', as it was called, was fine and white, and could be formed into delicate, elegant shapes. Once again, it was inspired by the Islamic potters' desire to copy Chinese porcelain ware. Other techniques that were developed at Kashan included lustreware and enamelled ceramics called *minai* (from the Persian word for enamel). Both of these techniques were used to produce high-quality luxury goods.

As well as bowls, plates, and other similar items usually associated with ceramics, the Kashan potters also worked on a larger scale. *Mihrabs* made entirely from large panels of ceramic were made for **mosques**. The *mihrabs* were covered with lustre glaze, and decorated with calligraphic inscriptions.

## Iznik

From the 15th century, production of high-quality blue-and-white pottery centred on Iznik in north-western Anatolia (Turkey), part of the expanding Ottoman Empire. After the Safavid defeat at the Battle of Chaldiran in 1514, Iranian artists were brought to work in the royal studios in Istanbul. Their influence is shown in designs including the Iranian *saz* style, which features delicately curving leaves with feathered edges.

The peak of achievement by the Iznik potters came in the second half of the

This fritware plate comes from Iznik. It has been painted and then glazed.

## Underglaze painting

The development of fritware led to a new technique of underglaze painting. This meant that the design was painted directly on to the body of the object, and then a clear glaze was applied over the top. Using this technique, potters created designs that were influenced by Chinese examples, often using blue motifs against the white background of the body material.

16th century. New colours had been added to the blue and white, usually black, green, and purple. A red **pigment**, called Iznik red, was developed during the 1550s. Iznik designs became extremely popular across Europe, and they were exported abroad, as well as being imitated in potteries in Italy and Hungary. The popularity of Iznik declined during the 18th century.

Kütahya is a well-known centre for ceramic production in modern-day Turkey. This woman is painting a ceramic jar with a fine brush.

Ceramics are still produced in local workshops in countries such as Iran and Pakistan, often using traditional designs and methods of working. The knowledge that is kept alive in such places is vital when a building is being restored, or when tiles are needed for a new construction. More large-scale production is found in Turkey, but Iznik continues to make pottery in traditional styles, mainly for export overseas. In the late 19th century, William De Morgan (see page 40) was invited by the Egyptian government to revitalize the ceramics industry, and he oversaw the establishment of a ceramics factory in Cairo. However, the outstanding figure in Egyptian ceramics in the 20th century was an Egyptian, Said al-Sadr. He trained in Britain, but studied the rich heritage of Islamic pottery and championed the study of ceramics in Egypt. He set up a ceramics centre and established a mixture of traditional and modern styles, looking back at old styles but making use of up-to-date techniques.

**43**

# Tiles

The manufacture of tiles to provide colour and decoration on buildings has long been one aspect of the art of the Islamic world. Both inside and outside walls are covered with **glazed** and unglazed tiles, usually highly decorated. While the actual structures of early Islamic buildings were often quite simple, their decoration became increasingly ornate, particularly in the eastern lands of the Islamic world.

This Moroccan tilemaker is at work on an ornate mosaic tile. Examples of his work are displayed on the wall.

## ◈ Ottoman tilework

Magnificent panels of tiles were made for the Ottoman **sultans** at the pottery workshops in Iznik in Turkey. The decoration on these tiles often used floral designs, and the *saz* designs seen on pottery and Ottoman textiles. The interior of the Baghdad Kiosk in the Topkapi Palace in Istanbul (shown opposite) is lavishly decorated with beautiful tilework showing the range of motifs and colours used by Ottoman tileworkers. As well as floral and geometric motifs there is a panel of calligraphy. Today, tiles are still made in Iznik, and are exported all over the world.

## Decorative techniques

Just as in pottery, different techniques have been developed over the centuries to decorate tiles. **Lustre** glazes were often used for tiles to decorate inside walls, turning them into sheets of gold or silver. Another method, known as **lajvardina**, made use of a blue glaze ornamented with red and white enamel and gold leaf. Other techniques allowed the use of several different colours on a tile without their running into one another. *Lakabi* was a style of decoration with raised ridges to separate different colours. In *cuerda seca* (dry cord), a type of greasy black paste was used to separate the colours. When the tiles were fired in the kiln, the paste burned off, leaving a black line between the colours.

There are several different styles for the decorative designs on tiles. Geometric designs are particularly associated with tilework of northern Africa. Elsewhere, geometric designs are combined with arabesque and floral ornament. **Calligraphic** inscriptions are an important decoration too.

Tiles are made in several different ways. Sometimes they are cut into shapes to form a mosaic pattern. Sometimes individual tiles form part of the larger pattern of a complete panel. In some cases, tiles are carved to form intricate decorative latticework. Glazed wall tiles continue to be made in many Islamic countries, often using modern production techniques.

## The Shah Mosque, Isfahan

Some of the most magnificent examples of tilework in the Islamic world are found in cities such as Isfahan and Samarkand. In Isfahan the **Shah Mosque** is covered in beautiful multi-coloured tilework, although the overall effect is one of blue. The most highly ornamented tilework is around the entrance to the mosque, where there are large panels of decorated tiles. Other parts of the mosque are less sumptuously decorated, probably due to shortage of money, in multicoloured glazed tiles.

The interior of the Baghdad Kiosk in the Topkapi Palace in Istanbul is lavishly decorated with beautiful tilework featuring floral and geometric motifs as well as a panel of calligraphy.

# Textiles and carpets

For centuries, the production and use of textiles has been very important across the Islamic world. Textiles have been used to make clothing, carpets, bags, tents, and furniture. The tradition of weaving tents originated with the **nomadic** tribes of the Islamic world – the Bedouin Arabs, the Turkmen, and the Mongols. In Muslim houses, carpets are spread on the floor and hung on walls to protect against extremes of temperature, while large woven bags are used for storage, and cushions are used for sitting.

## Materials

The importance of textiles is shown by the number of words that have passed down into the English language from Arabic or Persian origins: 'damask' comes from Damascus, the capital of Syria; 'muslin' from Mosul in Iraq; and taffeta from 'tafteh', the Persian word for 'woven'. The most common material in use from early to modern times is sheep's wool. Other materials are goat and camel hair, cotton, linen, flax, and, the most expensive of all, silk, made from the cocoons of silkworms. Silk is spoken of in the **Qur'an** as one of the luxuries to be enjoyed in Paradise.

Many textiles made for everyday use are plain, but patterned textiles are also very popular. For the most luxurious effect, the pattern is woven into the cloth as it is made on the loom. Patterns are also added after the cloth is made, by dying, printing, painting, or by embroidery. Traditions of producing luxurious cloth largely died out from the 19th century, as Islamic rulers adopted Western dress. However, carpets are still made in many places using traditional methods.

## Early examples

Very few textiles from early Islamic times have survived to the present day. Some have been excavated in archaeological digs, including the oldest-known example of a hand-knotted wool carpet. Known as the Pazyryk carpet, it is the oldest-known example of a hand-knotted carpet and dates back to the pre-Islamic era of the 4th and 5th centuries BCE. The carpet was found virtually intact in southern Siberia, preserved in the frozen chamber of a royal burial mound. It is now kept at the Hermitage Museum in St Petersburg, Russia. Other pieces of fabric were taken from the Islamic world to Europe as trophies. They were so highly regarded that they were often preserved in church treasuries, wrapped around precious objects such as relics, and have therefore survived until the present day.

## Kilims

A kilim is a flat-woven carpet or hanging (without a soft pile). Produced in many Islamic countries from northern Africa to Turkey and the Middle East, these flat-woven fabrics were originally woven to make saddlebags for animals, sacks, furnishings, and floor coverings. Kilims are traditionally died with vegetable dyes to produce bright colours. Designs vary from region to region, but they are often bold, with geometrical patterns. Today, Turkey specializes in arch (*mihrab*) designs, which are popular in many non-Islamic countries.

This Turkish woman is repairing a brightly decorated kilim.

## Persian carpets

Knotted carpets were once made across the Islamic world. Examples survive from Konya and Ushak in Anatolia, from Cairo in Egypt, and from Islamic Spain. In the 16th century, Safavid Iran became an important centre of carpet production. Under **Shah** Tahmasp and Shah Abbas, royal factories were set up for the manufacture of fine-quality carpets. Thousands of carpets were made for local use and for export to Europe, the Ottoman Empire, and India. Persian carpets are still very popular – there are centres of manufacture in Iran. Each has its own characteristic designs and methods of production.

## Ottoman textiles

Just like the Safavids, the Ottomans also set up royal workshops for the production of fine textiles and carpets. The Ottoman **sultans** wore simple robes called kaftans, which were made from sumptuous patterned silk, and velvets. For military campaigns, the Ottoman sultans used large tents, often decorated with beautiful **appliqué** designs. There was also a fine tradition of carpet-making, using both wool and silk.

## The DOBAG project

During the 19th century, traditional methods of carpet making were replaced by more commercial techniques in many parts of the Islamic world. Synthetic dyes were used instead of traditional plant dyes, and carpet production moved into factories. Nevertheless, the tradition of producing hand-knotted carpets did not completely die out, and fine wool carpets and kilims are still made for home use and for export. In some places, projects have been set up to revive traditional techniques and provide fair employment for carpet makers.

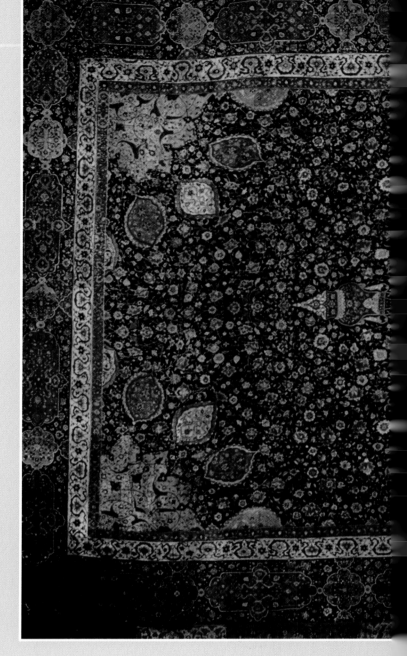

One example is the DOBAG project in Turkey. DOBAG stands for the Turkish words for Natural Dye Research and Development Project, and the project is run by the University of Marmara. Begun in 1982, this is the first women's rug-weaving co-operative in the Islamic world. The women make the rugs in their own homes, using only vegetable dyes to colour the wool. The designs of the rugs are unique, and have been passed down through families over generations.

 ## Carpet knots

Carpets are traditionally made by hand, by knotting pieces of wool around the backing yarns. Two different knots are used to make carpets in the Islamic world. The Turkish or Ghiordes knot is a **symmetrical** knot. It is generally used for carpets made in Turkey and the Caucasus (between the Black and Caspian seas). The Persian or Senneh knot is an assymetrical knot. It is associated with carpets from Iran and parts of Asia.

The Ardabil carpet (above), was woven in Persia between 1539 and 1540. It is made from wool and silk, and its design incorporates two **mosque** lamps hanging from the central medallion.

# Cross-currents

The term 'Islamic art' covers a wide range and huge variety of cultures. There are great differences, for example, in styles of architecture in Muslim Spain and Mughal India, although both were Islamic empires. Yet there are also features that make Islamic art and architecture recognizably Islamic in any part of the world: the use of **calligraphy**, for example, or the use of geometric and arabesque designs.

## Islam meets Hinduism

The most celebrated emperor of the Mughal Empire, Akbar, took a great interest in all religions. In the 1580s he even declared a new religion, which blended aspects of Islam with **Hinduism** and other faiths. The buildings commissioned by Akbar reflect this mixing of Islamic and local Hindu ideas. Akbar's most spectacular architectural achievement was Fatehpur Sikri, near Agra, which he began building in 1571 as a new capital for his empire. It was abandoned in the 1580s, but the buildings still stand today. The city is built from red sandstone, and the design combines Hindu styles and decorations with Islamic features.

## Islam in South-east Asia

Islam was taken to South-east Asia by sailors who crossed the Indian Ocean in search of trade. Conversion to Islam was slow and patchy, but by 1500 Muslims were established in many parts of the region, particularly Sumatra and Java. The traditions of Islam mixed with local cultures, as well as the Hindu and **Buddhist** religions, which also thrived in the region. For example, in Java **batik** cloth was produced – richly patterned with many different designs including butterflies, birds, and flowers. In areas where Islam was strongest, living beings were replaced by the geometrical patterns developed by Muslim artists.

This textile worker in Java, Indonesia, is at work on a piece of batik cloth. He is applying hot wax to the fabric using a press. When the fabric is dipped in dye, the areas covered in wax will not be coloured. The wax is removed by boiling the cloth.

## Islam and the West

In the West, there has long been an awareness of the riches of the Islamic world. From as early as the 1450s, paintings by European artists depict sumptuous carpets with distinctive patterns that betray their origins in the Islamic workshops of Turkey (Anatolia). In the 16th century, Hans Holbein, court painter to Henry VIII, included beautiful carpets in his portraits of court figures. However, it was during the 18th century that interest in Islamic art and architecture began to take off, as European visitors to Turkey told of the wonders they had seen there. Islamic monuments, such as the Taj Mahal at Agra, in India, inspired European architects who incorporated 'Muslim' elements into their work. In the 19th century, the English poet and designer William Morris took inspiration from the patterns of carpets from Persia and Turkey for his own work. Exhibitions of Islamic art were mounted in Europe during the 19th century, exciting great interest, and influencing painters such as Henri Matisse (1869–1954).

 **Matisse**

The French painter Henri Matisse visited several exhibitions of Islamic work, as well as travelling to Morocco in northern Africa, and to Cordoba and Granada in Spain. Inspired by what he saw, he incorporated elements from Islamic art into his painting. His use of bright, jewel-like colours, patterns, and a flattening of **perspective** all drew on his knowledge of Persian manuscript paintings and other Islamic work. His interest in the Islamic world continued throughout his life.

The Royal Pavilion in Brighton was redesigned and rebuilt between 1815 and 1822 by the British architect John Nash. Its style reflects the growing interest in Islamic art and architecture of the time.

# Further resources

## More books to read

Bloom, Jonathan and Sheila Blair, *Islamic Arts* (Phaidon Press, 1997)

Brend, Barbara, *Islamic Art* (The British Museum Press, 1991)

Morris, Neil, *The Atlas of Islam* (Barron's Educational Series, 2003)

Rice, David Talbot, *Islamic Art* (Thames and Hudson, 1975)

Wintle, Justin, *The Rough Guide History of Islam* (Rough Guides, 2003)

## Websites

*http://www.metmuseum.org/toah/hd/orna/hd_orna.htm*
New York Metropolitan Museum website with links to many aspects and periods of Islamic art

*http://www.metmuseum.org/explore/Flowers/HTM/cata_fs.htm*
New York Metropolitan Museum website about Mughal carpets

*http://www.themagiccarpet.biz*
Information about carpets and the DOBAG project

*http://www.lacma.org/islamic_art/intro.htm*
Los Angeles County Museum of Art website

*http://www.islamicart.com/*
General site about Islamic art

*http://www.demorgan.org.uk/collection/ceramics.htm*
Information about William De Morgan

*http://www.calligraphyislamic.com*
Information about Islamic calligraphy

## Places to visit

### UK

Ashmolean Museum, Oxford

British Museum, London

Fitzwilliam Museum, Cambridge

Oriental Museum, University of Durham

Royal Museum, Edinburgh

The Royal Pavilion, Brighton

Victoria and Albert Museum, London

### USA

Arthur M. Sackler Museum, Harvard University

Detroit Institute of Arts, Detroit

Los Angeles County Museum of Art

Metropolitan Museum of Art, New York

### Elsewhere

Davids Samling, Copenhagen, Denmark

Hermitage Museum, St Petersburg, Russia

Musée du Louvre, Paris, France

Museum of Islamic Art, Berlin, Germany

Museum of Islamic Art, Cairo, Egypt

Topkapi Sarayi, Istanbul, Turkey

# Glossary

**abstract**  in art describes something that is non-representational

*adhan*  call to prayer

**Allah**  Arabic word for God

**alloy**  mixture of two metals

**appliqué**  technique of sewing pieces of fabric and other decorative elements such as beads or sequins on to a fabric background to create an image

**batik**  technique of printing on fabric using wax

**Buddhism**  widespread Asian religion or philosophy

**Byzantine Empire**  the empire of Byzantium, the eastern Roman Empire. It dated from 330 CE, when the Roman emperor Constantine moved his capital to Byzantium and renamed it Constantinople (now Istanbul).

**calligraphy**  art of beautiful writing

**ceramic**  describes an object made from clay

**colony**  territory occupied and ruled by another state

**constellation**  group of stars as seen from Earth, many of which were named by the ancient Greeks

**cursive**  describes a flowing, handwriting style

**embossing**  type of decoration that is pushed out from the inside, standing proud from the outside surface of an ornament

**epic**  long poem that tells a story

**ewer**  large jug, often with a lid

**glaze**  glassy liquid that is applied to objects such as ceramics and glass

**griffin**  winged monster with the head of an eagle and the body of a lion

**gum arabic**  gum obtained from the acacia tree, used as a thickener in many products including ink

**harem**  women's quarters in a Muslim home, forbidden to all men except male relatives. The word comes from the Arabic *haram*, meaning 'sacred'.

**Hinduism**  major religious and cultural tradition of India. Hindus worship many gods and goddesses and believe that a person is reborn many times into many different lives.

**Ibrahim**  Abraham, the prophet

**illumination**  ornate decoration on a manuscript

**Ka'bah**  cube structure in Makkah towards which all Muslims direct their prayer

**Khalifah** (successor)  title given to the successors of the Prophet Muhammad

**lajvardina**  blue glaze ornamented with red and white enamel and gold leaf

**lamp-black**  black powder made from carbon, which is used as a pigment

**lithography**  method of printing from a stone or metal plate

**lustre** type of glaze that contains a metallic pigment

**madrasah** Islamic school or college

**mausoleum** large tomb

*mihrab* niche in the wall of a mosque that indicates the *qiblah* – the direction of prayer – towards Makkah

**minaret** tall tower from which the *adhan* (call to prayer) is given

*minbar* pulpit in a mosque from where the address is given during Friday prayers

**mosque** place where Muslims worship. From the Arabic *masjid*, meaning 'a place of bowing down'.

*muqarnas* style of ornament that hangs down, rather like a stalactite

**nomadic** describes people who move from one place to another, usually in search of grazing for their flocks

**oasis** fertile area with a water supply in an area of desert

**octagonal** eight-sided

**opulent** indicating great wealth

**patron** someone who pays an artist for a specific piece of work

**perspective** technique of optical illusion which allows an artist to create an impression of three-dimensional depth and space on a piece of paper

**pigment** substance that gives something colour

*qiblah* direction of prayer towards Makkah

**Qur'an** holy book of Islam, sacred to all Muslims

**Sasanian Empire** describes the empire of the Sassanids, a Persian dynasty, from the 3rd to the 7th centuries. At its greatest extent it stretched from Mesopotamia in the west to the Indus valley in the east. Its capital was at Ctesiphon.

**secular** non-religious

**shah** (ruler) from the Persian word meaning 'king'

**Shi'a Muslims** those who believe that leadership of the Islamic community passed directly to Ali, as the closest blood relative of the Prophet Muhammad, and then through Ali's descendants

**stucco** type of high-quality plaster

**sultan** name given to an Islamic ruler, particularly in the Ottoman Empire

**Sunni Muslims** those who believe in the successorship of the first four Khalifahs

**symmetrical** describes something that has symmetry – balance and proportion in its parts

**teak** type of hardwood that comes from native trees of South-east Asia

**vaulted** describes an arched roof structure

# Index

Abbasid dynasty 7–9, 16, 28, 30, 41
Akbar, Emperor 10, 20, 50
Alhambra, Granada 26, 27, 29
Anatolia 8, 10, 42; *see also*
    Turkey
Arabia 5
Arab–Israeli war 11
Ayyabids 34

Babur, Emperor 10
Baghdad 7, 9, 17, 18, 28
batik 50
books 9, 10, 17–19, 21, 26
Byzantine Empire 5, 10, 23, 28, 34

Cairo 28, 32, 35, 43, 48
calligraphy
    as decoration 14, 35, 41
    and mosques 28, 45
    tiles 11, 44, 45
    tools 13
carpets 46, 48–9, 51
carving 28–33
Casablanca 25
ceramics 40–5; *see also* tiles
China 9, 16, 31, 41, 42
Christianity 18, 23, 26, 38
Constantinople 5, 9, 10, 23;
    *see also* Istanbul
Cordoba 7, 8, 23, 30, 51

Damascus 6, 7, 16, 22, 23, 35, 46
De Morgan, William 40, 43
DOBAG project 48
Dome of the Rock, Jerusalem
    6, 7, 14, 23

Egypt 7, 8, 32, 34, 41, 43
Europe, influence 10, 11, 20, 36, 51

Fatimids 7–9, 32, 34, 41
Fes (Morocco) 44

gardens 27
Genghis Khan 9, 10
glass 32–5, 41
Grand Mosque, Makkah 5
Great Mosque, Casablanca 25
Great Mosque, Cordoba 7, 8, 23
Great Mosque, Damascus 22, 23
Great Mosque, Djenne 24

Great Mosque, Kairouan 30
Gulf war 11

Herat 19, 38

India 10, 31
Indonesia 36, 50
Iran 9, 11, 14, 18, 20, 32, 39, 42,
    43, 48; *see also* Persia
Iran–Iraq war 11
Isfahan, Iran 9, 27, 45
Istanbul 21, 23, 26, 44;
    *see also* Constantinople
ivory 30
Iznik 42, 44

jade 31, 32
jewellery 39

Kashan 8, 42
kilims 46–7, 48

lamps 35
lustre 34, 41, 42, 45

Madinah 6, 22
madrasahs 14, 17, 25
Makkah 5, 6
Mamluks 8, 17, 34
maps 21
metalworking 36–9
Mongol Empire 7, 9, 18, 20, 38, 46
Morocco 39, 44, 51
Mosque of Ibn Tulun, Cairo 28
mosques
    decoration 14, 42
    furnishings 17, 30, 35, 37
    modern 25
    types 22–5
    *see also specific mosques*
Mosul 38, 46
Mughal Empire 10, 18, 27, 31,
    39, 50
Muhammad, Prophet
    life 4, 6, 16, 22, 23, 39
    mission and views 5, 6, 12,
    25, 36

Ottoman Empire 9, 10, 14, 18, 26,
    32, 44, 48

painting 19, 20, 51
Pakistan 14, 39, 43
palaces 26, 28; *see also*
    Alhambra, Topkapi Sarayi
paper 16
papier mâché 31
patrons 4, 18, 30, 34, 36
Persia 5, 27, 51; *see also* Iran
portraits 18, 21

Qur'an
    calligraphy 12, 14, 15, 35
    illumination 8, 16–17
    and Paradise 27, 32, 46
    teaching of 14, 36

rock crystal 32–3
Roman Empire/Romans 5, 28
Royal Pavilion, Brighton 51

Safavid dynasty 9, 10, 19, 42, 48
Samarkand 9, 25, 31
Samarra 28
Sasanian Empire 5, 23, 28, 34
Saudi Arabia 5
Seljuks 7, 8, 25
Shah Mosque, Isfahan 27, 45
Sokullu Mehmet Pasha Mosque,
    Istanbul 23
Spain 8, 23, 26, 30, 48
stucco 26, 28, 29, 34
Syria 6, 23, 26, 32, 34, 38

Taj Mahal 10, 15, 25, 51
terrorism 11
textiles 46–9
tiles 11, 44–5
Timur (Tamerlane) 9, 10, 25, 31
Timurids 9, 31
tombs 15, 25
Topkapi Sarayi, Istanbul 10, 26,
    27, 44, 45
Turkey 11, 14, 43, 46, 48, 49, 51;
    *see also* Anatolia

Umayyad dynasty 6–8, 16, 22, 23,
    26, 28, 30

wood *see* carving

# The New Encyclopedia of Crochet Techniques

A comprehensive visual guide to traditional and contemporary techniques

Jan Eaton

Search Press

A QUARTO BOOK

Published in 2013 by Search Press Ltd
Wellwood
North Farm Road
Tunbridge Wells
Kent TN2 3DR

ISBN: 978-1-84448-922-0

Conceived, designed and produced by
Quarto Publishing plc
The Old Brewery
6 Blundell Street
London N7 9BH

QUA: ECR2

**PROJECT EDITOR:** Lindsay Kaubi
**ART EDITOR:** Julie Francis
**COPY EDITORS:** Pauline Hornsby, Helen Jordan
**ILLUSTRATORS:** Betty Barnden, Kuo Kang Chen, Coral Mula
**PHOTOGRAPHERS:** Martin Norris, Phil Wilkins
**PICTURE RESEARCHERS:** Sarah Bell, Claudia Tate

**CREATIVE DIRECTOR:** Moira Clinch
**PUBLISHER:** Paul Carslake

Colour separation by Pica Digital Pte Ltd, Singapore
Printed by 1010 Printing International Ltd, China

9 8 7 6 5 4 3 2 1

# CONTENTS

About this book ............................................ 6

**CHAPTER ONE:**
    **Crochet Essentials** .................. **8**

Equipment .................................................. 10
Yarns and threads ....................................... 12
Basic skills ................................................ 14
Foundation chains ....................................... 16
Turning and starting chains ........................ 17
Double crochet stitch .................................. 18
Half treble crochet stitch ............................ 19
Treble crochet stitch ................................... 20
Double treble crochet stitch ........................ 21
Measuring tension ....................................... 22
Joining, fastening off and
    weaving in yarns ................................... 24
Reading patterns and charts ........................ 26
Pressing and blocking .................................. 28
Seams ....................................................... 30

**CHAPTER TWO:**
    **Techniques and Stitches** ....... **32**

Stripe patterns .......................................... 34
Ridge stitches ............................................ 36
Shaping ..................................................... 38
Clusters .................................................... 40
Shell stitches ............................................ 42
Bobbles ..................................................... 44
Popcorns ................................................... 46
Puff stitches .............................................. 48
Loop stitches ............................................. 50
Openwork and lace stitches ......................... 52

Filet crochet .............................................. 56
Chevron patterns ........................................ 60
Spike stitches ............................................ 64
Raised stitches .......................................... 66
Jacquard patterns ...................................... 68
Intarsia patterns ........................................ 70
Tubular crochet .......................................... 72
Circular motifs ........................................... 74
Square motifs ............................................ 80
Hexagon motifs .......................................... 85
Tunisian crochet ........................................ 90
Broomstick crochet ..................................... 94
Hairpin crochet .......................................... 96
Edge finishes ............................................ 98
Buttonholes and button loops ..................... 100
Cords ...................................................... 102
Flowers .................................................... 104
Braids and insertions ................................ 106
Edgings .................................................... 108
Fringes and tassels ................................... 110
Surface crochet ........................................ 112
Applying beads ......................................... 114
Applying sequins ...................................... 116

**CHAPTER THREE: Projects** ......... **118**

Buttonhole bag .......................................... 120
Intarsia potholder ...................................... 121
Baby afghan .............................................. 122
Hexagon cushion ........................................ 124
Winter scarf .............................................. 126
Filet crochet wrap ...................................... 128
Striped bag ............................................... 130

**CHAPTER FOUR: Gallery** ............ **132**

Crochet in the home ................................... 134
Garments .................................................. 136
Scarves .................................................... 139
Head, nose, hands and toes ......................... 142
Bags and accessories ................................. 144
Whimsy ..................................................... 146

Care of crochet .......................................... 148
Abbreviations and symbols .......................... 150
Glossary ................................................... 153
Suppliers .................................................. 154
Index ....................................................... 158
Credits ..................................................... 160

# ABOUT THIS BOOK

THE BOOK BEGINS WITH CROCHET ESSENTIALS, A CHAPTER PACKED WITH THE BASICS OF CROCHET. ONCE YOU HAVE MASTERED THE BASICS, MOVE ON TO THE TECHNIQUES AND STITCHES CHAPTER, WHICH WILL EXPAND YOUR KNOWLEDGE AND SKILLS. EACH TECHNIQUE IS SELF-CONTAINED, SO YOU CAN EITHER DIP IN AND OUT OF THE CHAPTER OR WORK YOUR WAY FROM BEGINNING TO END. THE PROJECTS AND GALLERY CHAPTERS ARE INTENDED TO ENCOURAGE YOU TO PUT INTO PRACTICE THE SKILLS YOU HAVE LEARNED.

## CROCHET ESSENTIALS

Crochet Essentials guides you step-by-step through all the crochet basics in easy-to-follow sequences, progressing from equipment and materials and how to hold the hook and yarn to basic stitches, how to read patterns and how to stitch seams. This course in the essentials will direct you through your first steps in crochet.

Step-by-step sequences and clear, easy-to-follow illustrations accompany each skill.

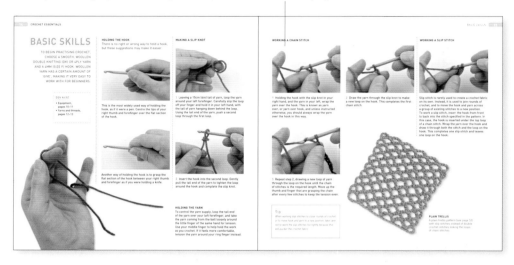

## TECHNIQUES AND STITCHES

From the easiest of striped patterns to the lacy delights of filet crochet, the Techniques and Stitches chapter demonstrates a wide range of crochet stitches and techniques. Beginning with simple patterns and shapes, it moves on to textured stitches and non-standard techniques such as hairpin and Tunisian crochet, and finally explains how to make embellishments like cords and fringes, and how to add beads and sequins. The accompanying Stitch Collections show how to put the techniques into practice.

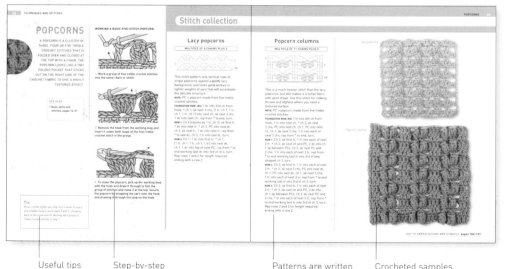

Useful tips are scattered throughout the book.

Step-by-step sequences explain how to work the stitch.

Patterns are written and charted.

Crocheted samples show the finished fabric.

## PROJECTS

This chapter features seven attractive projects, ranging from a simple scarf worked in a pretty lace stitch to a gorgeous striped bag crocheted entirely in the round using a selection of contrasting yarns. All of the projects encourage you to use and expand on the techniques you have learned in the previous chapter.

Clear instructions list materials, finished size, tension and how to make up the item.

Each project is illustrated with an inspirational picture of the finished item.

## GALLERY

This chapter showcases some of the different ways of using crochet fabric, from making stylish garments to creating home accessories. Crochet fabric is a textile with a huge range of possibilities – it can be light, delicate and lacy, chunky and textured, or smooth and patterned in a variety of ways. Organised into categories such as garments and bags, you can dip into the gallery anywhere for instant inspiration.

Each item is described with useful information on how it was created.

Vibrant colour pictures provide inspiration and ideas for colour schemes, stitches and possibilities for your own projects.

### SWATCH SIZES

Unless indicated otherwise, all of the crochet samples in this book were made using double knitting yarn and are shown in proportion to each other (approximately 80–85% actual size). This will help you to compare the sizes, textures and overall effect of the different stitch patterns in relation to each other.

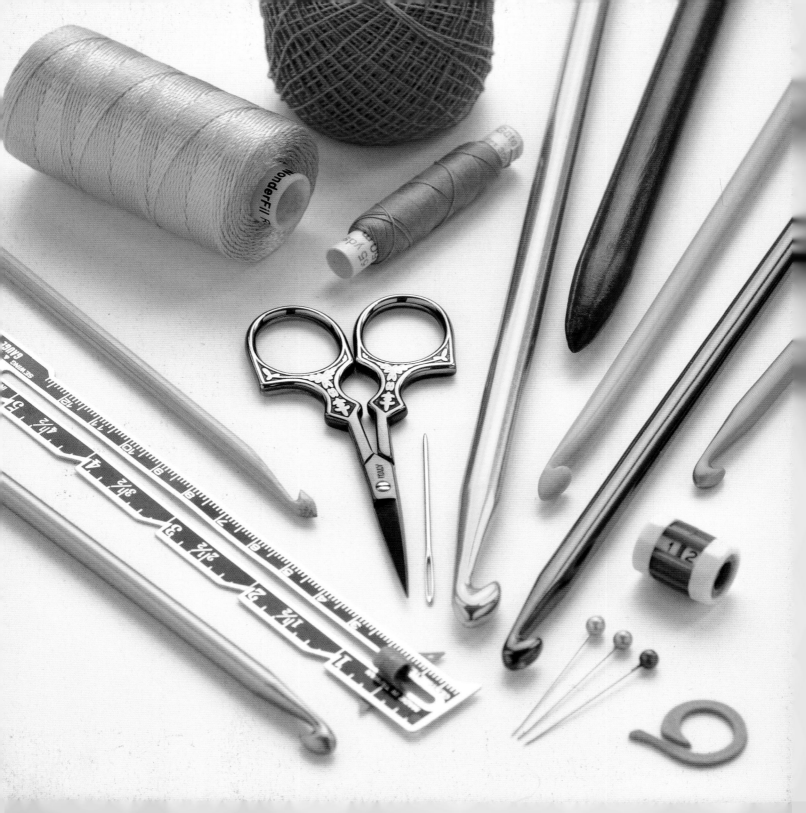

# CHAPTER ONE

## Crochet Essentials

This chapter contains all the key skills you need to get started with crochet. From choosing yarn and hooks to working the basic stitches and understanding both written and charted crochet patterns, this is the place to start, whether you are a beginner or someone who wants to freshen up existing crochet skills.

# EQUIPMENT

TO TAKE UP CROCHET, ALL YOU NEED IS A CROCHET HOOK AND A BALL OF YARN. HOOKS ARE AVAILABLE IN A WIDE RANGE OF SIZES AND MATERIALS. AS YOU PROGRESS IN THE CRAFT, YOU CAN COLLECT MORE EQUIPMENT AS YOU NEED IT.

## HOOKS

Hooks from different manufacturers, and those made from different materials, can vary widely in shape and size, even though they may all be branded with the same number or letter to indicate their size. Although the hook sizes quoted in pattern instructions are a very useful guide, you may find that you need to use smaller or larger hook sizes, depending on the brand, to achieve the correct tension for a pattern. The most important thing to consider when choosing a hook is how it feels in your hand, and the ease with which it works with your yarn.

When you have discovered your perfect brand of hook, it is useful to buy a range of several different sizes so that they are always available to you. Store your hooks in a clean container such as a cosmetic bag. If the hook you are using starts to feel greasy or sticky, wash it in warm water with a little detergent, rinse with clean water and dry thoroughly.

## COMMON HOOKS

The most common types of hooks are made from aluminium or plastic, and they come in a wide range of sizes to suit different yarn weights. Handmade wooden and horn hooks are also available, many featuring decorative handles.

## SMALL HOOKS

Small sizes of steel hooks are made for working crochet with fine cotton yarns (this type of fine work is sometimes called thread crochet). These hooks often have plastic handles to give a better grip.

## DOUBLE-ENDED HOOKS

These have a different size of hook at each end. This example has a thumb plate in the middle, but many double-ended hooks have a straight shaft and can be used for adapted Tunisian crochet patterns.

## SPECIALISED HOOKS

Specialist hooks with easy-to-hold handles are useful additions to a hook collection.

USEFUL YARN/HOOK COMBINATIONS
Refer to page 152 for recommended hook sizes to use with different weights of yarn to achieve commonly used tension ranges.

**LARGE KNITTING NEEDLES OR BROOMSTICK PINS**
Plastic needles are easier to manoeuvre when working broomstick crochet.

**STITCH MARKERS**
These can be looped through stitches to mark a particular point in a pattern.

**TAPE MEASURE**
Look for measures with both centimetres and inches marked along their length.

**LARGE-HEADED PINS**
Use these for securing fabric before seaming and for marking stitches.

**SCISSORS**
Small, sharp scissors are the most useful.

**NEEDLE CASE**
Use this to protect yarn needles and keep them safe.

**YARN NEEDLES**
These have blunt points and long eyes. Bent-tip and tapestry needles are both useful for seaming.

**FLEXIBLE TUNISIAN CROCHET HOOKS**
These are perfect for making large shawls and afghans worked in Tunisian crochet.

**TUNISIAN CROCHET HOOKS**
These look like knitting needles with a hook at one end.

# YARNS AND THREADS

YARNS COME IN A WIDE VARIETY OF MATERIALS, WEIGHTS, COLOURS AND PRICE RANGES.

There is a huge range of yarns available to use for crochet, from very fine cotton to chunky wool. Yarns can be made from one fibre or combine a mixture of two or three different fibres in varying proportions.

## NATURAL FIBRES

Woollen yarns and blended yarns with a high proportion of wool feel good to crochet with because they have a certain amount of stretch. Silk yarn has a delightful lustre, but it is less resilient than either wool or cotton and is more expensive. Yarns made from cotton and linen are durable and cool to wear, but may be blended with other fibres to add softness.

**HANDSPUN YARN**
Look for fibres you like working with and that have a tight, smooth twist if you require good stitch definition.

**WOOL**
Produces a light, stretchy fabric with good drape. [Sample made with 4mm (size F) hook.]

**ALPACA**
Produces a firm fabric with good stitch definition, but with more warmth and loft than cotton. [Sample made with 4mm (size F) hook.]

**MERCERISED COTTON**
Produces a firm fabric with good stitch definition. [Sample made with 4mm (size F) hook.]

**SILK**
Good stitch definition and drape.

**LINEN**
Crisp, with good stitch definition; the fabric softens with washing and wear. [Sample made with 4mm (size F) hook.]

**TWEED WOOL BLEND**
Light and stretchy, the fabric improves with age, but a strong tweed effect can dull the stitch definition. [Sample made with 4mm (size F) hook.]

## SYNTHETIC YARNS

Yarns made wholly from synthetic fibres, such as acrylic or nylon, are usually less expensive to buy than those made from natural fibres, but can pill when worn and lose their shape. A good solution is to choose a yarn with a small proportion of synthetic fibres combined with a natural fibre, such as wool or cotton.

Self-striping cotton

Fine crochet cotton

Silk rolls

Crochet cotton with lurex

### KID MOHAIR

The twist and treatment of mohair can make it more or less fluffy.

### KID MOHAIR/SILK BLEND

Produces a fine, open fabric with good drape and texture. [Sample made with 4mm (size F) hook. A smaller hook would produce better stitch definition, but the nature of the yarn would be lost.]

### FINE CROCHET COTTONS AND THREADS

A variety of fibres can be spun into threads and used for crochet. The nature of the fabric is dictated by the fibre content, but it is also influenced by hook size. Rolls of silk thread are perfect for tiny edgings and flowers. Shiny rayons are strong and durable. Cotton and lurex blends are available if you want glitter. [Sample made with 1.5mm (size 7) steel hook.]

Rayon

Fine crochet cotton

### SILK RIBBON YARN

Produces a chunky, open fabric with good drape and texture. [Sample made with 6.5mm (size K) hook.]

### SOCK YARN

The addition of some nylon to the wool or cotton strengthens the fabric but has little effect on the stitches. [Sample made with 3mm (size C/D) hook.]

### SILK AND BEADS

This yarn has been spun with a length of beaded thread. The random beading would be more visible on an open mesh fabric. [Sample made with 5mm (size H) hook.]

### UNUSUAL YARN COMBINATIONS

Spinners strive to intrigue and seduce crocheters with unusual yarns, and the only clues are the fibre content and the twist – sometimes only a swatch will reveal a yarn's true beauty.

# BASIC SKILLS

TO BEGIN PRACTISING CROCHET, CHOOSE A SMOOTH, WOOLLEN DOUBLE KNITTING (DK) OR 4PLY YARN AND A 4MM (SIZE F) HOOK. WOOLLEN YARN HAS A CERTAIN AMOUNT OF 'GIVE', MAKING IT VERY EASY TO WORK WITH FOR BEGINNERS.

### SEE ALSO
• Equipment, pages 10–11
• Yarns and threads, pages 12–13

## HOLDING THE HOOK

There is no right or wrong way to hold a hook, but these suggestions may make it easier.

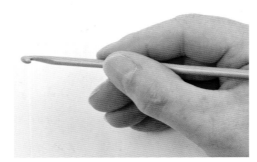

This is the most widely used way of holding the hook, as if it were a pen. Centre the tips of your right thumb and forefinger over the flat section of the hook.

Another way of holding the hook is to grasp the flat section of the hook between your right thumb and forefinger as if you were holding a knife.

## MAKING A SLIP KNOT

1 Leaving a 15cm (6in) tail of yarn, loop the yarn around your left forefinger. Carefully slip the loop off your finger and hold it in your left hand, with the tail of yarn hanging down behind the loop. Using the tail end of the yarn, push a second loop through the first loop.

2 Insert the hook into the second loop. Gently pull the tail end of the yarn to tighten the loop around the hook and complete the slip knot.

## HOLDING THE YARN

To control the yarn supply, loop the tail end of the yarn over your left forefinger, and take the yarn coming from the ball loosely around the little finger of the same hand for tension. Use your middle finger to help hold the work as you crochet. If it feels more comfortable, tension the yarn around your ring finger instead.

**WORKING A CHAIN STITCH**

**1** Holding the hook with the slip knot in your right hand, and the yarn in your left, wrap the yarn over the hook. This is known as yarn over, or yarn over hook, and unless instructed otherwise, you should always wrap the yarn over the hook in this way.

**2** Draw the yarn through the slip knot to make a new loop on the hook. This completes the first chain stitch.

**3** Repeat step 2, drawing a new loop of yarn through the loop on the hook until the chain of stitches is the required length. Move up the thumb and finger that are grasping the chain after every few stitches to keep the tension even.

**Tip**

*When working slip stitches to close rounds of crochet, or to move hook and yarn to a new position, take care not to work the slip stitches too tightly because this will pucker the crochet fabric.*

**WORKING A SLIP STITCH**

Slip stitch is rarely used to create a crochet fabric on its own. Instead, it is used to join rounds of crochet, and to move the hook and yarn across a group of existing stitches to a new position. To work a slip stitch, insert the hook from front to back into the stitch specified in the pattern. In this case, the hook is inserted under the top loop of a chain stitch. Wrap the yarn over the hook and draw it through both the stitch and the loop on the hook. This completes one slip stitch and leaves one loop on the hook.

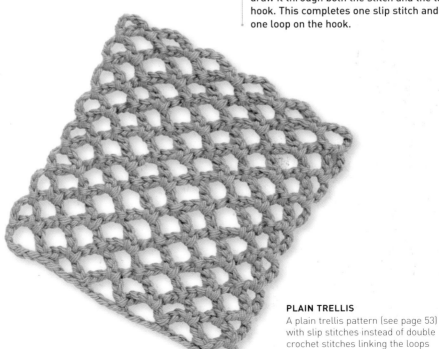

**PLAIN TRELLIS**
A plain trellis pattern (see page 53) with slip stitches instead of double crochet stitches linking the loops of chain stitches.

# FOUNDATION CHAINS

THE FOUNDATION CHAIN IS THE CROCHET EQUIVALENT OF CASTING ON IN KNITTING. IT IS THE FOUNDATION FROM WHICH YOUR CROCHET FABRIC GROWS.

### SEE ALSO

• Basic skills, pages 14–15

It is important to make sure that you have made the required number of chain stitches for the pattern you are going to work. The front of the foundation chain looks like a series of V-shapes or little hearts, while the back of the chain forms a distinctive 'bump' of yarn behind each V-shape. Count the stitches on either the front or back of the chain, whichever you find easier.

## COUNTING CHAINS

Count each V-shaped loop on the front of the chain as one chain stitch, except for the loop on the hook, which should not be counted. Alternatively, you may find it easier to turn the chain over and count the stitches on the back of the chain.

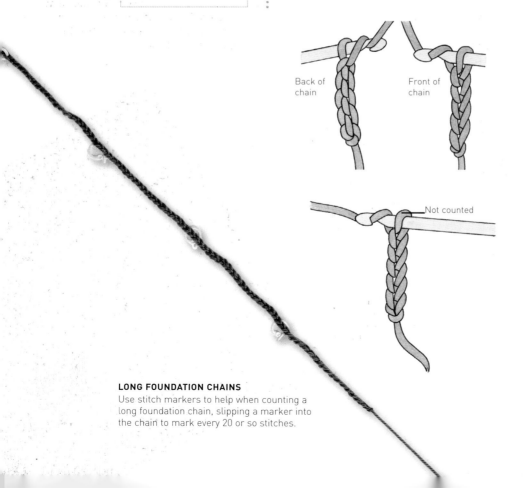

Back of chain

Front of chain

Not counted

**LONG FOUNDATION CHAINS**
Use stitch markers to help when counting a long foundation chain, slipping a marker into the chain to mark every 20 or so stitches.

## WORKING INTO THE FOUNDATION CHAIN

**1** The first row of stitches is worked into the foundation chain. The hook can be inserted into the chain in different ways, but the method described here is the easiest one for a beginner, although it does give the crochet a rather loose edge. Holding the chain with the front facing you, insert the hook from front to back under the top loop of the appropriate chain stitch and work the first stitch as specified in the pattern.

**2** To make a stronger, neater edge that can stand alone without an edge finish being needed, turn the chain so that the back of it is facing you. Work the first row of stitches as instructed in the pattern, inserting the hook through the 'bump' at the back of each chain stitch.

### Tip

*When working a foundation chain, most crocheters prefer to use a hook that is one size larger than the size used for the main crochet. This makes it easier to insert the hook when working the next row and stops the edge of the crochet from being too tight.*

# TURNING AND STARTING CHAINS

WHEN WORKING CROCHET IN ROWS OR ROUNDS, YOU WILL NEED TO WORK A SPECIFIC NUMBER OF EXTRA CHAIN STITCHES BEFORE BEGINNING EACH NEW ROW OR ROUND. THE EXTRA CHAINS ARE NEEDED TO BRING THE HOOK UP TO THE CORRECT HEIGHT FOR THE PARTICULAR CROCHET STITCH YOU WILL BE WORKING NEXT.

### SEE ALSO
• Basic skills, pages 14–15

When the work is turned in order to begin a new row, the extra chains are called a turning chain. When the extra chains are worked at the beginning of a new round, they are called a starting chain. The illustration below shows the correct number of chain stitches needed to make a turn for each type of crochet stitch. If you tend to work chain stitches very tightly, you may need to work an extra chain in order to stop the edges of your work from becoming too tight. If you tend to work your chains loosely, then you may decide to work one less chain than specified in the pattern.

| | |
|---|---|
| Double crochet stitch | 1 turning chain |
| Half treble crochet stitch | 2 turning chains |
| Treble crochet stitch | 3 turning chains |
| Double treble crochet stitch | 4 turning chains |

The turning or starting chain is usually counted as the first stitch of the row. For example, ch 3 (counts as 1 tr) at the beginning of a row or round means that the turning or starting chain contains three chain stitches, and these are counted as the equivalent of one treble crochet stitch. The exception is double crochet, when the single turning chain is ignored rather than being counted as a stitch. A turning or starting chain may be longer than the number required for the stitch, and in that case counts as one stitch plus a number of chains. For example, ch 5 (counts as 1 tr, ch 2) means that the turning or starting chain is the equivalent of one treble crochet stitch plus two chains.

At the end of the row or round, the final stitch is usually worked into the turning or starting chain of the previous row or round. The final stitch may be worked into the top chain stitch of the turning or starting chain, or into another specified stitch of the chain. For example, 1 tr into 3rd of ch 3 means that the final stitch is a treble crochet stitch and should be worked into the 3rd stitch of the turning or starting chain.

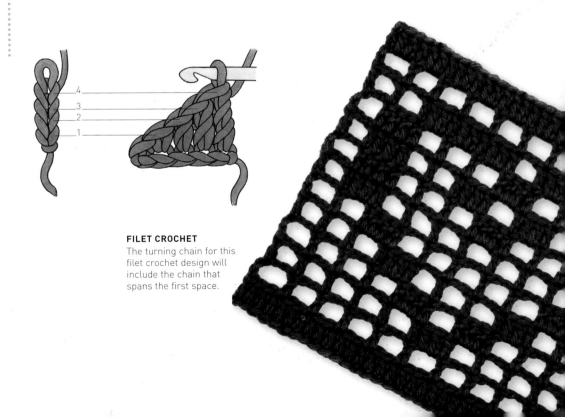

**FILET CROCHET**
The turning chain for this filet crochet design will include the chain that spans the first space.

# DOUBLE CROCHET STITCH

ONLY A SLIP STITCH OR CHAIN STITCH IS SHORTER THAN THE DOUBLE CROCHET STITCH. DOUBLE CROCHET CREATES A TIGHT, DENSE FABRIC.

**SEE ALSO**
..............
• Foundation and turning chains, pages 16–17

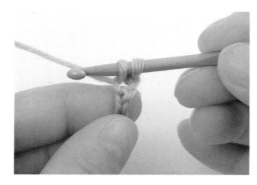

**1** Work the foundation chain, then insert the hook from front to back under the top loop of the second chain from the hook. Wrap the yarn over the hook and draw it through the chain, leaving two loops on the hook.

**2** To complete the stitch, wrap the yarn over the hook and draw it through both loops on the hook. Continue in this way along the row, working one double crochet stitch into each chain.

**3** At the end of the row, work one chain for the turning chain and turn (remember that this turning chain does not count as a stitch).

**4** Insert the hook from front to back under both loops of the first double crochet stitch at the beginning of the row and work a double crochet stitch. Continue in this way, working a double crochet stitch into each remaining stitch made on the previous row. At the end of the row, work the final double crochet into the last stitch of the row below, not into the turning chain.

# HALF TREBLE CROCHET STITCH

SLIGHTLY TALLER THAN THE DOUBLE CROCHET STITCH, THE HALF TREBLE CROCHET STITCH CREATES A FABRIC WITH A SOFT, DENSE TEXTURE.

### SEE ALSO
• Foundation and turning chains, pages 16–17

1  Work the foundation chain, then wrap the yarn over the hook and insert the hook from front to back under the top loop of the third chain from the hook.

2  Draw the yarn through the chain, leaving three loops on the hook.

3  Wrap the yarn over the hook and draw it through all three loops on the hook. This completes one half treble crochet stitch and leaves one loop on the hook.

4  Continue in this way along the row, working one half treble crochet stitch into each chain. At the end of the row, work two chains for the turning chain and turn.

5  Skipping the first half treble crochet stitch at the beginning of the row, wrap the yarn over the hook, insert the hook from front to back under both loops of the second half treble crochet stitch on the previous row, and work a half treble crochet stitch. Continue in this way, working a half treble crochet stitch into each remaining stitch made on the previous row. At the end of the row, work the last stitch into the top stitch of the turning chain.

# TREBLE CROCHET STITCH

TREBLE CROCHET IS A POPULAR STITCH THAT IS OFTEN USED IN FILET CROCHET AS WELL AS IN MANY OTHER CROCHET FABRICS.

**SEE ALSO**
• Foundation and turning chains, pages 16–17

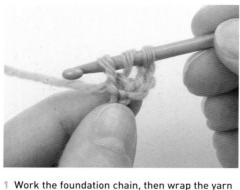

**1** Work the foundation chain, then wrap the yarn over the hook and insert the hook from front to back under the top loop of the fourth chain from the hook. Draw the yarn through the chain, leaving three loops on the hook.

**2** Wrap the yarn over the hook again and draw it through the first two loops on the hook, leaving two loops on the hook.

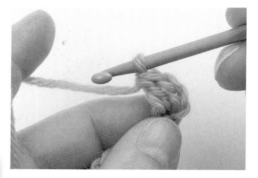

**3** Wrap the yarn over the hook once more and draw it through the two loops on the hook. This completes one treble crochet stitch and leaves one loop on the hook.

**4** Continue in this way along the row, working one treble crochet stitch into each chain. At the end of the row, work three chains for the turning chain and turn.

**5** Skipping the first treble crochet stitch at the beginning of the row, wrap the yarn over the hook, insert the hook from front to back under both loops of the second treble crochet stitch on the previous row, and work a treble crochet stitch. Continue in this way, working a treble crochet stitch into each remaining stitch made on the previous row. At the end of the row, work the last stitch into the top stitch of the turning chain.

# DOUBLE TREBLE CROCHET STITCH

DOUBLE TREBLE IS A TALL STITCH WITH A LOOSE TEXTURE. IT IS RARELY WORKED ON ITS OWN IN COMPLETE ROWS TO PRODUCE A FABRIC.

### SEE ALSO
• Foundation and turning chains, pages 16–17

**1** Work the foundation chain, then wrap the yarn over the hook twice and insert the hook from front to back under the top loop of the fifth chain from the hook. Wrap the yarn over the hook again and draw the yarn through the chain, leaving four loops on the hook.

**2** Wrap the yarn over the hook again and draw it through the first two loops on the hook (leaving three loops on the hook). Wrap the yarn over the hook again and draw it through the first two loops on the hook (leaving two loops on the hook).

**3** Wrap the yarn over the hook once more and draw it through the remaining two loops on the hook. This completes one double treble crochet stitch and leaves one loop on the hook.

**4** At the end of the row, work four chains for the turning chain and turn. Wrap the yarn twice over the hook and insert the hook from front to back under both loops of the second stitch on the previous row, and work a double treble crochet stitch as before. At the end of the row, work the last double treble crochet stitch into the top stitch of the turning chain.

# MEASURING TENSION

THE TERM 'TENSION' REFERS TO THE NUMBER OF STITCHES AND ROWS CONTAINED IN A GIVEN WIDTH AND LENGTH OF CROCHET FABRIC. CROCHET PATTERNS INCLUDE A RECOMMENDED TENSION FOR THE YARN THAT HAS BEEN USED TO MAKE THE ITEM SHOWN. IT IS IMPORTANT THAT YOU MATCH THIS TENSION EXACTLY SO THAT YOUR WORK COMES OUT THE RIGHT SIZE.

**SEE ALSO**

• Pressing and blocking, pages 28–29

Tension measurements are usually quoted as a specified number of stitches and rows to 10cm (4in) measured over a certain stitch pattern using a certain size of hook. The information may also include a measurement taken across one or more pattern repeats. Working to the suggested tension will ensure that the crochet fabric is neither too heavy and stiff, nor too loose and floppy. Yarn ball bands or tags may also quote a recommended tension as well as provide information on the yarn's fibre composition, length and aftercare. Always try to use the exact yarn quoted in the pattern instructions. Two yarns of the same weight and fibre content made by different manufacturers will vary slightly in thickness.

Tension can be affected by the type of yarn used, the size and brand of the crochet hook, the type of stitch pattern and the tension of an individual crocheter. No two people will crochet to exactly the same tension, even when working with the identical hook and yarn. How you hold the hook, and the rate at which the yarn flows through your fingers, will affect the tension you produce. Crochet fabric has less 'give' and elasticity than a comparable knitted fabric, so it is crucial to make and measure a tension swatch before you begin making any item. Accessories (bags, hats) and items of home furnishings (cushion covers, lace edgings) are often worked to a tighter tension than scarves, garments and afghans, which need a softer type of fabric with better drape.

**MAKING AND MEASURING A TENSION SAMPLE**
Refer to the pattern instructions to find the recommended tension. Working with the yarn and hook you will use for the item, make a generously sized sample 15–20cm (6–8in) wide. If you are working a stitch pattern, choose a number of foundation chains to suit the stitch repeat. Work in the required pattern until the piece is 15–20cm (6–8in) long. Fasten off the yarn. Block the tension sample using the method suited to the yarn composition and allow to dry.

**1** Lay the sample right side uppermost on a flat surface and use a ruler or tape measure to measure 10cm (4in) horizontally across a row of stitches. Mark this measurement by inserting two pins exactly 10cm (4in) apart. Make a note of the number of stitches (including partial stitches) between the pins. This is the number of stitches to 10cm (4in).

Recommended tension

50g • 1.75oz
100m • 110yds

55% Cotton • Coton
45% Nylon • Nylon

Purchase sufficient yarn of this dye lot because the next lot may differ slightly in shade.

**BALL BANDS**
Most yarn ball bands or tags carry information on recommended tension. However, this is only a guide. Project information and your own judgement are more important.

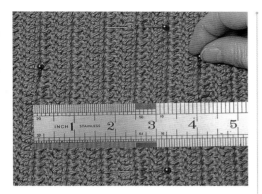

**2** Turn the sample on its side. Working in the same way, measure 10cm (4in) across the rows, again inserting two pins exactly 10cm (4in) apart. Make a note of the number of rows (including partial rows) between the pins. This is the number of rows to 10cm (4in).

When working a particular stitch pattern, tension information may be quoted as a multiple of the pattern repeat, rather than as a set number of rows and stitches. Work your tension sample in pattern, but this time count repeats instead of rows and stitches between the pins.

## HOW TO ADJUST THE TENSION

If you have more stitches or pattern repeats between the pins inserted in your tension sample, your tension is too tight and you should make another sample using a hook one size larger. If you have fewer stitches or pattern repeats between the pins inserted in your tension sample, your tension is too loose and you should make another sample using a hook one size smaller. Block the new sample and measure the tension as before. Repeat this process until your tension matches that given in the pattern.

## COMPARING TENSION

Each of the three swatches on the right has 20 stitches and nine rows of treble crochet worked in the same weight of yarn but using different sizes of hook. As well as altering the size of the swatch, the hook also affects the drape and handle of the crochet. Swatch 1 feels hard and stiff, while swatch 3 feels loose and floppy. Swatch 2 feels substantial but still has good drape.

### Tip

*The tension may vary slightly as you work on a project. On some days you may be tense and work more tightly, while on other days your attention may wander and your tension slacken. Check your tension periodically as you work.*

**SWATCH 1**
Double knitting yarn worked with a 3mm (size C/D) hook.

**SWATCH 2**
Double knitting yarn worked with a 4mm (size F) hook.

**SWATCH 2**
Double knitting yarn worked with a 5.5mm (size J) hook.

# JOINING, FASTENING OFF AND WEAVING IN YARNS

THERE ARE A NUMBER OF METHODS YOU CAN USE TO JOIN A NEW BALL OF YARN INTO YOUR CROCHET. THE METHOD YOU CHOOSE CAN DEPEND ON WHETHER YOU ARE CONTINUING IN THE SAME COLOUR OR INTRODUCING A NEW ONE.

## JOINING YARN

When working in one colour, try to join in a new ball of yarn at the end of the row rather than in the middle to make the join less noticeable. You can do this at the end of the row you are working by making an incomplete stitch and then using the new yarn to finish the stitch. Alternatively, join the new yarn at the beginning of the row you are about to work using the slip stitch method. When working colour patterns, join the new colour of yarn wherever the pattern or chart indicates by leaving the last stitch in the old colour incomplete and using the new colour to finish the stitch.

## JOINING A NEW YARN IN DOUBLE CROCHET

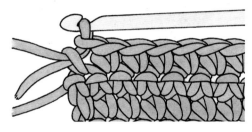

1  Join the new colour at the end of the last row worked in the previous colour. To work the last stitch, draw a loop of the old yarn through so that there are two loops on the hook. Loop the new yarn around the hook, then pull it through both loops on the hook. Turn and work the next row with the new colour.

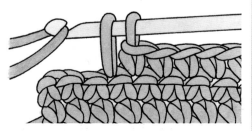

2  When working colour patterns, join the new yarn colour where the pattern or chart indicates. Leave the last stitch worked in the old colour incomplete and proceed as above.

## JOINING A NEW YARN IN TREBLE CROCHET

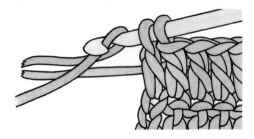

1  Join the new colour at the end of the last row worked in the previous colour. Leaving the last stage of the final stitch incomplete, loop the new yarn around the hook and pull it though the loops on the hook to complete the stitch.

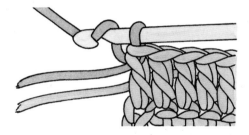

2  Turn and work the next row with the new colour. You may find it easier to knot the two loose ends together before you cut the yarn no longer in use, leaving an end of about 10cm (4in). Always undo the knot before weaving in the yarn ends.

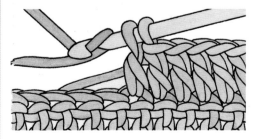

3  When working colour patterns, join the new yarn colour where the pattern or chart indicates. Leave the last stitch worked in the old colour incomplete and proceed as above.

## JOINING A NEW YARN USING SLIP STITCH

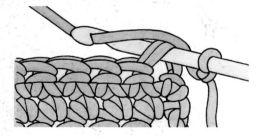

This method can be used when working any stitch. At the beginning of the row, make a slip knot in the new yarn and place it on the hook. Insert the hook into the first stitch of the row and make a slip stitch with the new yarn through both stitch and slip knot. Continue along the row using the new yarn.

## FASTENING OFF AND WEAVING IN YARN

It is very easy to fasten off yarn when you have finished a piece of crochet, but do not to cut the yarn too close to the work because you will need enough yarn to weave in the yarn end.

It is important to fasten off and weave in yarn ends securely so that they do not unravel in wear or during laundering. Try to do this as neatly as possible, so that the woven yarn does not show through on the front of the work.

### WEAVING IN YARN ENDS ON A STRIPE PATTERN

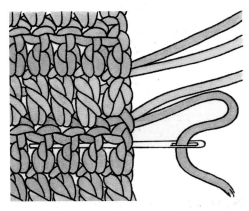

### FASTENING OFF YARN

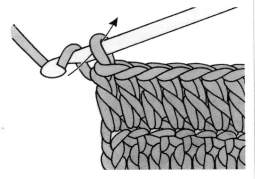

**1** Cut the yarn about 15cm (6in) from the last stitch. Wrap the yarn over the hook and draw the yarn end through the loop on the hook.

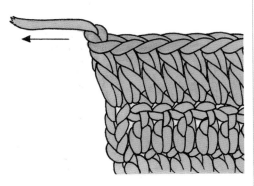

**2** Gently pull the yarn to tighten the last stitch, then weave in the yarn end on the wrong side of the work.

### WEAVING IN A YARN END AT THE TOP EDGE

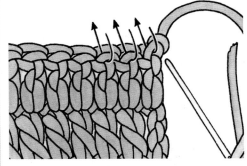

To weave in a yarn end along the top edge of a piece of crochet, start by threading the end into a yarn or tapestry needle. Take the needle through several stitches on the wrong side of the crochet, working stitch by stitch. Trim the remaining yarn.

### WEAVING IN A YARN END AT THE LOWER EDGE

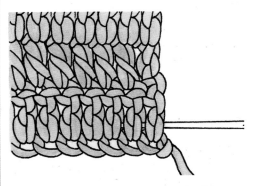

To weave in a yarn end along the lower edge of a piece of crochet, start by threading the end into a yarn or tapestry needle. Take the needle through several stitches on the wrong side of the crochet, then trim the remaining yarn.

When weaving in yarn ends on a stripe pattern, or when using more than one yarn colour, it pays to take a little more care in order to avoid the colours showing through on the right side of the fabric. Undo the knot securing the two yarn ends, thread the yarn or tapestry needle with one colour, and weave in the end on the wrong side of the same colour of stripe. Repeat with the second colour.

### DECORATIVE FEATURE
Yarns ends can become part of the design.

# READING PATTERNS AND CHARTS

CROCHET PATTERNS COME IN DIFFERENT FORMS. THERE IS THE WRITTEN TYPE WHERE YOU MUST FOLLOW THE WRITTEN INSTRUCTIONS LINE BY LINE. THE SAME INSTRUCTIONS CAN ALSO BE SHOWN AS A SYMBOL CHART, WHICH MAY ACCOMPANY WRITTEN INSTRUCTIONS OR REPLACE THEM ENTIRELY. A FILET CROCHET DESIGN IS USUALLY SHOWN AS A BLACK-AND-WHITE CHART GIVING THE POSITION OF THE BLOCKS AND SPACES THAT MAKE UP THE DESIGN. JACQUARD AND INTARSIA PATTERNS HAVE THEIR OWN TYPE OF CHARTS WHERE EACH STITCH IS REPRESENTED BY A BLOCK OF COLOUR, IN THE SAME WAY AS A CHART FOR A CROSS-STITCH DESIGN.

## SEE ALSO

• Filet crochet,
  pages 56–59
• Jacquard patterns,
  pages 68–69
• Intarsia patterns,
  pages 70–71
• Abbreviations and
  symbols, pages 150–151

## WRITTEN INSTRUCTIONS

At first sight the terminology of crochet can look rather complicated. The most important thing to remember when following a pattern is to check that you start off with the correct number of stitches in the foundation chain or ring, and then work through the instructions exactly as stated.

In a written pattern, square brackets and asterisks are used to make the pattern shorter and to avoid tedious repetition. Instructions may be phrased slightly differently depending on whether square brackets or asterisks are used, and both may be used together in the same pattern row of a complex design. The sequence of stitches enclosed inside square brackets must be worked as instructed.

For example, [1 tr into each of next 2 sts, ch 2] 3 times means that you will work the two treble crochet stitches and the two chains three times in all. The instruction may also be expressed like this: * 1 tr into each of next 2 sts, ch 2; rep from * twice. The information is exactly the same, but it is stated in a slightly different way.

You may also find asterisks used in instructions. These tell you how to work any stitches remaining after the last complete repeat of a stitch sequence is worked. For example, rep from * to end, ending with 1 tr into each of last 2 sts, turn, means that you have two stitches left at the end of the row after working the last repeat. In this case, work one treble crochet stitch into each of the last two stitches before turning to begin the next row.

You will also find round brackets in written instructions. They usually contain extra information, not instructions that have to be worked. For example, Row 1: (RS) means that the right side of the work is facing you as you work this row. Round brackets are also used to indicate the number of different sizes in which a garment pattern is worked, as well as the different numbers of stitches. In this case, it is helpful to read right through the pattern and highlight the corresponding numbers as an aid to easy reading. You may also find a number enclosed in round brackets at the end of a row

## WRITTEN PATTERNS

Written patterns use abbreviations to save space and avoid repetition.

**FOUNDATION RING:** Ch 6 and join with sl st to form a ring.
**ROUND 1:** Ch 3 (counts as 1 tr), 15 tr into ring, join with sl st into 3rd of ch 3. (16 tr)
**ROUND 2:** Ch 5 (counts as 1 tr, ch 2), [1 tr into next tr, ch 2] 15 times, join with sl st into 3rd of ch 5.
**ROUND 3:** Ch 3, 2 tr into ch 2 sp, ch 1, [3 tr, ch 1] into each ch 2 sp to end, join with sl st into 3rd of ch 3.
**ROUND 4:** * [Ch 3, 1 dc into next ch 1 sp] 3 times, ch 6 (corner sp made), 1 dc into next ch 1 sp; rep from * to end, join with sl st into first of ch 3.

Round brackets

Square brackets

Asterisks

or round – this indicates the total number of stitches you have worked in that particular row or round. For example, (12 tr) at the end of a round means that you have worked 12 treble crochet stitches in the round.

Each crochet stitch pattern worked in rows is written using a specific number of pattern rows and the sequence is repeated until the piece of crochet is the correct length. When working a complicated pattern, always make a note of exactly which row you are working because it is very easy to forget this if your crochet session gets interrupted.

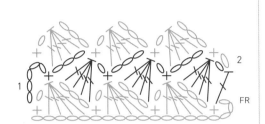

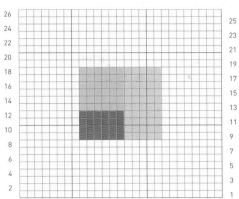

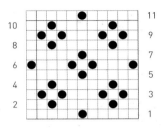

## SYMBOL CHARTS

Some crochet patterns use symbol charts to describe the method of working visually. Symbols indicate the different stitches and where and how they should be placed in relation to one another. A symbol chart will still contain some written instructions, but the stitch patterns are shown in a visual form and not written out line by line. Each row will either be shown in a colour that echoes the colour used for the swatch, or alternate rows will be in tints of the colour so that it is easier to follow progress along the row.

To use a symbol chart, first familiarise yourself with the different symbols. There is a key to the symbols used in the charts on pages 150–151. Each symbol represents a single instruction or stitch and indicates where to work the stitch. Follow the numerical sequence on the chart whether you are working in rows or rounds.

## COLOUR BLOCK CHARTS

Jacquard and intarsia patterns are shown as a coloured chart on a grid. Each coloured square on the chart represents one stitch and you should always work upwards from the bottom of the chart, reading odd-numbered (right side) rows from right to left and even-numbered (wrong side) rows from left to right.

Begin by working the foundation chain in the first colour, then work the pattern from the chart, starting at the bottom right-hand corner and joining in new colours as they occur in the design. On the first row, work the first stitch into the second chain from the hook, then work the rest of the row in double crochet.

## FILET CROCHET CHARTS

Filet crochet charts are numbered at the sides and you should follow the numbered sequence upwards from the bottom of the chart, working from side to side. Each open square on the chart represents one space and each solid square represents a block.

Tiny flowers pattern (see page 59) worked from a filet crochet chart.

Intarsia block (see page 71) worked from a colour block chart.

Angled clusters pattern (see page 40) worked from a symbol chart.

# PRESSING AND BLOCKING

A LIGHT PRESS ON THE WRONG SIDE WITH A COOL IRON IS OFTEN ALL THE TREATMENT THAT PIECES OF CROCHET NEED BEFORE BEING STITCHED TOGETHER, BUT SOME PIECES, SUCH AS GARMENT SECTIONS AND CROCHETED MOTIFS, WILL NEED MORE ATTENTION.

## BLOCKING A GARMENT AFTER ASSEMBLY

You can block a garment after assembly by immersing the crochet in cool water for a few minutes so that the water penetrates all of the yarn fibres. Do not lift the crochet out, but support it with your hand as you drain away the water. The aim is to avoid stretching the work. Gently squeeze out the excess water but do not wring. Roll the crochet in a towel to blot away excess moisture. Lay the crochet flat on a clean towel and pat it into shape. Leave it in a warm place, away from direct sunlight, to dry completely. This method is useful if you ever need to reshape a garment.

The process of blocking involves easing and pinning the crocheted pieces into the correct shape on a fabric-covered board, then either steaming with an iron or moistening with cold water, depending on the fibre content of the yarn. Always be guided by the information given on the ball band of the yarn because most synthetic fibres are easily damaged by heat. When in doubt, choose the cold water method for blocking synthetic fibres.

Yarns made from most natural fibres (cotton, linen and wool, but not silk, which is more delicate) can be blocked with warm steam. A large item, such as a blanket or throw made in one piece (or from motifs that have been joined together as you go), can be carefully pressed on the wrong side over a well-padded ironing board, using a light touch to avoid crushing the stitches. Do not steam or hot press a crochet piece made from yarns containing synthetic fibres such as nylon or acrylic – you will flatten it and make the yarn limp and lifeless. Instead, use a cool iron or the cold water blocking method.

To block garment pieces and large quantities of separate motifs, it is a good idea to make a blocking board. You can do this inexpensively by covering a 60 x 90cm (24 x 36in) piece of flat

## ROLLING IN A TOWEL

Shaped projects, such as hats and seamed items, may be blocked by soaking them in cold water and rolling them in a towel to remove the excess water. They can then be pulled and eased into shape and left to dry away from direct heat or sunlight. Hats may be placed over an upturned bowl or a hat stretcher to dry.

board (a lightweight pinboard made from cork is ideal) with one or two layers of quilter's wadding. Secure the wadding on the back of the board with staples or drawing pins, then cover with a layer of fabric and secure in the same way. Choose fabric made from cotton so that it can withstand the heat of the iron. A checked pattern is useful so that the lines can help you when pinning out straight edges.

Use plenty of rustproof pins to pin out the pieces, and make sure that the pins have glass rather than plastic heads because plastic will melt when heat is applied. When pinning out long pieces of crochet, such as edgings, work in sections and allow each section to dry completely before moving on to the next section.

## PINNING THE PIECES

Pin out the piece, inserting the pins through both the fabric and wadding layers. Be generous with the amount of pins you use around the edges, and gently ease the crochet into shape before inserting each pin. Unless the piece is heavily textured and needs blocking face up, you can block crochet with either the right side or wrong side facing upwards.

## BLOCKING NATURAL FIBRE YARNS

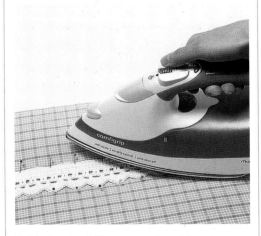

To block natural fibre yarns, pin out the pieces and hold a steam iron set at the correct temperature for the yarn about 2cm (¾in) above the surface of the crochet. Allow the steam to penetrate for several seconds. Work in sections and do not allow the iron to come into contact with the crochet surface. Lay the board flat and allow the crochet to dry before removing the pins.

## BLOCKING SYNTHETIC FIBRE YARNS

To block synthetic fibre yarns, pin out the pieces and use a spray bottle to mist the crochet with cold water until it is evenly moist all over, but not saturated. When blocking heavyweight yarns, gently pat the crochet with your hand to help the moisture penetrate more easily. Lay the board flat and allow the crochet to dry before removing the pins.

> ### Tip
> *If you are planning to block lots of pieces of crochet of the same size, such as square motifs to make an afghan, it is a good idea to make a special blocking board so that you can pin out six or more pieces at a time. Use a pencil to mark the outlines of several squares of the correct dimensions on a piece of plain, light-coloured fabric, allowing about 5cm (2in) of space between the squares for ease of pinning. Use the fabric to cover a blocking board as described opposite.*

# SEAMS

THERE ARE SEVERAL METHODS OF JOINING PIECES OF CROCHET BY SEWING OR USING A CROCHET HOOK. USE THE SAME YARN FOR BOTH CROCHET FABRIC AND SEAMS, UNLESS THE YARN IS THICK OR TEXTURED, IN WHICH CASE USE A FINER YARN OF MATCHING COLOUR.

SEE ALSO
• Basic skills and stitches, pages 14–21

**Tip**

*It is a good idea to try out some of the seams shown here before assembling a project. Crochet a couple of samples in your project stitch, then use contrasting yarn for seaming so that you can easily unpick the seam if you do not like the effect and wish to try a different method.*

## USING A YARN OR TAPESTRY NEEDLE

A back stitch or chain stitch seam is durable and good for joining irregular edges, but can be rather bulky, depending on the weight of the yarn. These methods are good for seaming loose-fitting garments such as winter sweaters and jackets. A woven seam gives a flatter finish because straight edges are joined edge to edge. Woven seams work best when making up fine work and baby garments.

### BACK STITCH SEAM

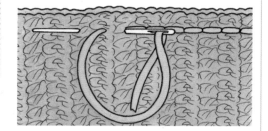

Place the pieces to be joined together with right sides facing and pin together, inserting the pins at right angles to the edge. Thread a yarn or tapestry needle with matching yarn and work a row of back stitches from right to left, one or two stitches away from the edge.

### CHAIN STITCH SEAM

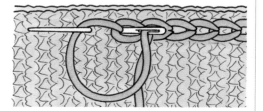

This is the stitched version of the slip stitch seam shown opposite. Place the pieces to be joined together with right sides facing and pin together, inserting the pins at right angles to the edge. Thread a yarn or tapestry needle with matching yarn and work a row of chain stitches from right to left, close to the edge.

### WOVEN SEAM

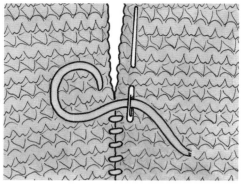

Place the pieces to be joined side by side on a flat surface with wrong sides facing upwards and row ends touching. Thread a yarn or tapestry needle with matching yarn and work a vertical row of evenly spaced stitches in a loose zigzag from edge to edge, carefully tightening the tension of the stitches as you work so that the edges pull together. For a double crochet fabric, pick up one stitch; for treble crochet, pick up half a stitch.

### JOINING UPPER OR LOWER EDGES

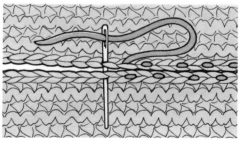

Place the pieces to be joined side by side on a flat surface with wrong sides facing upwards and edges touching. Thread a yarn or tapestry needle with matching yarn and work a horizontal row of evenly spaced stitches, working from edge to edge and carefully tightening the tension of the stitches as you work so that the edges pull together.

## USING A CROCHET HOOK

Double crochet seams are good for joining straight edges because they are less bulky than slip stitch seams. Double crochet seams can also be used on the right side of a garment – work the seams in contrasting yarn to make a decorative statement. Double crochet and chain seams, and alternating slip stitch seams, both give a flatter effect than double crochet seams, and have the advantage of being slightly stretchy.

### SLIP STITCH SEAM

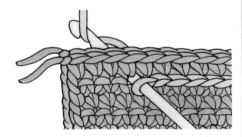

This is the crochet version of the chain stitch seam shown opposite. Place the pieces to be joined together with right sides facing and pin together, inserting the pins at right angles to the edge. Holding the yarn behind the work, insert the hook through both layers of fabric and draw a loop of yarn through both layers, leaving a loop on the hook. Repeat, working from right to left. Secure the yarn end carefully because slip stitch can unravel easily.

### DOUBLE CROCHET SEAM ALONG ROW EDGES

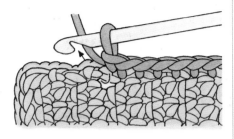

Place the pieces to be joined together with right sides facing for a concealed seam, or wrong sides facing for a decorative seam. Pin the layers together, inserting the pins at right angles to the edge. Holding the yarn behind the work, insert the hook through both layers of fabric and work a row of double crochet stitches close to the edge. Space the stitches so that the work remains flat without stretching or puckering.

### DOUBLE CROCHET SEAM ALONG UPPER OR LOWER EDGES

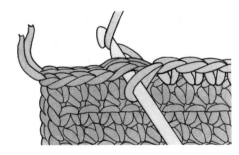

Place the pieces to be joined together with wrong sides facing and edges aligned. Pin the layers together, inserting the pins at right angles to the edge. Holding the yarn behind the work, insert the hook through corresponding stitches on both layers and work a row of double crochet stitches along the edge.

### DOUBLE CROCHET AND CHAIN SEAM

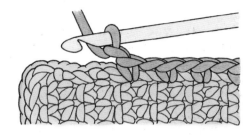

Place the pieces to be joined together with right sides facing and pin together, inserting the pins at right angles to the edge. Holding the yarn behind the work, insert the hook through both layers of fabric and work a double crochet stitch at the beginning of the seam. Work a chain, then work another double crochet stitch a short distance from the first. Repeat evenly along the edge, alternating double crochet stitches and chains, and ending with a double crochet stitch.

### ALTERNATING SLIP STITCH SEAM

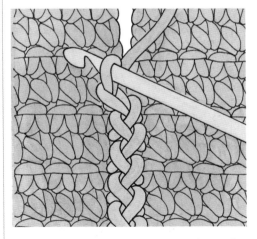

Place the pieces to be joined side by side on a flat surface with wrong sides facing upwards and row ends touching. Work a slip stitch at the bottom corner of the right-hand piece, then work another in the corresponding stitch on the left-hand piece. Continue to work slip stitches along the seam, alternating from side to side.

# CHAPTER TWO
......................
# Techniques and Stitches

This chapter takes you through a wide range of crochet techniques, from working in the round, colourwork and filet crochet to making sew-on embellishments and edgings. Throughout the chapter you will find special stitch collections featuring swatches and instructions for a variety of openwork, lace and textured stitch patterns.

# STRIPE PATTERNS

WORKING STRIPES OF COLOUR IS THE EASIEST WAY TO ADD PATTERN TO A PIECE OF CROCHET THAT IS WORKED IN ONE OF THE BASIC STITCHES. SIMPLE HORIZONTAL STRIPES WORKED IN TWO, THREE OR MORE COLOURS ADD ZING TO A PLAIN GARMENT OR ACCESSORY.

**SEE ALSO**
- Basic skills and stitches, pages 14–21
- Joining yarns, page 24

**USING DIFFERENT YARN WEIGHTS**
Calculate the tension and the number of stitches for the row or round for each yarn weight and work two stitches into one stitch or crochet two stitches together as required.

Stripes can be strongly contrasting in colour, worked in different shades of one colour for a more subtle effect, or combine one basic colour with one or more coordinating colours. Double crochet, half treble crochet and treble crochet all look good worked in stripes.

Working magic stripes is a fun way of using up oddments of yarn that are left over from making other projects. You can use any short lengths of yarn, depending on the width of crochet fabric you are making, but magic stripes look best when the colour changes at least once on every row. Choose yarns of similar weight and fibre composition when making garments, but for accessories and cushion covers you can combine different weights and textures.

## REDUCING THE NUMBER OF YARN ENDS

Instead of breaking off each colour of yarn when you change to another one, you can carry the colours not in use up the side of the work when working some stripe patterns. As well as being faster, this means that you have fewer yarn ends to deal with when you finish crocheting. You can do this when working a stripe pattern with an even number of rows using two colours, or an odd number of rows using three colours.

## WORKING STRIPES WITHOUT BREAKING OFF YARN

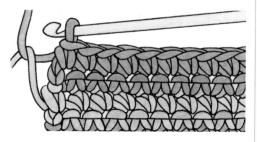

When working patterns of wide stripes that have an even number of rows, carry the colour not in use up the side of the work, but twist the two yarns together every two rows to avoid making big loops at the edge.

## CHANGING YARNS AT THE END OF A ROW

This method works with all crochet stitches.

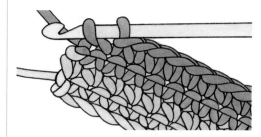

**1** Work the foundation chain and the first two rows using the first colour (yarn A). Join in the second colour (yarn B) without breaking off yarn A. Work to the last stitch, leaving two loops of yarn B on the hook.

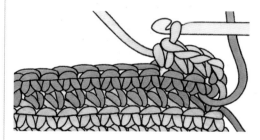

**2** Drop yarn B and pick up yarn A at the side of the work. Complete the stitch with yarn A, turn and work the next two rows using yarn A.

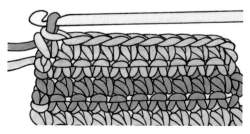

**3** At the end of the second row in yarn A, drop yarn A and complete the final stitch with yarn B. Continue working with yarn B for two rows, then repeat the two-row stripes, alternating the yarn colours as required.

# Stitch collection

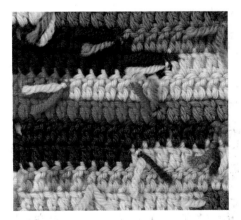

## Random stripes

ANY NUMBER OF CH PLUS TURNING CH

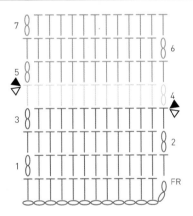

Worked in rows of half treble crochet stitches, the stripes are of different widths and arranged in a random colour sequence. Work several rows in yarn A, then continue working in the same stitch, changing colours randomly, after one, two, three or more rows have been worked.

## Repeating stripes

ANY NUMBER OF CH PLUS TURNING CH

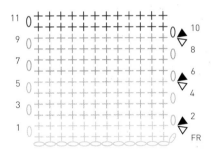

Worked in rows of double crochet stitches, the stripes are of different widths and arranged in a repeating colour sequence. Work two rows in yarn A, four in yarn B, four in yarn C and two in yarn D, then repeat the colour sequence from the beginning. This type of arrangement is also called a sequenced stripe pattern.

## Magic stripes

ANY NUMBER OF CH PLUS TURNING CH

Begin by winding all the yarn lengths into balls and knotting the ends together about 2cm (¾in) from the end, mixing colours at random. Work in rows of treble crochet stitches, pushing the knots through to the same side as you work. You can use either side of the crochet fabric as your right side.

# RIDGE STITCHES

UNLESS A PATTERN INSTRUCTS OTHERWISE, IT IS USUAL TO WORK MOST CROCHET STITCHES BY TAKING THE HOOK UNDER BOTH LOOPS OF THE STITCHES MADE ON THE PREVIOUS ROW. BY WORKING UNDER JUST ONE LOOP, EITHER THE BACK OR THE FRONT LOOP OF A STITCH, THE UNWORKED LOOP BECOMES A HORIZONTAL RIDGE, AND THE CHARACTER AND APPEARANCE OF EVEN THE MOST BASIC CROCHET FABRIC CHANGES.

### SEE ALSO
• Basic skills and stitches, pages 14–21

NEAT EDGES ON A RIDGE STITCH FABRIC
When working crochet stitches taller than double crochet into either the front or back loops of each stitch, you may find that the edges of the fabric become unstable and stretchy. To prevent this, try working into both loops of the first and last stitches on every row.

Ridge stitches are not used for decorative reasons but have practical uses. A row or round of ridge stitches will make the fabric easier to fold at this point, and so they are often used on flaps and collars. For small, fiddly shapes, rounds of stitches are often worked under the back loop only because it is easier to insert a hook under just one loop than under two. The ridges produced on treble crochet are less pronounced than those on double crochet, but the drape and the elasticity of the fabric are greatly improved.

## WORKING INTO THE FRONT LOOP OF DOUBLE CROCHET

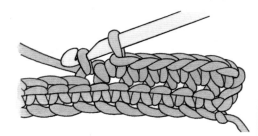

Insert the hook only under the front loop of the stitches on the previous row – the top loop nearest to you as you work the row.

## WORKING INTO THE BACK LOOP OF DOUBLE CROCHET

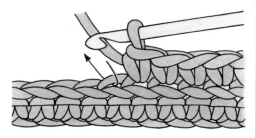

Insert the hook only under the back loop of the stitches on the previous row – the top loop farthest away from you as you work the row. Working into the back loops of a row of double crochet stitches creates a strongly ridged fabric.

## WORKING INTO THE FRONT LOOP OF TREBLE CROCHET

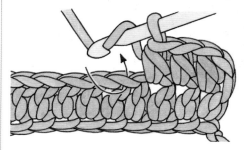

Work in the same way as for double crochet, but when you reach the end of the row, work under the back bump and front loop of the specified stitch of the turning chain.

## WORKING INTO THE BACK LOOP OF TREBLE CROCHET

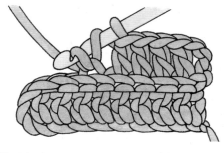

Work in the same way as for double crochet, but when you reach the end of the row, work under the back loop and back bump of the specified stitch of the turning chain.

# Stitch collection

## Wide ridges

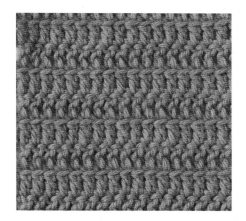

ANY NUMBER OF CHAINS PLUS 3

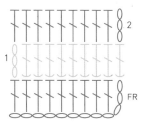

This stitch pattern has a ridged right side and smooth wrong side. The ridged side has fairly subtle ridges that are spaced widely apart.

**FOUNDATION ROW: (RS)** 1 tr into 4th ch from hook, 1 tr into each ch to end, turn.

**ROW 1:** Ch 3 (counts as 1 tr), 1 tr into front loop of each tr to end working last tr into 3rd of beg skipped ch 3, turn.

**ROW 2:** Ch 3 (counts as 1 tr), 1 tr into both loops of each tr to end working last tr into 3rd of ch 3, turn.

Rep rows 1 and 2 for length required, ending with a row 1.

## Faux ribbing

ANY NUMBER OF CHAINS PLUS 1

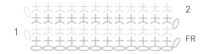

This stitch looks rather like knitted ribbing and both sides are identical. It can be worked in narrow bands to edge cuffs and hems on a crochet garment, or used as a textured pattern stitch in its own right.

**FOUNDATION ROW:** 1 dc into 2nd ch from hook, 1 dc into each ch to end, turn.

**ROW 1:** Ch 1, 1 dc into back loop of each dc to end, turn.

Rep row 1 for length required.

## Simple ridges

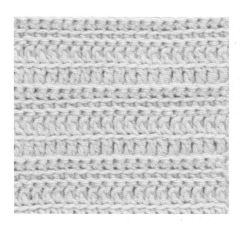

ANY NUMBER OF CHAINS PLUS 3

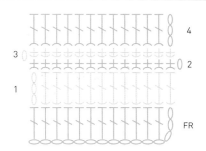

This stitch pattern has a ridged side and a smooth side.

**FOUNDATION ROW:** 1 tr into 4th ch from hook, 1 tr into each ch to end, turn.

**ROW 1:** Ch 3 (counts as 1 tr), 1 tr into front loop of each tr to end working last tr into 3rd of beg skipped ch 3, turn.

**ROW 2:** Ch 1, 1 dc into back loop of each tr to end working last dc into 3rd of ch 3, turn.

**ROW 3:** Ch 1, 1 dc into front loop of each dc to end, turn.

**ROW 4:** Ch 3 (counts as 1 tr), 1 tr into back loop of each dc to end, turn.

Rep rows 1–4 for length required, ending with a row 2.

**KEY TO ABBREVIATIONS AND SYMBOLS pages 150–151**

# SHAPING

THERE ARE SEVERAL DIFFERENT METHODS OF SHAPING YOUR CROCHET GARMENTS BY INCREASING AND DECREASING THE NUMBER OF STITCHES.

**SEE ALSO**

• Basic skills and stitches, pages 14–21

**MITRED BLOCK**
Working an internal decrease (dc3tog) at the centre of every row creates a neat square of double crochet.

### MAKING A NEAT EDGE

To make a neat edge at the beginning of a row, work the first stitch and then work the increase. At the end of a row, work until two stitches remain (the last stitch will probably be the turning chain from the previous row). Work the increase into the penultimate stitch, then work the last stitch as usual.

Adding or subtracting one or two stitches at intervals along a row of crochet is the easiest way of shaping. This process is known as working internal increases or decreases. When groups of stitches are added or subtracted at the beginning and end of specified rows, this is known as working external increases or decreases. The methods can be used with double, half treble, treble and double treble crochet stitches.

### WORKING A SINGLE INTERNAL INCREASE

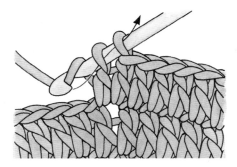

The simplest method of working a single increase (adding a single stitch) at intervals along a row of crochet is by working two stitches into one stitch on the previous row.

### WORKING A DOUBLE INTERNAL INCREASE

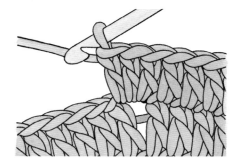

To work a double increase (adding two stitches) at intervals along the row, work three stitches into one stitch on the previous row.

### WORKING AN INTERNAL DECREASE IN DOUBLE CROCHET

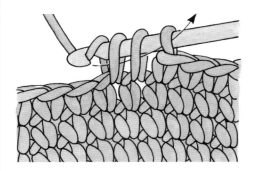

Decrease one double crochet stitch by working two stitches together (dc2tog). Leave the first stitch incomplete so that there are two loops on the hook, then draw the yarn through the next stitch so that you have three loops on the hook. Yarn over and pull through all three loops to finish the decrease. Two stitches can be decreased in the same way by working three stitches together (dc3tog).

### WORKING AN INTERNAL DECREASE IN TREBLE CROCHET

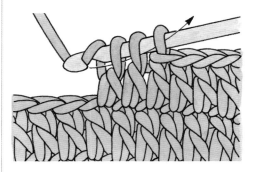

Decrease one treble crochet stitch by working two stitches together (tr2tog). Leave the first stitch incomplete so that there are two loops on the hook, then work another incomplete stitch so that you have three loops on the hook. Yarn over and pull through all three loops to finish the decrease. Two stitches can be decreased in the same way by working three treble crochet stitches together (tr3tog).

## WORKING AN EXTERNAL INCREASE

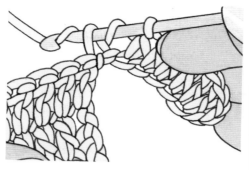

**1** To increase several stitches at one time, you will need to add extra foundation chains at the appropriate end of the row. To add stitches at the beginning of a row, work the required number of extra chains at the end of the previous row. Do not forget to add the correct number of turning chains for the stitch you are using.

**2** Turn and work back along the extra chains, then work along the rest of the row in the usual way. In this case, the stitches have been worked into one loop of the extra chains, but for easier seaming and a firmer edge, work into the bump on the reverse of the chains.

## WORKING AN EXTERNAL DECREASE

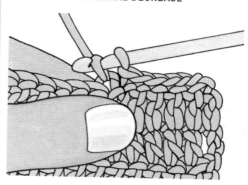

To decrease several stitches at one time at the beginning of a row, turn at the end of the previous row and work a slip stitch into each of the stitches to be decreased, then work the appropriate turning chain and continue along the row. To decrease at the end of a row, simply leave the stitches to be decreased unworked, turn work the appropriate turning chain and continue along the row.

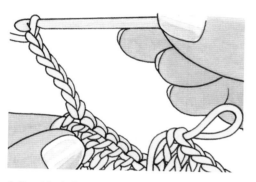

**3** To add stitches at the end of a row, leave the last few stitches of the row unworked and remove the hook. Join a length of yarn to the last stitch of the row and work the required number of extra chains, then fasten off the yarn. Insert the hook back into the row and continue, working extra stitches across the chains. Turn and work the next row in the usual way.

**EXTERNAL INCREASES AND DECREASES**
These have been used to add or subtract groups of stitches at the beginning and end of rows.

**INTERNAL INCREASES AND DECREASES**
These have been used at the beginning and end of rows to shape the edges. They are commonly used on garments.

# CLUSTERS

CLUSTERS ARE GROUPS OF TWO, THREE OR MORE STITCHES THAT ARE JOINED TOGETHER AT THE TOP BY LEAVING THE LAST LOOP OF EACH STITCH ON THE HOOK, THEN DRAWING THE YARN THROUGH ALL THE LOOPS TO SECURE THE STITCH. THIS TECHNIQUE CAN BE USED AS A WAY OF DECREASING ONE OR MORE STITCHES, BUT CLUSTERS CAN ALSO MAKE ATTRACTIVE STITCH PATTERNS IN THEIR OWN RIGHT.

**SEE ALSO**
• Shaping, pages 38–39

**Tip**

*Clusters come in different sizes because they can be worked over two, three or more stitches. Try practising two-stitch clusters first, then move on to making larger ones.*

## WORKING A BASIC TREBLE CROCHET CLUSTER

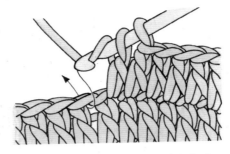

**1** To work a two-stitch treble crochet cluster, wrap the yarn over the hook and work the first stitch, omitting the last stage to leave two loops on the hook.

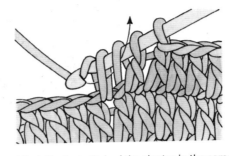

**2** Work the last stitch of the cluster in the same way, resulting in three loops on the hook.

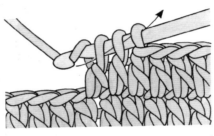

**3** Wrap the yarn over the hook, then draw the yarn through all three loops on the hook to complete the cluster and secure the loops.

## Angled clusters

MULTIPLE OF 5 CHAINS PLUS 4

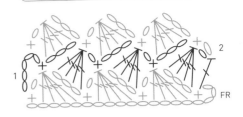

Rows of clusters face in opposite directions, making a beautifully textured crochet fabric. Try working this stitch in two-row stripes of contrasting colours.
**NOTE:** CL = cluster made from four treble crochet stitches worked together (tr4tog).
**FOUNDATION ROW: (RS)** 1 dc into 4th ch from hook, * ch 3, CL over next 4 chs, ch 1, 1 dc into next ch; rep from * to end, turn.
**ROW 1:** Ch 5, 1 dc into first CL, * ch 3, CL into next ch 3 sp, ch 1, 1 dc into next CL; rep from * to last ch 3 sp, ch 3, CL into last ch 3 sp, ch 1, 1 tr into last dc, turn.
**ROW 2:** Ch 1, 1 dc into first CL, * ch 3, CL into next ch 3 sp, ch 1, 1 dc into next CL; rep from * ending last rep with 1 dc into sp made by ch 5, turn.
Rep rows 1 and 2 for length required, ending with a row 2.

# Trinity stitch

**MULTIPLE OF 2 CHAINS**

Trinity stitch is usually worked in one colour and the crochet fabric looks the same on both sides, making this stitch ideal for items such as scarves where both sides can be seen.

**NOTE:** CL = cluster made from three double crochet stitches worked together (dc3tog).

**FOUNDATION ROW:** 1 dc into 2nd ch from hook, CL inserting hook first into same ch as previous dc, then into each of next 2 chs, * ch 1, CL inserting hook first into same ch as 3rd st of previous CL, then into each of next 2 chs; rep from * to last ch, ch 1, 1 dc into same ch as 3rd st of previous CL, turn.

**ROW 1:** Ch 1, 1 dc into first dc, ch 1, CL inserting hook first into first ch 1 sp, then into top of next CL, then into next ch 1 sp, * ch 1, CL inserting hook first into same ch 1 sp as 3rd st of previous CL, then into top of next CL, then into next ch 1 sp; rep from * to end working 3rd st of last CL into last dc, 1 dc into same place, turn. Rep row 1 for length required.

Angled clusters

Trinity stitch

# SHELL STITCHES

SHELL STITCHES ARE FORMED FROM THREE OR MORE STITCHES THAT SHARE THE SAME CHAIN, STITCH OR CHAIN SPACE, RESULTING IN A TRIANGULAR GROUP OF STITCHES THAT LOOKS LIKE A CLAM SHELL. USUALLY, CHAINS OR STITCHES AT EITHER SIDE OF A SHELL ARE SKIPPED TO COMPENSATE FOR THE SHELL, AND EACH STITCH MAKING UP A SHELL IS COUNTED AS ONE STITCH. LARGE GROUPS OF STITCHES FORMED INTO SHELLS ARE KNOWN AS FAN STITCHES.

**SEE ALSO**

• Basic skills and stitches, pages 14–21

**Tip**

*When the first row of a stitch pattern requires you to work fairly large shells directly into the foundation chain, it is a good idea to use a size larger hook when making the chain.*

## WORKING A BASIC TREBLE CROCHET SHELL

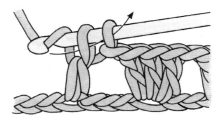

1 Skip the stated number of chains or stitches and work the first treble crochet of the shell into the correct chain or stitch.

2 Work the second treble crochet of the group into the same place as the previous stitch. In the three-stitch shell shown, this stitch forms the centre stitch of the shell.

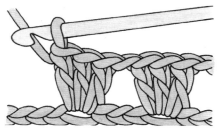

3 Work the remaining stitches of the shell into the same place as the previous stitches.

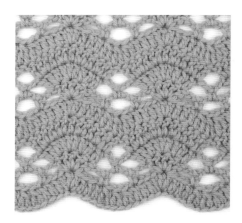

## Generous shells

MULTIPLE OF 13 CHAINS PLUS 4

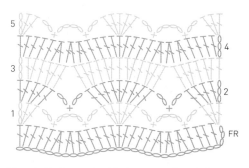

The shell shapes in this large-scale stitch are formed over the course of several rows. Delicate areas of trellis pattern separate each shell to give a lacy touch and lighten the effect.

**FOUNDATION ROW: (RS)** 1 tr into 4th ch from hook, 1 tr into each of next 3 chs, [tr2tog over next 2 chs] 3 times, 1 tr into each of next 3 chs, * 3 tr into next ch, 1 tr into each of next 3 chs, [tr2tog over next 2 chs] 3 times, 1 tr into each of next 3 chs; rep from * to last ch, 2 tr into last ch, turn.

**ROW 1:** Ch 3, 2 tr into first tr, ch 2, sk next 3 tr, 1 dc into next tr, ch 4, sk next 3 tr, 1 dc into next tr, ch 2, * sk next 3 tr, 5 tr into next tr, ch 2, sk next 3 tr, 1 dc into next tr, ch 4, sk next 3 tr, 1 dc into next tr, ch 2; rep from * to last 3 tr, sk last 3 tr, 3 tr into beg skipped ch 3, turn.

**ROW 2:** Ch 3, 1 tr into first tr, 2 tr into next tr, 1 tr into next tr, ch 2, sk next ch 2 sp, 1 dc into next ch 4 sp, ch 2, sk next dc, 1 tr into next tr, 2 tr into next tr, * 3 tr into next tr, 2 tr into next tr, 1 tr into next tr, ch 2, sk next ch 2 sp, 1 dc into next ch 4 sp, ch 2, sk next dc, 1 tr into next tr, 2 tr into next tr; rep from * to turning ch, 2 tr into 3rd of ch 3, turn.

**ROW 3:** Ch 3, [2 tr into next tr, 1 tr into next tr] twice, sk next dc, 1 tr into next tr, * [2 tr into next tr, 1 tr into next tr] 4 times, sk next dc, 1 tr into next tr; rep from * to last 3 tr, 2 tr into next tr, 1 tr into next tr, 2 tr into last tr, 1 tr into 3rd of ch 3, turn.

**ROW 4:** Ch 3, 1 tr into each of first 4 tr, [tr2tog over next 2 tr] 3 times, 1 tr into each of next 3 tr, * 3 tr into next tr, 1 tr into each of next 3 tr, [tr2tog over next 2 tr] 3 times, 1 tr into each of next 3 tr; rep from * to turning ch, 2 tr into 3rd of ch 3, turn.

**ROW 5:** Ch 3, 2 tr into first tr, ch 2, sk next 3 tr, 1 dc into next tr, ch 4, sk next 3 tr, 1 dc into next tr, ch 2, * sk next 3 tr, 5 tr into next tr, ch 2, sk next 3 tr, 1 dc into next tr, ch 4, sk next 3 tr, 1 dc into next tr, ch 2; rep from * to last 3 tr, sk last 3 tr, 3 tr into 3rd of ch 3, turn.

Rep rows 2–5 for length required, ending with a row 4.

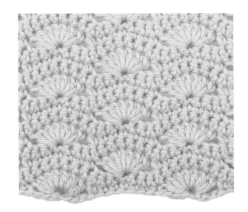

# Alternate shells

> **MULTIPLE OF 14 CHAINS PLUS 4**

This solidly worked stitch has rows of alternately spaced seven-stitch shells, divided by rows of double crochet. Work this stitch in a solid colour or use a hand-painted yarn to get a different look.

**FOUNDATION ROW: (RS)** 3 tr into 4th ch from hook, * sk next 3 chs, 1 dc into each of next 7 chs, sk next 3 chs, 7 tr into next ch; rep from * ending last rep with 4 tr into last ch, turn.

**ROW 1:** Ch 1, 1 dc into each st to end working last dc into 3rd of beg skipped ch 3, turn.

**ROW 2:** Ch 1, 1 dc into each of first 4 sts, sk next 3 sts, 7 tr into next st, sk next 3 sts, 1 dc into each of next 7 sts; rep from * to last 11 sts, sk next 3 sts, 7 tr into next st, sk next 3 sts, 1 dc into each of last 4 sts, sk turning ch 1, turn.

**ROW 3:** Ch 1, 1 dc into each st to end, sk turning ch 1, turn.

**ROW 4:** Ch 3, 3 tr into first st, * sk next 3 sts, 1 dc into each of next 7 sts, sk next 3 sts, 7 tr into next st; rep from * ending last rep with 4 tr into last st, sk turning ch 1, turn.

**ROW 5:** Ch 1, 1 dc into each st to end working last dc into 3rd of ch 3, turn.

Rep rows 2–5 for length required, ending with a row 5.

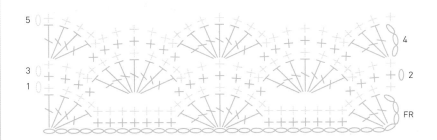

# BOBBLES

A BOBBLE IS A GROUP OF STITCHES, USUALLY TREBLE CROCHET STITCHES, WORKED INTO THE SAME STITCH AT THE BASE AND CLOSED AT THE TOP. WHEN CALCULATING YARN REQUIREMENTS FOR A PROJECT, REMEMBER THAT BOBBLES USE UP MORE YARN THAN MOST OTHER STITCHES.

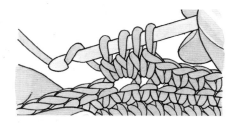

**SEE ALSO**
.................
• Basic skills and stitches, pages 14–21

Made from three, four or five stitches, bobbles are usually worked on wrong side rows and surrounded by flat, solidly worked stitches to throw them into high relief.

**WORKING A BASIC FIVE-STITCH BOBBLE**

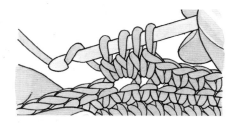

**1** On a wrong side row, work to the position of the bobble. Wrap the yarn over the hook and work the first stitch, omitting the last stage to leave two loops on the hook. Work the second and third stitches in the same way. You now have four loops on the hook.

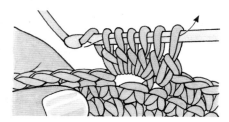

**2** Work the remaining two stitches of the bobble in the same way, resulting in six loops on the hook.

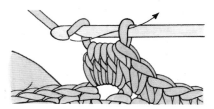

**3** Wrap the yarn over the hook and draw it through all six loops to secure them and complete the bobble. As you do so, gently poke the bobble through to the right side with the tip of a finger.

**Tip**
*When working the right side row following a wrong side bobble row, take care to work one stitch into the securing stitch at the top of each bobble.*

## Stitch collection

### All-over bobbles

MULTIPLE OF 3 CHAINS

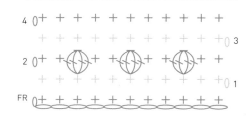

Four-stitch bobbles set against a double crochet background produces a wonderfully textured piece of crochet. This type of stitch is good for making home furnishings such as cushion covers because the fabric is substantial and will keep its shape well.

**NOTE:** MB = make bobble from four treble crochet stitches.

**FOUNDATION ROW: (WS)** 1 dc into 2nd ch from hook, 1 dc into each ch to end, turn.

**ROW 1:** Ch 1, 1 dc into each dc to end, turn.

**ROW 2:** Ch 1, 1 dc into each of first 2 dc, * MB, 1 dc into each of next 2 dc; rep from * to end, turn.

**ROW 3:** Ch 1, 1 dc into each st to end, turn.

**ROW 4:** Ch 1, 1 dc into each dc to end, turn. Rep rows 1–4 for length required, ending with a row 4.

# Alternate bobbles

MULTIPLE OF 4 CHAINS PLUS 3

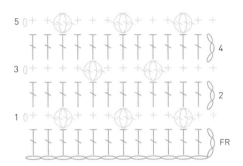

Make a softer feeling fabric by working a row of treble crochet stitches between the bobble rows instead of the more usual double crochet. To make a flatter fabric, simply work three stitches for each bobble instead of four.

**NOTE:** MB = make bobble from four treble crochet stitches.

**FOUNDATION ROW: (RS)** 1 tr into 4th ch from hook, 1 tr into each ch to end, turn.

**ROW 1:** Ch 1, 1 dc into each of first 2 tr, * MB, 1 dc into each of next 3 tr; rep from * to last 3 sts, MB, 1 dc into next tr, 1 dc into 3rd of beg skipped ch 3, turn.

**ROWS 2 AND 4:** Ch 3 (counts as 1 tr), 1 tr into each st to end, turn.

**ROW 3:** Ch 1, 1 dc into each of first 4 tr, * MB, 1 dc into each of next 3 tr; rep from * ending with 1 dc into 3rd of ch 3, turn.

**ROW 5:** Ch 1, 1 dc into each of first 2 tr, * MB, 1 dc into each of next 3 tr; rep from * to last 3 sts, MB, 1 dc into next tr, 1 dc into 3rd of ch 3, turn.

Rep rows 2–5 for length required, ending with a row 4.

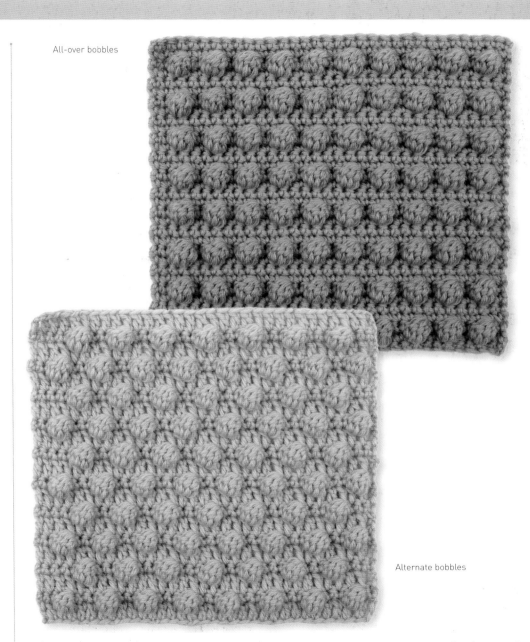

All-over bobbles

Alternate bobbles

# POPCORNS

A POPCORN IS A CLUSTER OF THREE, FOUR OR FIVE TREBLE CROCHET STITCHES THAT IS FOLDED OVER AND CLOSED AT THE TOP WITH A CHAIN. THE POPCORN LOOKS LIKE A TINY FOLDED POCKET THAT STICKS OUT ON THE RIGHT SIDE OF THE CROCHET FABRIC TO GIVE A HIGHLY TEXTURED EFFECT.

**SEE ALSO**
• Basic skills and stitches, pages 14–21

**Tip**
*If you crochet tightly, you may find it easier to use a size smaller hook to work steps 2 and 3, changing back to the usual size for working each group of treble crochet stitches in step 1.*

## WORKING A BASIC FIVE-STITCH POPCORN

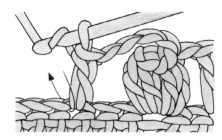

**1** Work a group of five treble crochet stitches into the same chain or stitch.

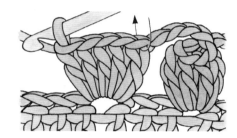

**2** Remove the hook from the working loop and insert it under both loops of the first treble crochet stitch in the group.

**3** To close the popcorn, pick up the working loop with the hook and draw it through to fold the group of stitches and close it at the top. Secure the popcorn by wrapping the yarn over the hook and drawing it through the loop on the hook.

## Stitch collection

### Lacy popcorns

**MULTIPLE OF 8 CHAINS PLUS 2**

This stitch pattern sets vertical rows of single popcorns against a pretty lacy background, and looks good worked in lighter weights of yarn that will accentuate the delicate structure.

**NOTE:** PC = popcorn made from five treble crochet stitches.

**FOUNDATION ROW: (RS)** 1 dc into 2nd ch from hook, * ch 1, sk next 3 chs, [1 tr, ch 1, 1 tr, ch 1, 1 tr, ch 1] into next ch, sk next 3 chs, 1 dc into next ch; rep from * to end, turn.

**ROW 1:** Ch 6 (counts as 1 tr, ch 3), sk first tr, 1 dc into next tr, * ch 3, PC into next dc, ch 3, sk next tr, 1 dc into next tr; rep from * to last dc, ch 3, 1 tr into last dc, turn.

**ROW 2:** Ch 1, 1 dc into first tr, * ch 1, [1 tr, ch 1, 1 tr, ch 1, 1 tr] into next dc, ch 1, 1 dc into top of next PC; rep from * to end working last dc into 3rd of ch 6, turn. Rep rows 1 and 2 for length required, ending with a row 2.

# Popcorn columns

MULTIPLE OF 11 CHAINS PLUS 5

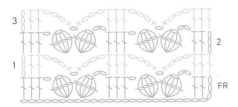

This is a much heavier stitch than the lacy popcorns, but still makes a crochet fabric with good drape. Use this stitch for making throws and afghans where you need a textured surface.

**NOTE:** PC = popcorn made from five treble crochet stitches.

**FOUNDATION ROW: (RS)** 1 tr into 4th ch from hook, 1 tr into next ch, * ch 2, sk next 3 chs, PC into next ch, ch 1, PC into next ch, ch 1, sk next 3 chs, 1 tr into each of next 3 chs; rep from * to end, turn.

**ROW 1:** Ch 3, sk first tr, 1 tr into each of next 2 tr, * ch 3, sk next ch and PC, 2 dc into ch 1 sp between PCs, ch 3, sk next PC and 2 chs, 1 tr into each of next 3 tr; rep from * to end working last tr into 3rd of beg skipped ch 3, turn.

**ROW 2:** Ch 3, sk first tr, 1 tr into each of next 2 tr, * ch 2, sk next 3 chs, PC into next dc, ch 1, PC into next dc, ch 1, sk next 3 chs, 1 tr into each of next 3 tr; rep from * to end working last tr into 3rd of ch 3, turn.

**ROW 3:** Ch 3, sk first tr, 1 tr into each of next 2 tr, * ch 3, sk next ch and PC, 2 dc into ch 1 sp between PCs, ch 3, sk next PC and 2 chs, 1 tr into each of next 3 tr; rep from * to end working last tr into 3rd of ch 3, turn. Rep rows 2 and 3 for length required, ending with a row 2.

Lacy popcorns

Popcorn columns

# PUFF STITCHES

PUFF STITCHES ARE SOFT, FLUFFY GROUPS OF STITCHES THAT ARE LESS TEXTURED THAN EITHER BOBBLES OR POPCORNS. A PUFF STITCH IS MADE FROM THREE OR MORE HALF TREBLE CROCHET STITCHES THAT ARE WORKED INTO THE SAME CHAIN OR STITCH. PUFF STITCHES NEED A LITTLE PRACTICE TO WORK SUCCESSFULLY.

### SEE ALSO

- Bobbles, pages 44–45
- Popcorns, pages 46–47

**Tip**

*Puff stitches can be a little tricky to work, especially for a beginner. It is a good idea to practise them using a smooth, chunky yarn and large hook until you understand the stitch construction.*

### WORKING A BASIC PUFF STITCH

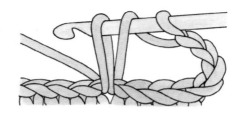

1 Wrap the yarn over the hook, insert the hook into the specified chain or stitch, wrap the yarn over the hook again and draw a loop through so that there are three loops on the hook.

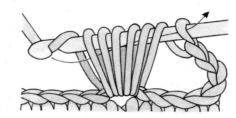

2 Repeat step 1 twice more, each time inserting the hook into the same place, so that there are seven loops on the hook. Wrap the yarn over the hook again and draw it through all the loops on the hook.

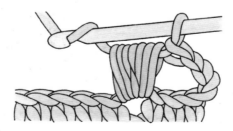

3 A chain stitch is often worked to close the puff stitch and secure the loops. Wrap the yarn over the hook and draw it through the loop on the hook to complete the securing chain stitch.

## Stitch collection

## Puff stitch stripes

**MULTIPLE OF 2 CHAINS PLUS 2**

This stitch makes a softly textured crochet fabric that is perfect for making baby blankets and small afghans when worked in baby yarn. You can use either side of the work as the right side.

**NOTE:** PS = puff stitch made from three half treble crochet stitches closed with one chain stitch.

**FOUNDATION ROW:** 1 dc into 2nd ch from hook, * ch 1, sk next ch, 1 dc into next ch; rep from * to end, turn.

**ROW 1:** Ch 2 (counts as 1 htr), * PS into next ch 1 sp, ch 1, sk next dc; rep from * to last ch 1 sp, PS into last ch 1 sp, 1 htr into last dc, turn.

**ROW 2:** Ch 1, 1 dc into first htr, * ch 1, sk next st, 1 dc into next ch 1 sp; rep from * to end working last dc into 2nd of ch 2, turn.

Rep rows 1 and 2 for length required, ending with a row 2.

# Puff stitch waves

MULTIPLE OF 17 CHAINS PLUS 2

Puff stitches combined with groups of decreases make this pretty ripple pattern. It looks attractive worked in a solid colour or in two-row stripes of closely toning colours.

**NOTE:** PS = puff stitch made from three half treble crochet stitches closed with one chain stitch.

tr2tog = work two treble crochet stitches together.

**FOUNDATION ROW: (RS)** 1 tr into 4th ch from hook, [tr2tog over next 2 chs] twice, * [ch 1, PS into next ch] 5 times, ch 1, ** [tr2tog over next 2 chs] 6 times; rep from * ending last rep at ** when 6 chs rem, [tr2tog over next 2 chs] 3 times, turn.

**ROW 1:** Ch 1, 1 dc into each st and ch 1 sp to end excluding beg skipped ch 3, turn.

**ROW 2:** Ch 3, sk first dc, 1 tr into next dc, [tr2tog over next 2 dc] twice, * [ch 1, PS into next dc] 5 times, ch 1, ** [tr2tog over next 2 dc] 6 times; rep from * ending last rep at ** when 6 dc rem, [tr2tog over next 2 dc] 3 times, sk turning ch 1, turn. Rep rows 2 and 3 for length required, ending with a row 2.

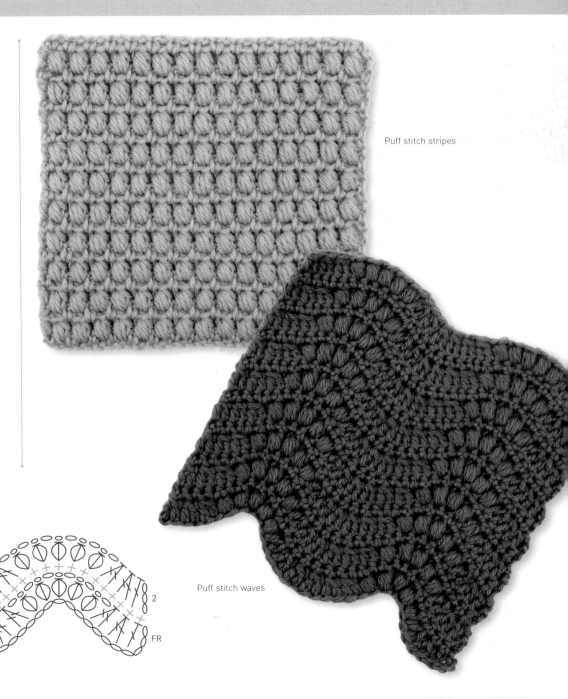

Puff stitch stripes

Puff stitch waves

# LOOP STITCHES

LOOP STITCHES FALL INTO TWO CATEGORIES. THE FIRST IS WHERE EXTENDED LOOPS ARE MADE FROM THE WORKING YARN (LOOP STITCH). THE SECOND IS WHERE SHORT LENGTHS OF CROCHET CHAIN ARE FORMED INTO LOOPS (ASTRAKHAN STITCH). BOTH TYPES OF STITCH MAKE A DELIGHTFUL TEXTURE AND ARE GOOD FOR MAKING ACCESSORIES SUCH AS SCARVES AND HATS, OR FOR WORKING COLLARS AND CUFFS TO TRIM A PLAIN GARMENT.

**SEE ALSO**

• Basic skills and stitches, pages 14–21

## WORKING A LOOP STITCH

Loop stitches are often worked on wrong side rows of double crochet by extending a loop of yarn with your finger. You may need some practice before you are able to make all the loops the same size. Loop stitches can be worked into every stitch along the row.

1 With the wrong side of the work facing you, insert the hook into the next stitch as usual. Using one finger, pull up the working yarn to make a loop of the desired size, pick up both strands of the loop with the hook and draw them through the crochet fabric.

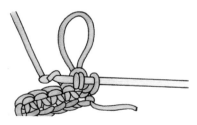

2 Take your finger out of the yarn loop and wrap the working yarn over the hook.

3 Carefully draw the yarn through all three loops on the hook.

## WORKING ASTRAKHAN STITCH

Astrakhan stitch is worked back and forth without turning the work. Loops of crochet chain are made on right side rows by working into the front loops of the previous plain row. Each following plain row is worked into the back loops of the previous plain row.

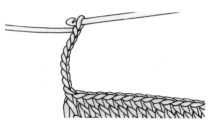

1 **PLAIN ROW:** Work a row of treble crochet stitches. At the end of the row, work the number of chains specified in the pattern. Do not turn.

2 **LOOP ROW:** Working from left to right, and keeping the crochet chain behind the hook, work a slip stitch into the front loop of the next treble crochet made on the previous row. Repeat along the row and do not turn at the end of the row.

3 **PLAIN ROW:** Working from right to left behind the chain loops made on the previous row, work a treble crochet stitch into the back loop of each stitch made on the first plain row.

# Stitch collection

## Banded loop stitch

> MULTIPLE OF 8 CHAINS PLUS 2

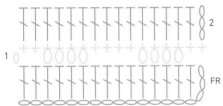

Loop stitches are worked in groups of four to make vertical bands of texture that contrast well with the plain background.

**FOUNDATION ROW: (RS)** 1 tr into 4th ch from hook, 1 tr into each ch to end, turn.

**ROW 1:** Ch 1, 1 dc into each of first 2 tr, * loop stitch into each of next 4 tr, 1 dc into each of next 4 tr; rep from * to last 6 sts, loop stitch into each of next 4 tr, 1 dc into next tr, 1 dc into 3rd of beg skipped ch 3, turn.

**ROW 2:** Ch 3 (counts as 1 tr), 1 tr into each st to end, sk turning ch 1, turn.

Rep rows 1 and 2 for length required, ending with a row 1.

## Astrakhan stitch

> ANY NUMBER OF CHAINS PLUS 2

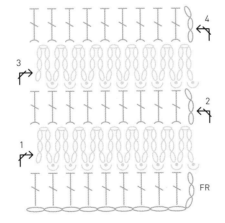

Loops of crochet chains are worked on alternate rows to create this highly textured stitch. It is worked without turning at the end of the rows.

**FOUNDATION ROW: (RS)** 1 tr into 4th ch from hook, 1 tr into each ch to end. Do not turn.

**ROW 1: (LOOP ROW)** Working from left to right, sk first tr, * ch 7, sl st into front loop of next tr to right; rep from * to end working last sl st into both loops of 3rd of beg skipped ch 3. Do not turn.

**ROW 2: (PLAIN ROW)** Working from right to left behind loops made on previous row, ch 3, sk first st, * 1 tr into back loop of next tr worked on foundation row; rep from * to end. Do not turn.

**ROW 3: (LOOP ROW)** Working from left to right, * ch 7, sk first tr, sl st into front loop of next tr to right; rep from * to end working last sl st into both loops of 3rd of ch 3. Do not turn.

**ROW 4: (PLAIN ROW)** Working from right to left behind loops made on previous row, ch 3, sk first st, * 1 tr into back loop of next tr worked on last but one row; rep from * to end. Do not turn.

Rep rows 3 and 4 for length required, ending with a row 4.

# OPENWORK AND LACE STITCHES

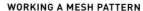

THESE VERSATILE STITCHES CAN BE USED TO MAKE ACCESSORIES SUCH AS SHAWLS AND WRAPS, AS WELL AS LIGHTWEIGHT, SIMPLY SHAPED SUMMER GARMENTS. THEY ARE STRAIGHTFORWARD TO WORK, BUT IT IS ESSENTIAL TO MAKE THE CORRECT NUMBER OF CHAINS IN THE FOUNDATION CHAIN.

**SEE ALSO**
• Basic skills and stitches, pages 14–21
• Surface crochet, pages 112–113

**PLAIN TRELLIS WORKED IN THE ROUND**
The number of chain stitches in each loop increases by one chain stitch for each new round.

## WORKING A TRELLIS PATTERN

Although similar in construction, trellis patterns have longer chain spaces than mesh patterns, with the chain spaces curving upwards to create delicate arches. The chain spaces are usually anchored by double crochet stitches worked into the space below each arch.

## WORKING A MESH PATTERN

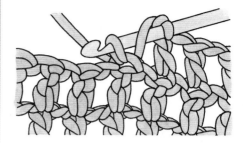

1 When working a mesh pattern, take care to insert the hook into the correct place. In this example, the hook is inserted into the top of each stitch made on the previous row.

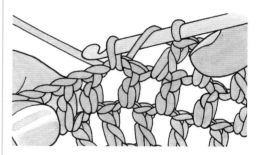

2 Some mesh patterns are made by inserting the hook into the chain spaces between stitches worked on the previous row. Do not insert the hook directly into the chain, but into the space below it.

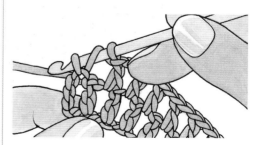

3 When working the last stitch of the row, work it into the third stitch of the turning chain rather than into the chain space. This makes a neater, more stable edge.

# Stitch collection

## Plain trellis

**MULTIPLE OF 4 CHAINS PLUS 2**

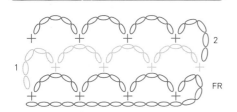

This easy-to-work stitch is lovely when used to make a lightweight wrap, scarf or stole. It is reversible, so you can choose which side you prefer as the right side.
**FOUNDATION ROW:** 1 dc into 6th ch from hook, * ch 5, sk next 3 chs, 1 dc into next ch; rep from * to end, turn.
**ROW 1:** * Ch 5, 1 dc into next ch 5 sp; rep from * to end, turn.
Rep row 1 for length required.

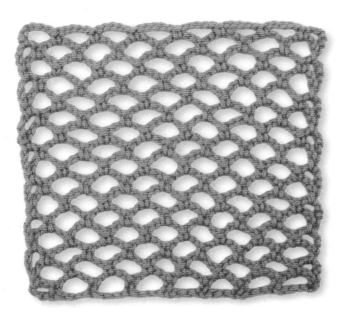

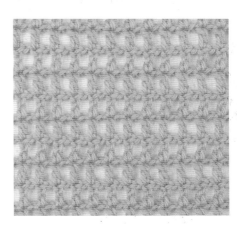

## Openwork mesh

**MULTIPLE OF 2 CHAINS PLUS 4**

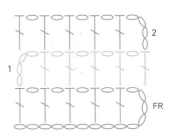

This stitch is very easy to work and is a good introduction to openwork stitch patterns for the beginner. It also makes a good background stitch for surface crochet.
**FOUNDATION ROW: (RS)** 1 tr into 6th ch from hook, * ch 1, sk next ch, 1 tr into next ch; rep from * to end, turn.
**ROW 1:** Ch 4 (counts as 1 tr, ch 1), * 1 tr into next tr, ch 1; rep from * to end working last tr into 2nd of beg skipped ch 5, turn.
**ROW 2:** Ch 4 (counts as 1 tr, ch 1), * 1 tr into next tr, ch 1; rep from * to end working last tr into 3rd of ch 3, turn.
Rep row 2 for length required.

**KEY TO ABBREVIATIONS AND SYMBOLS** pages 150–151

## Stitch collection

### Fancy openwork

> MULTIPLE OF 18 CHAINS PLUS 8

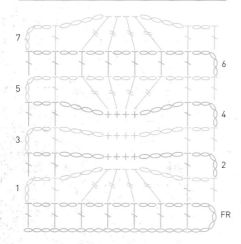

Fancy openwork

A more challenging stitch to work than either of the previous ones, the resulting crochet fabric is soft and delicate with good drape. Choose which side you prefer as the right side.

**FOUNDATION ROW:** 1 tr into 8th ch from hook, * ch 2, sk next 2 chs, 1 tr into next ch; rep from * to end, turn.

**ROW 1:** Ch 5 (counts as 1 tr, ch 2), sk first tr, 1 tr into next tr, * ch 4, 1 dtr into each of next 4 tr, ch 4, 1 tr into next tr, ch 2, 1 tr into next tr; rep from * to end working last tr into 3rd of beg skipped ch 7, turn.

**ROW 2:** Ch 5, sk first tr, 1 tr into next tr, * ch 4, 1 dc into each of next 4 dtr, ch 4, 1 tr into next tr, ch 2, 1 tr into next tr; rep from * to end working last tr into 3rd of ch 5, turn.

**ROWS 3 AND 4:** Ch 5, sk first tr, 1 tr into next tr, * ch 4, 1 dc into each of next 4 dc, ch 4, 1 tr into next tr, ch 2, 1 tr into next tr; rep from * to end working last tr into 3rd of ch 5, turn.

**ROW 5:** Ch 5, sk first tr, 1 tr into next tr, * ch 2, [1 dtr into next dc, ch 2] 4 times, 1 tr into next tr, ch 2, 1 tr into next tr; rep from * to end working last tr into 3rd of ch 5, turn.

**ROW 6:** Ch 5, sk first tr, 1 tr into next tr, * ch 2, [1 tr into next dtr, ch 2] 4 times, 1 tr into next tr, ch 2, 1 tr into next tr; rep from * to end working last tr into 3rd of ch 5, turn.

**ROW 7:** Ch 5, sk first tr, 1 tr into next tr, * ch 4, 1 dtr into each of next 4 tr, ch 4, 1 tr into next tr, ch 2, 1 tr into next tr; rep from * to end working last tr into 3rd of ch 5, turn.

Rep rows 2–7 for length required, ending with a row 6.

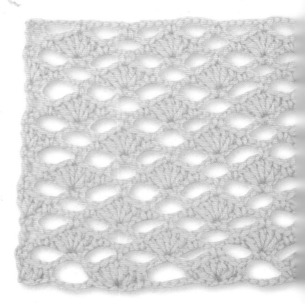

Seashore trellis

## Seashore trellis

> MULTIPLE OF 12 CHAINS PLUS 4

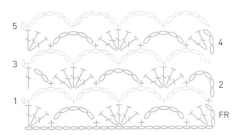

A combination of a trellis pattern and shell stitches, this stitch works well for a scarf or baby shawl. Choose a lightweight yarn to enhance the beauty of the stitch pattern.

**FOUNDATION ROW: (RS)** 2 tr into 4th ch from hook, * sk next 2 chs, 1 dc into next ch, ch 5, sk next 5 chs, 1 dc into next ch, sk next 2 chs, 5 tr into next ch; rep from * to end working only 3 tr into last ch, turn.

**ROW 1:** Ch 1, 1 dc into first tr, * ch 5, 1 dc into next ch 5 sp, ch 5, 1 dc into 3rd tr of next 5 tr group; rep from * to end working last dc into 3rd of beg skipped ch 3, turn.

**ROW 2:** * Ch 5, 1 dc into next ch 5 sp, 5 tr into next dc, 1 dc into next ch 5 sp; rep from * ending with ch 2, 1 tr into last dc, turn.

**ROW 3:** Ch 1, 1 dc into first tr, * ch 5, 1 dc into 3rd tr of next 5 tr group, ch 5, 1 dc into next ch 5 sp; rep from * to end, turn.

**ROW 4:** Ch 3, 2 tr into first dc, * 1 dc into next ch 5 sp, ch 5, 1 dc into next ch 5 sp, 5 tr into next dc; rep from * to end working only 3 tr into last dc, turn.

**ROW 5:** Ch 1, 1 dc into first tr, * ch 5, 1 dc into next ch 5 sp, ch 5, 1 dc into 3rd tr of next 5 tr group; rep from * to end working last dc into 3rd of ch 3, turn.

Rep rows 2–5 for length required, ending with a row 4.

## Fan lace

> MULTIPLE OF 12 CHAINS PLUS 3

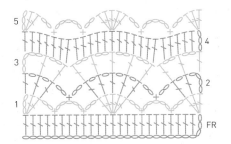

This attractive, large-scale lace pattern is deceptively easy to work in double and treble crochet stitches. Work it in a soft cotton or cotton blend yarn to make a pretty wrap to wear on summer evenings.

**FOUNDATION ROW: (RS)** 1 tr into 4th ch from hook, 1 tr into each ch to end, turn.

**ROW 1:** Ch 3, 2 tr into first tr, ch 2, sk next 3 tr, 1 dc into next tr, ch 5, sk next 3 tr, 1 dc into next tr, ch 2, sk next 3 tr, * 5 tr into next tr, ch 2, sk next 3 tr, 1 dc into next tr, ch 5, sk next 3 tr, 1 dc into next tr, ch 2, sk next 3 tr; rep from * ending with 3 tr into 3rd of beg skipped ch 3, turn.

**ROW 2:** Ch 4, sk first tr, 1 tr into next tr, ch 1, 1 tr into next tr, ch 2, sk next 2 sp, 1 dc into next ch 5 sp, ch 2, * [1 tr into next tr, ch 1] 4 times, 1 tr into next tr, ch 2, sk next 2 sp, 1 dc into next ch 5 sp, ch 2; rep from * to last 2 tr, [1 tr into next tr, ch 1] twice, 1 tr into 3rd of ch 3, turn.

**ROW 3:** Ch 5, sk first tr, 1 tr into next tr, ch 2, 1 tr into next tr, * sk next dc, [1 tr into next tr, ch 2] 4 times, 1 tr into next tr; rep from * to last dc, sk last dc, [1 tr into next tr, ch 2] twice, 1 tr into 3rd of ch 4, turn.

**ROW 4:** Ch 3, 2 tr into next ch 2 sp, 1 tr into next tr, 2 tr into next ch 2 sp, sk next tr, 1 tr into next tr, * [2 tr into next ch 2 sp, 1 tr into next tr] 3 times, 2 tr into next ch 2 sp, sk next tr, 1 tr into next tr; rep

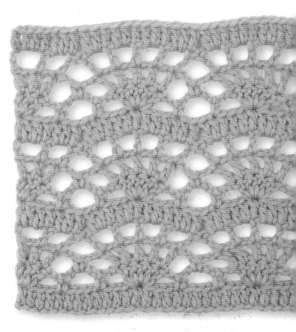

from * to last ch 2 sp, 2 tr into last ch 2 sp, 1 tr into next tr, 2 tr into sp formed by ch 5, sk first 2 chs of ch 5, 1 tr into 3rd of ch 5, turn.

**ROW 5:** Ch 3, 2 tr into first tr, ch 2, sk next 3 tr, 1 dc into next tr, ch 5, sk next 3 tr, 1 dc into next tr, ch 2, sk next 3 tr, * 5 tr into next tr, ch 2, sk next 3 tr, 1 dc into next tr, ch 5, sk next 3 tr, 1 dc into next tr, ch 2, sk next 3 tr; rep from * ending with 3 tr into 3rd of ch 3, turn.

Rep rows 2–5 for length required, ending with a row 4.

# FILET CROCHET

FILET CROCHET IS AN OPENWORK TYPE OF CROCHET CHARACTERISED BY A MESH BACKGROUND ON WHICH THE PATTERN IS PICKED OUT IN SOLID BLOCKS OF STITCHES. IT IS TRADITIONALLY WORKED IN FINE COTTON THREAD, BUT ALSO LOOKS EFFECTIVE WORKED IN YARN.

**SEE ALSO**

• Openwork and lace stitches, pages 52–55

## FILET CROCHET PATTERNS

Filet crochet patterns are always worked from a chart that shows the pattern as it will appear on the right side of the work. The chart rows are numbered at the sides, and you follow the numbered sequence, working upwards from the bottom of the chart (row 1) and from side to side (see diagram below).

A filet crochet 'unit' comprises a beginning treble crochet, either two chains for a space or two treble crochet stitches for a block, and an ending treble crochet. The ending treble crochet stitch is also the beginning treble crochet of the next unit.

## HEART MOTIF

Filet crochet lends itself to working simplified motifs such as this heart, which can be worked as a single motif or turned on its side and repeated to make a lovely border.

## WORKING THE FIRST ROW

Filet crochet charts begin with the first row, so the foundation chain is not shown. To calculate the number of chains to make, you will need to multiply the number of squares across the chart by three and add one. For example, for a chart that is 20 squares across, make a foundation chain 61 chains long (20 x 3 + 1). You also need to add the correct number of turning chains, depending on whether the first chart row begins with a space or a block. After making the foundation chain, start to follow the chart from the bottom right-hand corner, working along the row of squares marked 1. Follow the directions for the first square, depending on whether the first square is a space or a block.

Each filled square represents one block, which is made by working four treble crochet stitches.

Two blocks together on the chart are filled by seven treble crochet stitches.

Read even-numbered (wrong side) rows from left to right.

Read odd-numbered (right side) rows from right to left.

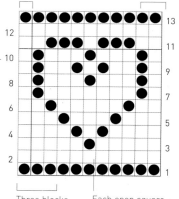

Three blocks together are filled by ten treble crochet stitches.

Each open square represents one space, which is made by working two treble crochet stitches separated by two chains.

## STARTING THE FIRST ROW WITH A SPACE

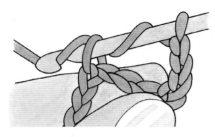

When the first square is a space, add four turning chains and work the first treble crochet stitch into the eighth chain from the hook. Continue working spaces and blocks along the row, reading the chart from right to left.

## STARTING THE FIRST ROW WITH A BLOCK

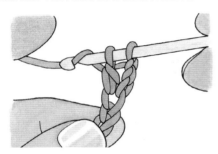

1 When the first square on the chart is a block, add two turning chains and work the first treble crochet stitch into the fourth chain from the hook.

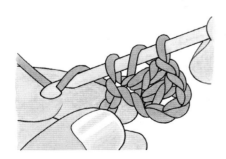

2 Work one treble crochet stitch into each of the next two chains to complete the first block. Continue along the row, reading the chart from right to left.

## WORKING THE REST OF THE CHART ROWS

At the end of the first row, turn the work and follow the second row of the chart, reading from left to right. Work spaces and blocks at the beginning and end of the second and subsequent rows as follows.

## WORKING A SPACE OVER A SPACE ON THE PREVIOUS ROW

1 At the beginning of a row, work five turning chains (these count as one treble crochet stitch and two chains), skip the first stitch and the next two chains, then work one treble crochet stitch into the next treble crochet stitch. Continue across the row, working the spaces and blocks from the chart.

2 At the end of a row, finish by working one treble crochet stitch into the last treble crochet stitch, then work two chains, skip two chains and work one treble crochet stitch into the third of the five turning chains, then turn.

## WORKING A SPACE OVER A BLOCK ON THE PREVIOUS ROW

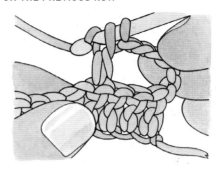

1 At the beginning of a row, work five turning chains (these count as one treble crochet stitch and two chains), skip the first three stitches, then work one treble crochet stitch into the next treble crochet stitch. Continue across the row, working spaces and blocks from the chart.

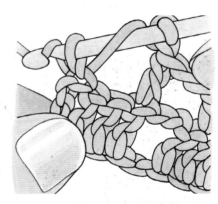

2 At the end of a row, work to the last four stitches. Work one treble crochet stitch into the next stitch, work two chains, skip two stitches and work one treble crochet stitch into the top of the three turning chains to complete the block, then turn.

## WORKING A BLOCK OVER A SPACE ON THE PREVIOUS ROW

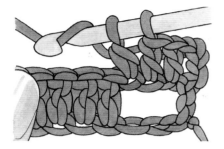

**1** At the beginning of a row, work three turning chains (these count as one treble crochet stitch), then skip one stitch, work one treble crochet stitch into each of the next two chains and one treble crochet stitch into the next stitch to complete the block. Continue across the row, working spaces and blocks from the chart.

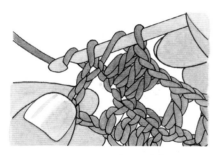

**2** At the end of a row, finish by working one treble crochet stitch into the last treble crochet stitch and one treble crochet stitch into each of the next three chains of the turning chain, then turn.

## WORKING A BLOCK OVER A BLOCK ON THE PREVIOUS ROW

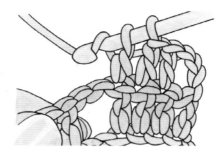

**1** At the beginning of a row, work three turning chains (these count as one treble crochet stitch), then skip one stitch and work one treble crochet stitch into each of the next three treble crochet stitches to complete the block. Continue across the row, working spaces and blocks from the chart.

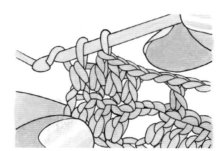

**2** At the end of a row, finish by working one treble crochet stitch into each of the last three treble crochet stitches and one treble crochet stitch into the top of the three turning chains, then turn.

# Stitch collection

## Checquerboard

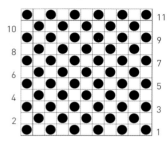

This pattern is one of the simplest designs for filet crochet, consisting of alternating blocks and spaces. It is a great, easy-to-work stitch for making lightweight blankets and throws.

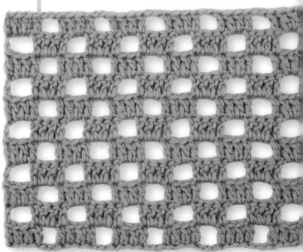

## Tiny flowers

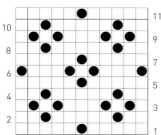

This design has a lighter feel than the chequerboard pattern. Groups of four blocks are arranged to make stylised flowers at regular intervals across the plain mesh background.

## Sitting cat

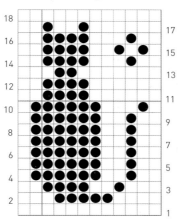

This cat motif would look pretty repeated several times across the border of a baby shawl or snuggle blanket. Use a lightweight baby yarn and a fairly small hook to make the most of the design.

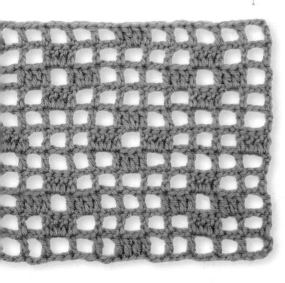

# CHEVRON PATTERNS

CHEVRON PATTERNS ARE WORKED IN A SIMILAR WAY TO PLAIN HORIZONTAL STRIPES, BUT IN THIS TYPE OF STRIPE PATTERN EXTRA STITCHES ARE ADDED AND SUBTRACTED AT REGULAR INTERVALS ALONG EACH ROW.

**SEE ALSO**
- Basic skills and stitches, pages 14–21
- Stripe patterns, pages 34–35

The adding and subtracting of stitches forms a pattern of regular peaks and troughs, separated by blocks of stitches, and creates attractive patterns often known as ripple patterns. The peaks and troughs can form sharp points or gentle waves, depending on the pattern, and the effect can vary when the number of stitches in the blocks between the peaks and troughs is changed.

With basic chevron patterns, the pattern repeat is usually set on the first row after you have worked the foundation row of stitches into the foundation chain. This row is then repeated until the work is the required length. More complex chevron patterns, combining smooth, textured and lace stitches, are made up of peaks and troughs in a similar way, but each pattern repeat may take several rows to complete. Join new colours at the end of rows in the same way as when working simple stripe patterns.

**CHEVRON EDGING**
Working one or two rows of a chevron pattern creates a useful edging, such as this two-row double crochet chevron pattern (see step-by-step sequence, right).

**RIC RAC EDGING**
To create this ric rac pattern, work three double crochet stitches into one chain, one double crochet into the next chain, then skip the following chain and work one double crochet stitch into the chain after that. Repeat this sequence to the end of the chain. This edging, worked in fine cotton, is ideal for trimming fabric projects.

## WORKING A CHEVRON PATTERN IN DOUBLE CROCHET

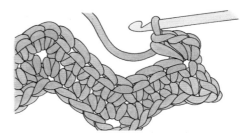

**1** To keep the peaks and troughs of chevron stripe patterns correctly spaced, you may need to work one or more extra stitches at the beginning or end (or both) of every row. In this easy pattern, two double crochet stitches are worked into the first stitch of every row.

**2** To make the bottom V-shapes of the chevron pattern (the troughs), skip two double crochet stitches (sk next 2 dc) at the bottom of the troughs, then continue working the next block of stitches.

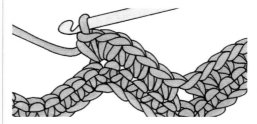

**3** To make the top V-shapes of the chevrons (the peaks), work three double crochet stitches into the same stitch (3 dc into next dc) at the top of the peaks.

# Stitch collection

## Double crochet chevrons

MULTIPLE OF 11 CHAINS PLUS 2

**YARN:** Worked in three colours, A, B and C. Using yarn A, make the required length of foundation chain.

**FOUNDATION ROW: (RS)** 2 dc into 2nd ch from hook, * 1 dc into each of next 4 chs, sk next 2 chs, 1 dc into each of next 4 chs, 3 dc into next ch; rep from * ending last rep with 2 dc into last ch, turn.

**ROW 1:** Ch 1, 2 dc into first dc, * 1 dc into each of next 4 dc, sk next 2 dc, 1 dc into each of next 4 dc, 3 dc into next dc; rep from * ending last rep with 2 dc into last dc, turn.
Rep row 1, changing yarns in the following colour sequence:

        4 rows in yarn A
        4 rows in yarn B
        4 rows in yarn C
Repeat for length required.

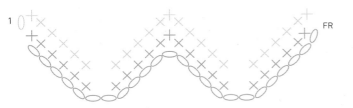

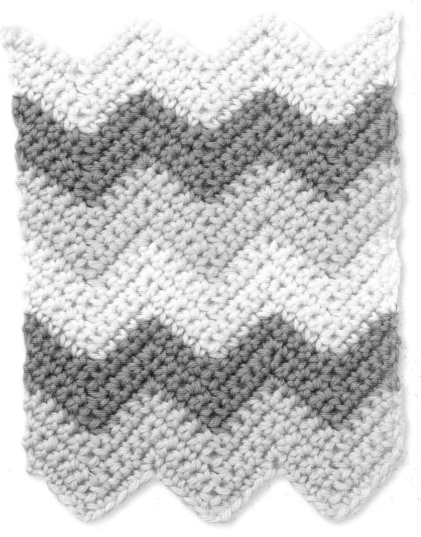

## WORKING A CHEVRON PATTERN IN TREBLE CROCHET

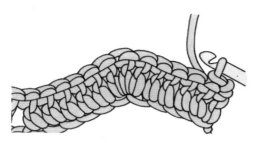

1 Instead of working extra stitches at the beginning of a row, you may be instructed to work one or more slip stitches in order to move the yarn and hook to the correct place for working the row. In this pattern, turn and work a slip stitch into the second treble crochet stitch of the row (sl st into 2nd tr) before working the turning chain.

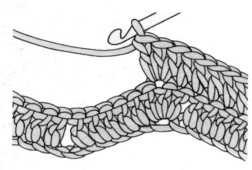

2 Three stitches are worked into the same stitch on the previous row to form the peaks. Work the block of stitches before the peak, then work three treble crochet stitches into the next treble crochet stitch (3 tr into next tr). The troughs are made in the same way as the double crochet pattern (see page 60), by simply skipping two stitches at the bottom of the troughs.

## WORKING A WAVE PATTERN IN TREBLE CROCHET

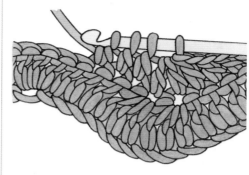

1 Soft waves are made by working two sets of increases and decreases into the peaks and troughs instead of one. To make the troughs, work three treble crochet stitches together over the six stitches (tr3tog over next 6 sts) at the bottom of each trough.

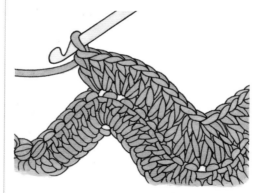

2 To make the peaks, work three treble crochet stitches into each of the central two stitches (3 tr into each of next 2 tr) at the top of the peaks.

## Treble crochet chevrons

MULTIPLE OF 13 CHAINS

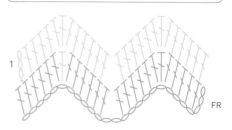

YARN: Worked in two colours, A and B. Using yarn A, make the required length of foundation chain.

FOUNDATION ROW: (RS) 1 tr into 4th ch from hook, 1 tr into each of next 3 chs, * 3 tr into next ch, 1 tr into each of next 5 chs, sk next 2 chs, 1 tr into each of next 5 chs; rep from * to last 6 chs, 3 tr into next ch, 1 tr into each of next 5 chs, turn.

ROW 1: Sl st into 2nd tr, ch 3, 1 tr into each of next 4 tr, * 3 tr into next tr, 1 tr into each of next 5 tr, sk next 2 tr, 1 tr into each of next 5 tr; rep from * to last 6 sts, 3 tr into next tr, 1 tr into each of next 5 tr, turn.

Rep row 1, changing yarns in the following colour sequence:
     2 rows in yarn A
     2 rows in yarn B
Repeat for length required.

# Wavy chevrons

> **MULTIPLE OF 14 CHAINS PLUS 3**

**YARN:** Worked in three colours, A, B and C. Using yarn A, make the required length of foundation chain.

**FOUNDATION ROW: (RS)** 2 tr into 4th ch from hook, 1 tr into each of next 3 chs, [dc3tog over next 3 chs] twice, 1 tr into each of next 3 chs, * 3 tr into each of next 2 chs, 1 tr into each of next 3 chs, [dc3tog over next 3 chs] twice, 1 tr into each of next 3 chs; rep from * to last ch, 3 tr into last ch, turn.

**ROW 1:** Ch 3, 2 tr into first tr, 1 tr into each of next 3 tr, dc3tog twice, 1 tr into each of next 3 tr, * 3 tr into each of next 2 tr, 1 tr into each of next 3 tr, dc3tog twice, 1 tr into each of next 3 tr; rep from * to beg skipped chs, 3 tr into 3rd of beg skipped ch 3, turn. Join yarn B but do not break off yarn A.

**ROW 2:** Ch 3, 2 tr into first tr, 1 tr into each of next 3 tr, dc3tog twice, 1 tr into each of next 3 tr, * 3 tr into each of next 2 tr, 1 tr into each of next 3 tr, dc3tog twice, 1 tr into each of next 3 tr; rep from * to turning ch, 3 tr into 3rd of ch 3, turn.

Rep row 2, changing yarns in the following colour sequence:

      1 row (foundation row) in yarn A
      [1A, 1B, 1A, 1C, 2A] rep to end
Repeat for length required.

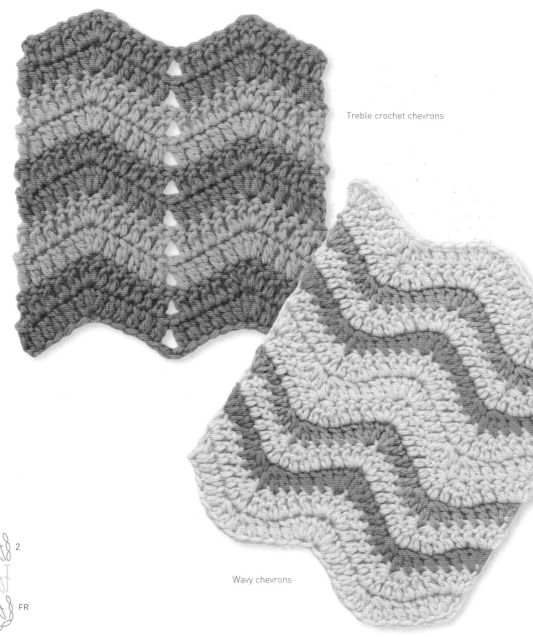

Treble crochet chevrons

Wavy chevrons

# SPIKE STITCHES

SPIKE STITCHES (ALSO CALLED DROPPED STITCHES) ARE WORKED OVER THE TOP OF OTHER STITCHES TO ADD COLOUR OR TEXTURE TO CROCHET. THE STITCHES ARE WORKED SINGLY OR IN GROUPS OVER ONE OR MORE ROWS, AND ARE USUALLY WORKED IN DOUBLE CROCHET.

### SEE ALSO
• Stripe patterns, pages 34–35

As well as making interesting colour patterns when worked in two or more contrasting colours, spike stitches also create a thick, densely worked fabric, without much drape, which is good for making adult outerwear and accessories such as hats and bags.

**WORKING A BASIC DOUBLE CROCHET SPIKE STITCH**

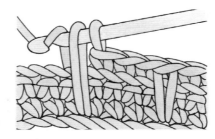

**1** Insert the hook into the work the specified number of rows below the next stitch as directed in the pattern instructions, taking the point right through the fabric to the wrong side. Wrap the yarn over the hook and draw through, lengthening the loop to the height of the working row.

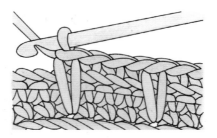

**2** To finish the spike, complete the stitch in the usual way. When working spike stitches, take care not to pull the loop too tight because this will distort the fabric.

**FABRIC WEIGHT**
Spike stitches create a thick fabric.

## Spiked stripes

**MULTIPLE OF 8 CHAINS PLUS 1**

Stripes of contrasting colours show off spike stitches to perfection. Here, the colour changes after every two rows, with the colour not in use being carried loosely up the side to avoid lots of yarn ends.

**YARN:** Worked in two colours, A and B.

**NOTE:** SP = spike stitch made by inserting hook into work two rows below next stitch and working a double crochet stitch.

Using yarn A, make the required length of foundation chain.

**FOUNDATION ROW: (RS)** 1 dc into 2nd ch from hook, 1 dc into each ch to end, turn.

**ROW 1:** Ch 1, 1 dc into each dc to end, turn. Join yarn B but do not break off yarn A.

**ROW 2:** Using yarn B, ch 1, * 1 dc into each of next 3 dc, SP twice, 1 dc into each of next 3 dc; rep from * to end, turn.

**ROW 3:** Using yarn B, ch 1, 1 dc into each dc to end, turn.

**ROW 4:** Using yarn A, ch 1, * 1 dc into each of next 3 dc, SP twice, 1 dc into each of next 3 dc; rep from * to end, turn.

Rep rows 1–4 for length required, ending with a row 1.

### Tip
*When first trying out spike stitches, it is easier to see exactly what is happening if you work each row using a contrasting colour of yarn.*

## Alternate spikes

MULTIPLE OF 2 CHAINS

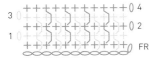

This lovely stitch makes a thick, textured fabric. Worked in one colour, the fabric is reversible, so you can choose which side of the work you like best and use that as the right side.

**NOTE:** SP = spike stitch made by inserting hook into work one row below next stitch and working a double crochet stitch.

**FOUNDATION ROW:** 1 dc into 2nd ch from hook, 1 dc into each ch to end, turn.

**ROW 1:** Ch 1, 1 dc into first dc, * SP, 1 dc into next dc; rep from * to end, turn.

**ROW 2:** Ch 1, 1 dc into each of first 2 dc, * SP, 1 dc into next dc; rep from * to last dc, 1 dc into last dc, turn.

Rep row 2 for length required.

Alternate spikes

Spiked stripes

# RAISED STITCHES

STITCHES MADE WITH THIS TECHNIQUE ARE KNOWN BY SEVERAL DIFFERENT NAMES: RAISED STITCHES, POST STITCHES OR RELIEF STITCHES. THEY CREATE A HEAVILY TEXTURED SURFACE, MADE BY INSERTING THE HOOK AROUND THE POST (STEM) OF THE STITCHES ON THE PREVIOUS ROW AND THEN WORKING A TREBLE CROCHET STITCH. THE HOOK CAN BE INSERTED FROM THE FRONT OR THE BACK OF THE WORK, GIVING A DIFFERENT EFFECT EACH WAY.

**Tip**

*If you are finding it difficult to figure out where to insert your hook, try practising this technique on a larger scale by using a thick yarn and large hook.*

## INSERTING THE HOOK

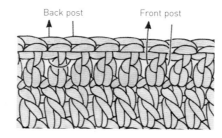

When working a front post stitch, insert the hook into the front of the fabric, around the back of the post and return to the front of the work. When working a back post stitch, insert the hook from the back of the fabric, around the front of the post and return to the back of the work.

## WORKING A RAISED STITCH FROM THE FRONT

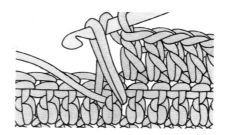

Wrap the yarn over the hook, insert the hook as described above, wrap the yarn over the hook again and draw up a loop at the front of the work. Complete the treble crochet stitch as usual.

## WORKING A RAISED STITCH FROM THE BACK

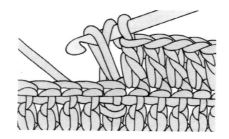

Wrap the yarn over the hook, insert the hook as described above, wrap the yarn over the hook again and draw up a loop at the back of the work. Complete the treble crochet stitch as usual.

## Raised columns

**MULTIPLE OF 8 CHAINS PLUS 2**

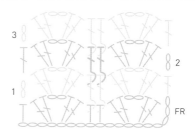

Raised stitches look good when combined with other decorative crochet stitches, particularly those with a flatter surface. Here, vertical rows of raised stitches combine well with simple treble crochet shells.

**NOTE:** FP = raised treble crochet stitch worked around the front post (front raised treble crochet stitch).
BP = raised treble crochet stitch worked around the back post (back raised treble crochet stitch).

**FOUNDATION ROW: (RS)** 2 tr into 6th ch from hook, * ch 2, 2 tr into next ch, sk next 2 chs, 1 htr into each of next 2 chs, sk next 2 chs, 2 tr into next ch; rep from * to last 3 chs, sk next 2 chs, 1 htr into last ch, turn.

**ROW 1:** Ch 2, sk htr and next 2 tr, * [2 tr, ch 2, 2 tr] into next ch 2 sp, sk next 2 tr, BP around each of next 2 htr; rep from * ending last rep with 1 tr into 5th of beg skipped ch 5, turn.

**ROW 2:** Ch 2, sk first 3 tr, * [2 tr, ch 2, 2 tr] into next ch 2 sp, sk next 2 tr, FP around each of next 2 tr; rep from * ending last rep with 1 tr into 2nd of ch 2, turn.

**ROW 3:** Ch 2, sk first 3 tr, * [2 tr, ch 2, 2 tr] into next ch 2 sp, sk next 2 tr, BP around each of next 2 tr; rep from * ending last rep with 1 tr into 2nd of ch 2, turn.

Rep rows 2 and 3 for length required, ending with a row 3.

Raised columns using double knitting yarn and a standard hook.

Raised columns using medium-weight yarn and an extra large hook.

# Basketweave

MULTIPLE OF 8 CHAINS PLUS 4

This heavily worked stitch looks like a woven basket. It is perfect for making cushion covers and thick, warm throws and blankets, but you should be aware that it will use up yarn very quickly.

**NOTE:** FP = raised treble crochet stitch worked around the front post (front raised treble crochet stitch).
BP = raised treble crochet stitch worked around the back post (back raised treble crochet stitch).

**FOUNDATION ROW:** 1 tr into 4th ch from hook, 1 tr into each ch to end, turn.

**ROW 1:** Ch 2, sk first tr, * FP around each of next 4 tr, BP around each of next 4 tr; rep from * ending last rep with 1 tr into 3rd of beg skipped ch 3, turn.

**ROWS 2–4:** Ch 2, sk first tr, * FP around each of next 4 tr, BP around each of next 4 tr; rep from * ending last rep with 1 tr into 2nd of ch 2, turn.

**ROWS 5–8:** Ch 2, sk first tr, * BP around each of next 4 tr, FP around each of next 4 tr; rep from * ending last rep with 1 tr into 2nd of ch 2, turn.

**ROW 9:** Ch 2, sk first tr, * FP around each of next 4 tr, BP around each of next 4 tr; rep from * ending last rep with 1 tr into 2nd of ch 2, turn.
Rep rows 2–9 for length required, ending with a row 4.

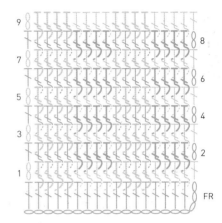

**KEY TO ABBREVIATIONS AND SYMBOLS** pages 150–151

# JACQUARD PATTERNS

JACQUARD PATTERNS ARE WORKED IN TWO OR MORE COLOURS FROM A CHART, USUALLY IN DOUBLE CROCHET. THIS TYPE OF CROCHET CREATES A COLOURFUL, STURDY FABRIC WITH A WOVEN LOOK TO IT.

Begin by working the foundation chain in the first colour. Calculate the number of chains to make according to the number of times you intend to repeat the pattern, then add one turning chain. On the first row, work the first double crochet stitch into the second chain from the hook, then work the rest of the row in double crochet. Each square represents one stitch. When changing yarns, carry the yarn not in use loosely across the back of the work and pick it up again when it is needed. This is called stranding and it works well when the areas of colour are narrow.

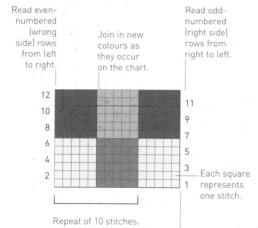

Read even-numbered (wrong side) rows from left to right.

Join in new colours as they occur on the chart.

Read odd-numbered (right side) rows from right to left.

Each square represents one stitch.

Repeat of 10 stitches.

Start at bottom right-hand corner and work upwards.

## WORKING A TWO-COLOUR JACQUARD PATTERN

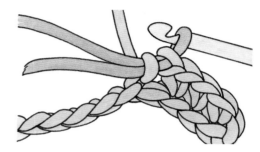

**1** Make the required length of foundation chain in yarn A, turn and begin to work the first row of the chart. When you reach the last stitch worked in yarn A, omit the final stage of the double crochet stitch, leaving two loops on the hook.

**2** Join yarn B by drawing a loop of the new colour through the two loops on the hook. This completes the last double crochet stitch worked in yarn A. Do not break off yarn A.

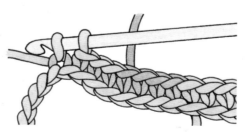

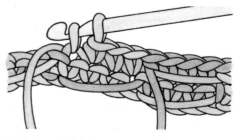

**3** Continue to work across the chart in yarn B. When you reach the last stitch worked in yarn B, change back to yarn A by carrying it loosely behind the work. Draw a loop of it through to finish the last stitch worked in yarn B and complete the colour change. Continue changing yarns in this way across the row, repeating the pattern as indicated on the chart.

**4** At the end of the row, turn and work the chart in the opposite direction from left to right. At the colour changes, bring the old colour forwards and take the new one to the back, ready to complete the stitch partially worked in the old colour. Carry the colour not in use loosely along the wrong side of the work.

# Stitch collection

## Jacquard stripes

2          1

◼ Yarn A
◼ Yarn B

Repeat of 8 stitches

Working several repeats of this simple
stripe pattern makes a good practice piece.
It is important to carry the yarn not in use
loosely across the wrong side of the work
to avoid it pulling and distorting the pattern.

## Jacquard checks

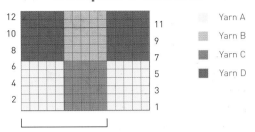

12        11
10        9
8        7
6        5
4        3
2        1

◻ Yarn A
◼ Yarn B
◼ Yarn C
◼ Yarn D

Repeat of 10 stitches

This chequerboard pattern uses four
different yarns and looks best when four
shades of the same colour are selected.
Choose one light shade, one dark and
two slightly contrasting mid-tones.

KEY TO ABBREVIATIONS AND SYMBOLS pages 150–151

# INTARSIA PATTERNS

INTARSIA CROCHET PRODUCES A DESIGN THAT IS VISIBLE ON BOTH SIDES OF THE FABRIC. INTARSIA PATTERNS ARE WORKED IN TWO OR MORE COLOURS FROM A CHART.

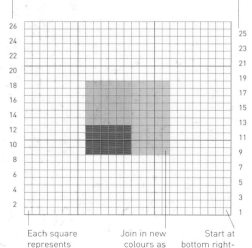

### SEE ALSO

• Jacquard patterns, pages 68–69

Read even-numbered (wrong side) rows from left to right.

Read odd-numbered (right side) rows from right to left.

Each square represents one stitch.

Join in new colours as they occur on the chart.

Start at bottom right-hand corner and work upwards.

The main difference between intarsia and jacquard is that, in intarsia, the colour areas are larger and may be irregularly shaped, so colours not in use cannot be carried across the back of the work. Instead, work each colour area using a separate ball of yarn. Work the foundation chain in the first colour, working the same number of chains as the number of squares across the chart and adding one chain for turning. If you are working a repeating intarsia pattern, calculate the number of chains to make at the start of the project in the same way as for a jacquard pattern.

## WORKING AN INTARSIA PATTERN

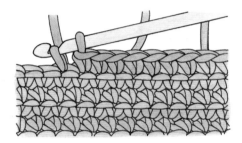

1 Make the required length of foundation chain in yarn A, turn and work the plain rows at the bottom of the chart in double crochet. Work the first multicoloured row, beginning with yarn A. At the colour changes, omit the final stage of the stitch before the change, leaving two loops on the hook. Join the next yarn by drawing a loop of the new colour through the two loops. This completes the last stitch worked in the first yarn. Continue in this way along the row.

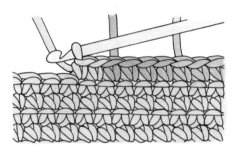

2 When you reach the last colour change in the row, where the chart indicates a change back to yarn A, work with another ball of the same yarn, not the one you used to begin the row.

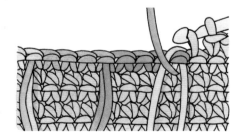

3 At the end of the row, turn and work from the chart in the opposite direction, from left to right. At each colour change, bring the old colour forwards and take the new one to the back, ready to complete the stitch partially worked in the old colour. Make sure that you loop the new yarn around the old one on the wrong side of the work to prevent holes.

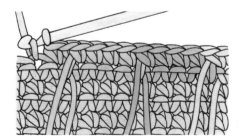

4 At the end of wrong side rows, make sure that all of the yarns are back on the wrong side of the work.

# Stitch collection

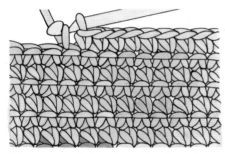

**5** When you reach new areas of colour farther up the chart, join in the yarns as before, making sure that you work each colour change into the last stitch of the previous colour.

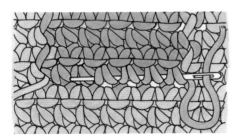

**6** When you reach the point in the chart where all the stitches in a row are worked in yarn A, work across all the stitches using the original ball of this colour.

**7** Take extra care when dealing with all the yarn ends on a piece of intarsia. Carefully weave each end into an area of crochet worked in the same colour so that it will not be visible on the right side.

## Intarsia blocks

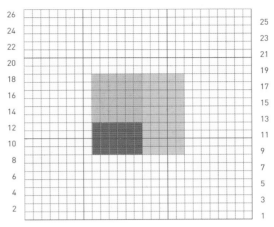

☐ Yarn A
▨ Yarn B
▨ Yarn C
▨ Yarn D

This simple block pattern will give you experience in working intarsia colour changes. It is worked in four colours, A, B, C and D. You can work the chart exactly as it is, or repeat it several times to make a bigger piece of crochet.

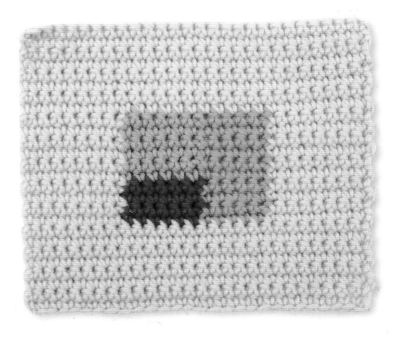

# TUBULAR CROCHET

TUBULAR CROCHET IS WORKED IN THE ROUND USING AN ORDINARY CROCHET HOOK. ALTHOUGH THE ROUNDS ARE WORKED AND JOINED IN A SIMILAR WAY TO THOSE USED FOR MAKING A CIRCULAR MOTIF, THE EFFECT HERE IS VERY DIFFERENT.

**SEE ALSO**
...........
• Circular motifs, pages 74–79

This type of crochet forms a cylinder that can be as wide or narrow as you wish. This handy technique means that you can make an item such as a hat in one piece without a seam. Cylinders can also be combined with motifs or flat pieces of crochet to make garments and accessories.

Tubular crochet can be worked in three different ways, but each one begins with a length of chain joined into a ring. You can work rounds of double crochet stitches without making a join; this forms a spiral shape. When using taller stitches such as treble crochet, each round is joined to make a seam. If you turn the work at the end of each round, you will produce a straight seam; if you continue working in the same direction on every round, the seam will spiral around the cylinder.

## WORKING A SPIRAL CYLINDER IN DOUBLE CROCHET

**1** Make the required length of chain and join it into a ring with a slip stitch. Turn and work one row of double crochet stitches into the chain. Join the round by working a double crochet into the first stitch of the round.

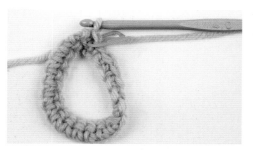

**2** Insert a ring marker into the double crochet stitch just worked to mark the beginning of a new round. Continue working the new round, working a double crochet into each stitch of the previous round.

Double crochet cylinder worked in a spiral.

**3** When you reach the marker, do not join the round. Instead, remove the marker and work the marked stitch.

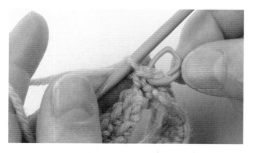

**4** Replace the marker in the new stitch to mark the start of the new round. Continue working around and around, moving the marker each time you reach it, until the cylinder is the required length, then fasten off the yarn.

## WORKING A TREBLE CROCHET CYLINDER WITHOUT TURNS

1  Make the required length of chain and join it into a ring with a slip stitch.

2  Work three chains (or the correct number of chains for the stitch you are using) to start the first round.

3  Work one treble crochet stitch into each chain until you reach the end of the round.

4  Join the first round by working a slip stitch into the third of the three starting chains.

5  Work the next and subsequent rounds in treble crochet stitch, joining each round with a slip stitch as before. When all the rounds have been worked, fasten off the yarn.

Treble crochet cylinder worked without turns.

Treble crochet cylinder worked with turns.

## WORKING A TREBLE CROCHET CYLINDER WITH TURNS

1  Work the foundation chain and first round of stitches as described in steps 1–4 of making a treble crochet cylinder without turns. Work three chains to begin the second round.

2  Turn the cylinder to reverse the direction to begin the second round. You will be working this round from the inside of the cylinder.

3  Work one treble crochet stitch into each stitch until you reach the end of the round. Join the round by working a slip stitch into the third of the three turning chains. Turn and work three chains, then work the next round from the outside of the cylinder. Continue in this way, making sure that you turn the work at the beginning of every round.

# CIRCULAR MOTIFS

WORKING CROCHET IN FLAT ROUNDS RATHER THAN BACKWARDS AND FORWARDS IN STRAIGHT ROWS OFFERS A NEW RANGE OF POSSIBILITIES FOR MAKING COLOURFUL AND INTRICATE PIECES OF CROCHET CALLED MOTIFS OR MEDALLIONS.

**SEE ALSO**
• Basic skills and stitches, pages 14–21
• Joining yarns, page 24

**A MOTIF WITH MANY USES**
Circular motifs are often worked in a variety of yarns and sizes to make items such as coasters and table mats.

Crochet motifs are worked outwards from a central ring and the number of stitches on each round increases. Evenly spaced increases result in a flat, circular motif, but when the increases are grouped together to make corners, the resulting motif can be a square, hexagon or other flat shape. Motifs can be solid, textured or lacy in appearance. They are joined together using a variety of techniques to make afghans, shawls and wraps, as well as simply shaped garments.

## WORKING IN ROUNDS

The usual way of starting to work a motif is to make a short length of chain and join it into a ring. The ring can be made any size, depending on the pattern instructions, and can leave a small or large hole at the centre of the motif.

### MAKING A RING OF STITCHES

1 Work the number of chains stated in the pattern and join into a ring by working a slip-stitch into the first stitch of this chain.

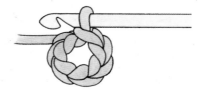

2 Gently tighten the first stitch by pulling the loose yarn end with your left hand. The foundation ring is now complete.

### WORKING INTO THE RING

1 After making the foundation ring, you are ready to begin the first round of the pattern. Work the number of starting chains stated in the pattern – three chains are shown here and will count as one treble crochet stitch.

2 Inserting the hook into the space at the centre of the ring each time, work the correct number of stitches into the ring as stated in the pattern. Count the stitches at the end of the round to make sure that you have worked the correct number.

3 Join the first and last stitches of the round together by working a slip stitch into the top of the starting chain.

## MAKING A YARN RING

This alternative method of making a foundation ring is useful because the yarn end is enclosed in the first round of stitches and will not need weaving in later.

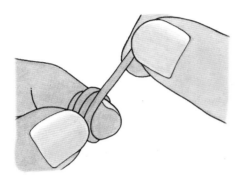

**1** Hold the yarn end between the thumb and forefinger of your left hand and wind the yarn several times around the tip of your forefinger.

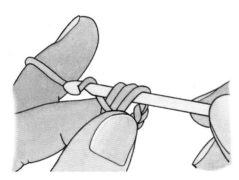

**2** Carefully slip the yarn ring off your finger. Inserting the hook into the ring, pull a loop of yarn through and work a double crochet stitch to secure the ring. Work the specified number of starting chains and the first round of pattern into the ring in the usual way.

## FASTENING OFF

For a really neat edge on the final round, use this method of sewing the first and last stitches together in preference to using a slip stitch.

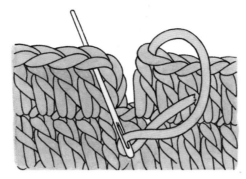

**1** Cut the yarn, leaving an end of about 10cm (4in), and draw it through the last stitch. With right side facing, thread the yarn end into a yarn or tapestry needle and take the needle under both loops of the stitch next to the starting chain.

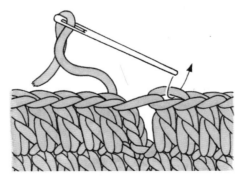

**2** Pull the needle through and insert it into the centre of the last stitch of the round. On the wrong side, pull the needle through to complete the stitch. Adjust the length of the stitch to close the round, then weave in the end on the wrong side in the usual way.

## JOINING ROUND MOTIFS

Circular motifs join less easily than motifs with straight sides because of their curved shape. They look best arranged in rows and sewn together with a few stitches where the curves touch.

# Stitch collection

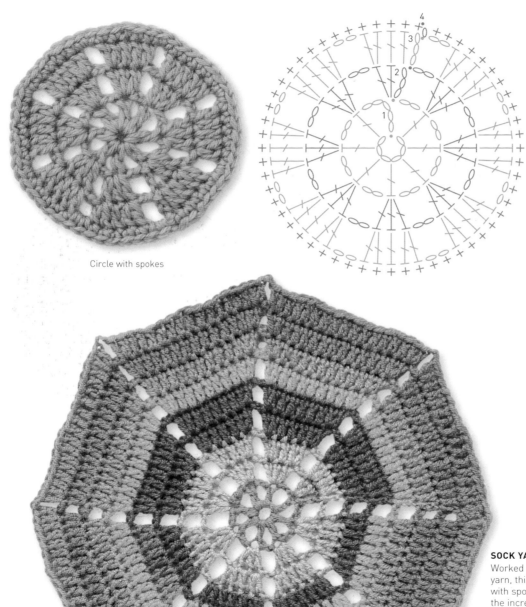

Circle with spokes

## Circle with spokes

**FOUNDATION RING:** Ch 6 and join with sl st to form a ring.

**ROUND 1:** Ch 5 (counts as 1 tr, ch 2), [1 tr, ch 2] into ring 7 times, join with sl st into 3rd of ch 5. (8 spaced tr)

**ROUND 2:** Ch 3 (counts as 1 tr), 2 tr into same place, ch 2, [3 tr into next tr, ch 2] 7 times, join with sl st into 3rd of ch 3.

**ROUND 3:** Ch 3 (counts as 1 tr), 1 tr into same place, 1 tr into next tr, 2 tr into next tr, ch 2, [2 tr into next tr, 1 tr into next tr, 2 tr into next tr, ch 2] 7 times, join with sl st into 3rd of ch 3.

**ROUND 4:** Ch 1, 1 dc into each tr to end working 2 dc into each ch 2 sp, join with sl st into first dc.

Fasten off yarn.

**SOCK YARN VARIATION**
Worked in self-striping sock yarn, this variation of the circle with spokes continues to work the increases in the pattern set to create an octagon.

# Treble crochet circle

**FOUNDATION RING:** Ch 6 and join with sl st to form a ring.

**ROUND 1:** Ch 3 (counts as 1 tr), 15 tr into ring, join with sl st into 3rd of ch 3. (16 tr)

**ROUND 2:** Ch 3 (counts as 1 tr), 1 tr into same place, 2 tr into each tr to end, join with sl st into 3rd of ch 3. (32 tr)

**ROUND 3:** Ch 3 (counts as 1 tr), 1 tr into same place, * [1 tr into next tr, 2 tr into next tr]; rep from * to last tr, 1 tr into last tr, join with sl st into 3rd of ch 3. (48 tr)

**ROUND 4:** Ch 3 (counts as 1 tr), 1 tr into same place, * [1 tr into each of next 2 tr, 2 tr into next tr]; rep from * to last 2 tr, 1 tr into each of last 2 tr, join with sl st into 3rd of ch 3. (64 tr)

Fasten off yarn.

This circle can be made larger than shown by working one more treble crochet stitch between the increases on each subsequent round.

Treble crochet circle

**STRIPED VARIATION**

Work the treble crochet circle using a different yarn colour on every round. Leave a 10cm (4in) end of yarn at each colour change, and weave in the yarn ends on the wrong side when the circle is complete.

# Stitch collection

## Sunburst circle

**YARN:** Worked in three colours, A, B and C.

**NOTE:** beg CL = beginning cluster made from two treble crochet stitches worked together (tr2tog).

CL = cluster made from three treble crochet stitches worked together (tr3tog).

**FOUNDATION RING:** Using yarn A, ch 4 and join with sl st to form a ring.

**ROUND 1:** Ch 1, 6 dc into ring, join with sl st into first dc.

**ROUND 2:** Ch 1, 2 dc into each dc to end, join with sl st into first dc. (12 dc)

**ROUND 3:** Ch 1, 2 dc into each dc to end, join with sl st into first dc. (24 dc)
Break off yarn A and join yarn B to any dc.

**ROUND 4:** Ch 3 (counts as 1 tr), beg CL into same dc, ch 2, sk next dc, * CL into next dc, ch 2, sk next dc; rep from * 10 times, join with sl st into top of beg CL.
Break off yarn B and join yarn C to any ch 2 sp.

**ROUND 5:** Ch 3 (counts as 1 tr), beg CL into same sp, ch 3, * CL into next ch 2 sp, ch 3; rep from * 10 times, join with sl st into top of beg CL.

**ROUND 6:** Ch 3, 2 tr into top of beg CL, 3 tr into next ch 3 sp, * 3 tr into top of next CL, 3 tr into next ch 3 sp; rep from * 10 times, join with sl st into 3rd of ch 3.
Fasten off yarn.

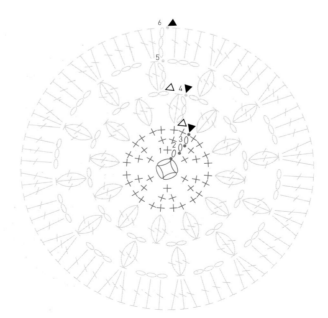

# Cluster circle

**NOTE:** beg CL = beginning cluster made from three treble crochet stitches worked together (tr3tog).

CL = cluster made from four treble crochet stitches worked together (tr4tog).

**FOUNDATION RING:** Ch 6 and join with sl st to form a ring.

**ROUND 1:** Ch 1, 12 dc into ring, join with sl st into first dc.

**ROUND 2:** Ch 4 (counts as 1 tr, ch 1), * 1 tr into next dc, ch 1; rep from * 10 times, join with sl st into 3rd of ch 4. (12 spaced tr)

**ROUND 3:** Sl st into next ch 1 sp, ch 3 (counts as 1 tr), beg CL into same sp, ch 3, * CL into next ch 1 sp, ch 3; rep from * 10 times, join with sl st into top of beg CL. (12 clusters)

**ROUND 4:** Sl st into next ch 3 sp, ch 3 (counts as 1 tr), beg CL into same sp, * ch 2, 1 tr into top of next CL, ch 2, ** CL into next ch 3 sp; rep from * 10 times and from * to ** once again, join with sl st into top of beg CL.

**ROUND 5:** Ch 1, 3 dc into each ch 2 sp to end, join with sl st into first dc.
Fasten off yarn.

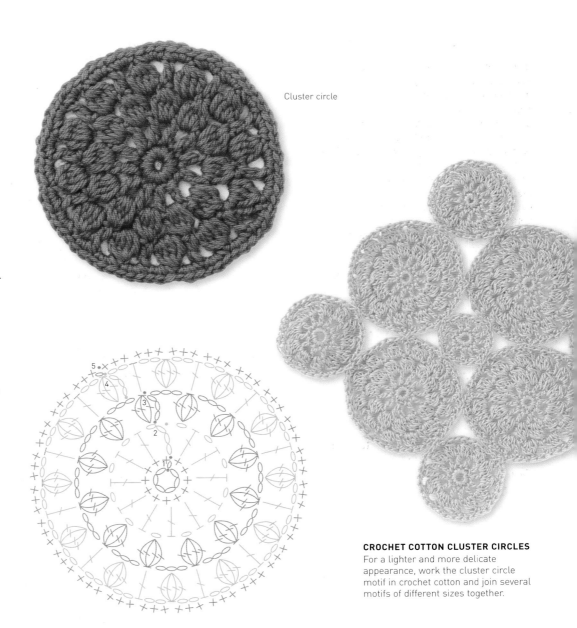

Cluster circle

**CROCHET COTTON CLUSTER CIRCLES**
For a lighter and more delicate appearance, work the cluster circle motif in crochet cotton and join several motifs of different sizes together.

KEY TO ABBREVIATIONS AND SYMBOLS **pages 150–151**

# SQUARE MOTIFS

SQUARE MOTIFS ARE WORKED IN A SIMILAR WAY TO CIRCULAR MOTIFS, STARTING AT THE CENTRE WITH A FOUNDATION RING AND WORKING OUTWARDS IN ROUNDS.

**SEE ALSO**
...............
- Basic skills and stitches, pages 14–21
- Circular motifs, pages 74–79

Extra stitches or chains are worked at regular intervals on some of the rounds to form corners. Some motifs, such as the granny square (see page 84), begin with a small circle at the centre. Others, such as the circle in a square (see page 83), have several rounds worked before the corners are made.

**JOINING MOTIFS WITH A NEEDLE**

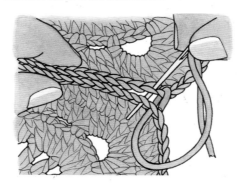

1 Lay out the motifs in the correct order, with right sides facing upwards. Using a yarn or tapestry needle and working in horizontal rows, stitch the motifs together, beginning with the top row of motifs. Begin stitching at the right-hand edge of the first two motifs, sewing into the back loops of corresponding stitches.

**JOINING SQUARE MOTIFS**
Square motifs can be stitched together or joined with rows of slip stitches or double crochet. For the neatest join, work the stitches through the back loops of the crochet. To make a stronger but more visible join, work the stitches through both loops.

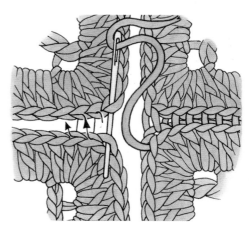

2 Continue stitching the first two motifs together, making sure that you join only the back loops of each edge together, until you reach the left-hand corner. Align the next two motifs, carry the yarn firmly across and join them together in the same way. For extra strength, you can work two stitches into the corner loops before and after carrying the yarn across. Continue joining motifs along the row, then secure the yarn ends carefully at the beginning and end of the stitching. Repeat until all the horizontal edges of the motifs are joined.

3 Turn the crochet so that the unstitched (vertical) edges of the motifs are now horizontal. Working in the same way as before, join the remaining edges together with horizontal rows of stitching. When working the corners, take the needle under the stitch made on the previous row of stitching.

**Tip**
*When joining two differently coloured squares by stitching them together, use a yarn that matches one of the squares so that the stitches are less noticeable.*

## JOINING MOTIFS WITH SLIP STITCH

Joining motif edges by slip stitching them together with a crochet hook makes a firm seam with an attractive ridge on the right side. To add interest, use a contrasting yarn colour to work the slip stitch rows.

## JOINING MOTIFS WITH DOUBLE CROCHET

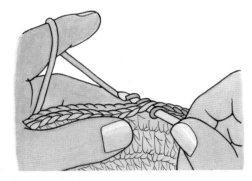

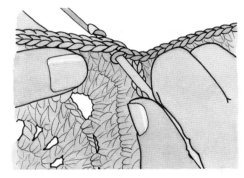

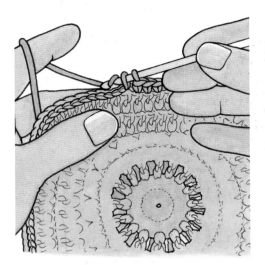

1  Lay out the motifs in the correct order. Working all the horizontal seams first, place the first two motifs together, wrong sides facing, and work a row of slip stitch through both loops of each motif.

2  When you reach the corner, align the next two motifs, carry the yarn firmly across and join them together in the same way. Continue joining motifs along the row, keeping your tension even. Secure the yarn ends carefully, then repeat until all the horizontal edges of the motifs are joined.

Double crochet can also be used to join edges together, and it makes a strong but rather bulky, thick seam. Work as for joining with slip stitch, but place the motifs right sides together and work rows of double crochet through both loops of the crochet edge.

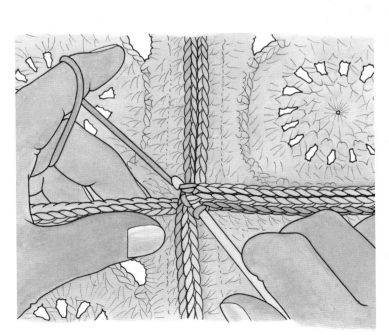

3  Turn the work so that the remaining (vertical) edges of the motifs are now horizontal. Working in the same way as before, join the remaining edges together with horizontal rows of slip stitch. When working the corners, carry the yarn firmly across the ridge.

## Tip

*If you are finding it difficult to insert your hook through the edges of the squares when joining motifs, use a slightly smaller hook or one that has a more pointed tip.*

# Stitch collection

## Croydon square

**YARN:** Worked in three colours, A, B and C.

**NOTE:** beg CL = beginning cluster made from two treble crochet stitches worked together (tr2tog).

CL = cluster made from three treble crochet stitches worked together (tr3tog).

**FOUNDATION RING:** Using yarn A, ch 4 and join with sl st to form a ring.

**ROUND 1:** Ch 4 (counts as 1 tr, ch 1), [1 tr into ring, ch 1] 11 times, join with sl st into 3rd of ch 4. (12 spaced tr)

**ROUND 2:** Ch 3 (counts as 1 tr), beg CL into same sp, [ch 3, CL into next ch 1 sp] 11 times, ch 3, join with sl st into top of beg CL.

**ROUND 3:** Sl st into centre st of next ch 3 sp, ch 1, 1 dc into same sp, [ch 5, 1 dc into next ch 3 sp] 11 times, ch 5, join with sl st into first dc.
Break off yarn A and join yarn B to centre st of any ch 5 sp.

**ROUND 4:** Ch 3 (counts as 1 tr), 4 tr into same sp, * ch 1, 1 dc into next ch 5 sp, ch 5, 1 dc into next ch 5 sp, ch 1, ** [5 tr, ch 3, 5 tr] into next ch 5 sp; rep from * twice and from * to ** once again, 5 tr into next ch 5 sp, ch 3, join with sl st into 3rd of ch 3.
Break off yarn B and join yarn C to any ch 3 sp.

**ROUND 5:** Ch 3 (counts as 1 tr), [1 tr, ch 2, 2 tr] into same sp, * 1 tr into each of next 4 tr, ch 4, 1 dc into next ch 5 sp, ch 4, sk next tr, 1 tr into each of next 4 tr, ** [2 tr, ch 2, 2 tr] into next ch 3 sp; rep from * twice and from * to ** once again, join with sl st into 3rd of ch 3.

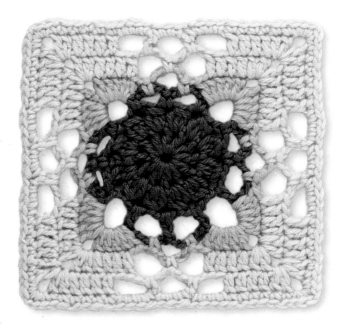

**ROUND 6:** Sl st into next tr and next ch 2 sp, ch 3 (counts as 1 tr), [1 tr, ch 2, 2 tr] into same sp, * 1 tr into each of next 4 tr, [ch 4, 1 tr into next ch 4 sp] twice, ch 4, sk next 2 tr, 1 tr into each of next 4 tr, ** [2 tr, ch 2, 2 tr] into next ch 2 sp; rep from * twice and from * to ** once again, join with sl st into 3rd of ch 3.

**ROUND 7:** Ch 1, 1 dc into same place, 1 dc into each tr to end working 4 dc into each ch 4 sp along sides and 3 dc into each ch 2 corner sp, join with sl st into first dc.
Fasten off yarn.

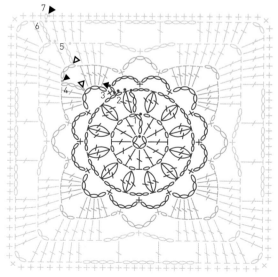

## Circle in a square

**FOUNDATION RING:** Ch 6 and join with sl st to form a ring.

**ROUND 1:** Ch 3 (counts as 1 tr), 15 tr into ring, join with sl st into 3rd of ch 3. (16 tr)

**ROUND 2:** Ch 5 (counts as 1 tr, ch 2), [1 tr into next tr, ch 2] 15 times, join with sl st into 3rd of ch 5.

**ROUND 3:** Ch 3, 2 tr into ch 2 sp, ch 1, [3 tr, ch 1] into each ch 2 sp to end, join with sl st into 3rd of ch 3.

**ROUND 4:** * [Ch 3, 1 dc into next ch 1 sp] 3 times, ch 6 (corner sp made), 1 dc into next ch 1 sp; rep from * to end, join with sl st into first of ch 3.

**ROUND 5:** Ch 3, 2 tr into first ch 3 sp, 3 tr into each of next two ch 3 sps, * [5 tr, ch 2, 5 tr] into corner sp, ** 3 tr into each of next three ch 3 sps; rep from * twice and from * to ** once again, join with sl st into 3rd of ch 3.

**ROUND 6:** Ch 3, 1 tr into each tr to end working [1 tr, 1 dtr, 1 tr] into each ch 2 corner sp, join with sl st into 3rd of ch 3. Fasten off yarn.

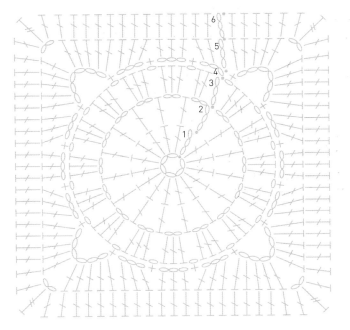

KEY TO ABBREVIATIONS AND SYMBOLS **pages 150–151**

## Stitch collection

### Granny square

**YARN:** Worked in four colours, A, B, C and D.

**FOUNDATION RING:** Using yarn A, ch 6 and join with sl st to form a ring.

**ROUND 1:** Ch 3 (counts as 1 tr), 2 tr into ring, ch 3, * 3 tr into ring, ch 3; rep from * twice, join with sl st into 3rd of ch 3.

Break off yarn A and join yarn B to any ch 3 sp.

**ROUND 2:** Ch 3 (counts as 1 tr), [2 tr, ch 3, 3 tr] into same sp (corner made), * ch 1, [3 tr, ch 3, 3 tr] into next ch 3 sp; rep from * twice, ch 1, join with sl st into 3rd of ch 3.

Break off yarn B and join yarn C to any ch 3 corner sp.

**ROUND 3:** Ch 3 (counts as 1 tr), [2 tr, ch 3, 3 tr] into same sp, * ch 1, 3 tr into next ch 1 sp, ch 1, ** [3 tr, ch 3, 3 tr] into next ch 3 corner sp; rep from * twice and from * to ** once again, join with sl st into 3rd of ch 3.

Break off yarn C and join yarn D to any ch 3 corner sp.

**ROUND 4:** Ch 3 (counts as 1 tr), [2 tr, ch 3, 3 tr] into same sp, * [ch 1, 3 tr] into each ch 1 sp along side of square, ch 1, ** [3 tr, ch 3, 3 tr] into next ch 3 corner sp; rep from * twice and from * to ** once again, join with sl st into 3rd of ch 3.

Break off yarn D and join yarn A to any ch 3 corner sp.

**ROUND 5:** Ch 3 (counts as 1 tr), [2 tr, ch 3, 3 tr] into same sp, * [ch 1, 3 tr] into each ch 1 sp along side of square, ch 1, ** [3 tr, ch 3, 3 tr] into next ch 3 corner sp; rep from * twice and from * to ** once again, join with sl st into 3rd of ch 3.

**ROUND 6:** Sl st into next ch 3 corner sp, ch 3 (counts as 1 tr), [2 tr, ch 3, 3 tr] into same sp, * [ch 1, 3 tr] into each ch 1 sp along side of square, ch 1, ** [3 tr, ch 3, 3 tr] into next ch 3 corner sp; rep from * twice and from * to ** once again, join with sl st into 3rd of ch 3. Fasten off yarn.

**KEY TO ABBREVIATIONS AND SYMBOLS** pages 150–151

# HEXAGON MOTIFS

HEXAGON MOTIFS ARE WORKED IN A SIMILAR WAY TO CIRCULAR AND SQUARE MOTIFS, BUT THEY NEED DIFFERENT SEQUENCES OF INCREASES TO MAKE SIX CORNERS. HEXAGON MOTIFS WITH A SOLIDLY CROCHETED LAST ROUND CAN BE STITCHED OR CROCHETED TOGETHER TO MAKE LARGE PIECES OF CROCHET SUCH AS AFGHANS, THROWS AND SHAWLS IN THE SAME WAY AS SQUARE MOTIFS.

### SEE ALSO
• Basic skills and
  stitches, pages 14–21
• Circular motifs,
  pages 74–79
• Square motifs,
  pages 80–84

The centres of hexagon motifs may have a circular or hexagonal shape, depending on the pattern. When working a motif with a hexagonal centre, remember that you will be working six corners rather than the four needed for a square, so you need to work the foundation ring fairly loosely in order to make sure that the finished hexagon will lie flat.

**BEGINNING WITH A HEXAGONAL CENTRE**

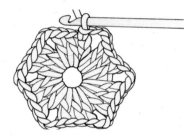

**1** Work the foundation ring, then work six groups of stitches separated by chain spaces as indicated in the pattern to make a hexagon shape. Join the round with a slip stitch in the usual way.

**2** On the second round, work two groups of stitches separated by a chain space into each of the chain spaces on the previous round to continue making a hexagon shape. Work additional rows as indicated in the pattern.

You can join hexagons into long strips and then join the strips together, or simply lay out the pieces in the required arrangement and join the edges that touch with separate seams. Pay special attention to securing the yarn ends neatly at the beginning and end of each seam. When joining motifs that have a lacy last round, such as the classic hexagon (see page 87), you can crochet these together as you work.

**BEGINNING WITH A CIRCULAR CENTRE**

**1** Work the foundation ring, then work the number of stitches indicated in the pattern. The stitches form a circle, and they may be solidly worked or separated by a single chain space. Join the round with a slip stitch in the usual way.

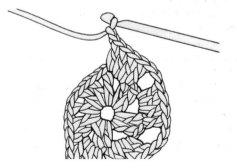

**2** On the second round, work groups of stitches separated by chain spaces into the previous round. This creates a hexagon shape in which the corners are formed by chain spaces rather than by groups of stitches. The chain spaces act as a foundation for corners worked on the next and subsequent rounds.

## JOINING HEXAGONS AS YOU WORK

To begin, work one complete motif, then join the edges of additional motifs to the original one as you work the final rounds.

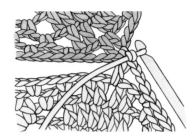

1  Work the second motif until you reach the last round. Work in pattern along the first side, then work the first treble crochet stitch of the corner group. Align the edges of both motifs and join by working a double crochet stitch into the chain space of the corner on the first hexagon.

2  Return to the second hexagon and work a treble crochet stitch into it to complete the corner.

3  Continue working around the second hexagon, joining the chain spaces of each hexagon together by working one chain, one double crochet into the opposite chain space and one double chain until you reach the next corner. At the corner, work the first treble crochet stitch of the pattern, then one double crochet stitch into the chain space of the first hexagon.

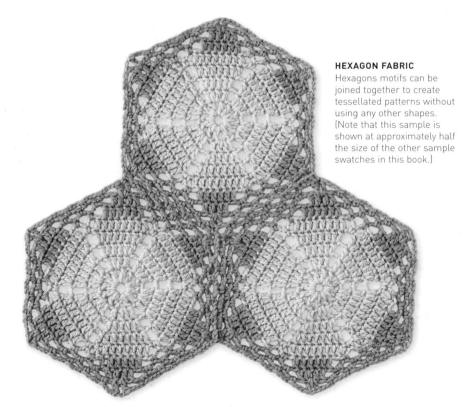

### HEXAGON FABRIC

Hexagons motifs can be joined together to create tessellated patterns without using any other shapes. (Note that this sample is shown at approximately half the size of the other sample swatches in this book.)

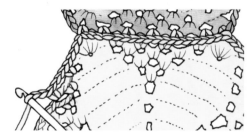

4  Work one treble crochet stitch to complete the corner, then work the remainder of the last round as instructed in the pattern. Fasten off the yarn. Join other hexagons to the first two in the same way, joining one, two or more edges as required.

### Tip

*You can join the first few hexagons to make a strip and use this as a base for attaching the remaining motifs if you are making a rectangular piece, or begin with one motif and let your piece grow outwards from the centre.*

# Stitch collection

## Classic hexagon

**YARN:** Worked in three colours, A, B and C.

**FOUNDATION RING:** Using yarn A, ch 6 and join with sl st to form a ring.

**ROUND 1:** Ch 4 (counts as 1 tr, ch 1), [1 tr into ring, ch 1] 11 times, join with sl st into 3rd of ch 4. (12 spaced tr)

**ROUND 2:** Ch 3 (counts as 1 tr), 2 tr into next ch 1 sp, 1 tr into next tr, ch 2, * 1 tr into next tr, 2 tr into next ch 1 sp, 1 tr into next tr, ch 2; rep from * 4 times, join with sl st into 3rd of ch 3.

**ROUND 3:** Ch 3, 1 tr into same place, 1 tr into each of next 2 tr, 2 tr into next tr, ch 2, * 2 tr into next tr, 1 tr into each of next 2 tr, 2 tr into next tr, ch 2; rep from * 4 times, join with sl st into 3rd of ch 3. Break off yarn A and join yarn B.

**ROUND 4:** Ch 3, 1 tr into same place, 1 tr into each of next 4 tr, 2 tr into next tr, ch 2, * 2 tr into next tr, 1 tr into each of next 4 tr, 2 tr into next tr, ch 2; rep from * 4 times, join with sl st into 3rd of ch 3.

**ROUND 5:** Ch 3, 1 tr into each of next 7 tr, * ch 3, 1 dc into next ch 2 sp, ch 3, 1 tr into each of next 8 tr; rep from * 4 times, ch 3, 1 dc into next ch 2 sp, ch 3, join with sl st into 3rd of ch 3.
Break off yarn B and join yarn C into top of next tr.

**ROUND 6:** Ch 3, 1 tr into each of next 5 tr, * ch 3, [1 dc into next ch 3 sp, ch 3] twice, sk next tr, 1 tr into each of next 6 tr; rep from * 4 times, ch 3, [1 dc into next ch 3 sp, ch 3] twice, join with sl st into 3rd of ch 3.

**ROUND 7:** Sl st into next tr, ch 3, 1 tr into each of next 3 tr, * ch 3, [1 dc into next ch 3 sp, ch 3] 3 times, sk next tr, 1 tr into each of next 4 tr; rep from * 4 times, ch 3, [1 dc into next ch 3 sp, ch 3] 3 times, join with sl st into 3rd of ch 3.

**ROUND 8:** Sl st between 2nd and 3rd tr of group, ch 4 (counts as 1 tr, ch 1), 1 tr into same place, * ch 3, [1 dc into next ch 3 sp, ch 3] 4 times, [1 tr, ch 1, 1 tr] between 2nd and 3rd tr of group; rep from * 4 times, ch 3, [1 dc into ch 3 sp, ch 3] 4 times, join with sl st into 3rd of ch 4.
Fasten off yarn.

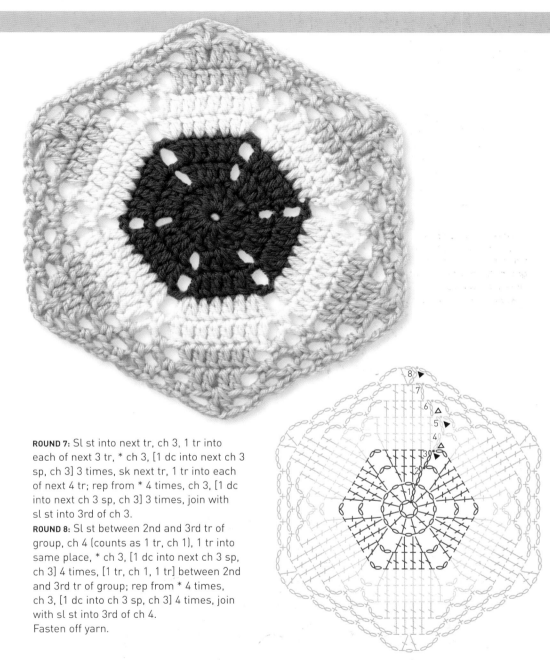

# Stitch collection

## Wheel hexagon

**FOUNDATION RING:** Ch 6 and join with sl st to form a ring.

**ROUND 1:** Ch 6 (counts as 1 dtr, ch 2), 1 dtr into ring, * ch 2, 1 dtr into ring; rep from * 9 times, ch 2, join with sl st into 4th of ch 6. (12 spaced dtr)

**ROUND 2:** Sl st into next ch 2 sp, ch 3 (counts as 1 tr), [1 tr, ch 2, 2 tr] into same ch 2 sp as sl st, * 3 tr into next ch 2 sp, [2 tr, ch 2, 2 tr] into next ch 2 sp; rep from * 4 times, 3 tr into next ch 2 sp, join with sl st into 3rd of ch 3.

**ROUND 3:** Ch 3 (counts as 1 tr), 1 tr into next tr, * [2 tr, ch 3, 2 tr] into next ch 2 sp, 1 tr into each of next 7 tr; rep from * 4 times, [2 tr, ch 3, 2 tr] into next ch 2 sp, 1 tr into each of next 5 tr, join with sl st into 3rd of ch 3.

**ROUND 4:** Ch 3 (counts as 1 tr), 1 tr into each of next 3 tr, * 3 tr into next ch 3 sp, 1 tr into each of next 11 tr; rep from * 4 times, 3 tr into next ch 3 sp, 1 tr into each of next 7 tr, join with sl st into 3rd of ch 3.
Fasten off yarn.

**SMALL WHEEL HEXAGON**
You can often reduce the size of a motif by simply omitting the final round. To make this small wheel hexagon, omit round 4 and work 2 tr, ch 1, 2 tr into the corner spaces on round 3 (instead of 2 tr, ch 3, 2 tr). This sample has been worked in Aran-weight yarn (rather than double knitting) to give a slightly bulkier appearance, despite the smaller size.

Wheel hexagon

# Granny hexagon

**YARN:** Worked in three colours, A, B and C.

**FOUNDATION RING:** Using yarn A, ch 8 and join with sl st to form a ring.

**ROUND 1:** Ch 3 (counts as 1 tr), 2 tr into ring, ch 3, * 3 tr into ring, ch 3; rep from * 4 times, join with sl st into 3rd of ch 3. Break off yarn A and join yarn B to any ch 3 sp.

**ROUND 2:** Ch 3 (counts as 1 tr), [2 tr, ch 3, 3 tr] into same sp (corner made), * ch 1, [3 tr, ch 3, 3 tr] into next ch 3 sp (corner made); rep from * 4 times, ch 1, join with sl st into 3rd of ch 3. Break off yarn B and join yarn C to any corner sp.

**ROUND 3:** Ch 3, [2 tr, ch 3, 3 tr] into same sp, * ch 1, 3 tr into next ch 1 sp, ch 1, [3 tr, ch 3, 3 tr] into next corner sp; rep from * 4 times, ch 1, 3 tr into next ch 1 sp, ch 1, join with sl st into 3rd of ch 3. Break off yarn C and join yarn B to any corner sp.

**ROUND 4:** Ch 3, [2 tr, ch 3, 3 tr] into same sp, * [ch 1, 3 tr into each ch 1 sp] along side of hexagon, ch 1, [3 tr, ch 3, 3 tr] into next corner sp; rep from * 4 times, [ch 1, 3 tr into each ch 1 sp] along side of hexagon, ch 1, join with sl st into 3rd of ch 3. Break off yarn B and join yarn A to any corner sp.

**ROUND 5:** Ch 3, [2 tr, ch 3, 3 tr] into same sp, * [ch 1, 3 tr into each ch 1 sp] along side of hexagon, ch 1, [3 tr, ch 3, 3 tr] into next corner sp; rep from * 4 times, [ch 1, 3 tr into each ch 1 sp] along side of hexagon, ch 1, join with sl st into 3rd of ch 3.

**ROUND 6:** Ch 1, 1 dc into each tr to end working 1 dc into each ch 1 sp along sides of hexagon and 3 dc into each ch 3 corner sp, join with sl st into first dc. Fasten off yarn.

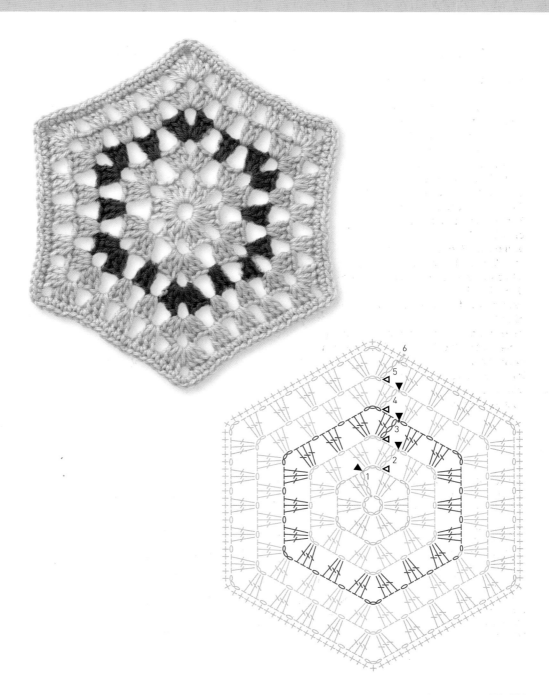

# TUNISIAN CROCHET

OFTEN REFERRED TO AS AFGHAN STITCH, TUNISIAN CROCHET COMBINES THE TECHNIQUES OF BOTH CROCHET AND KNITTING TO PRODUCE A STRONG, ELASTIC FABRIC.

## SEE ALSO

• Basic skills and stitches, pages 14–21

Tunisian crochet hooks look like long knitting needles with a hook at one end, and they are available in a range of sizes and lengths. The length of the hook determines how wide the crochet fabric can be. Flexible hooks are also available. These consist of a short hooked needle joined to a length of flexible cord with a stopper at the end. Flexible hooks come in longer lengths than ordinary Tunisian hooks, and enable you to work wider pieces of crochet. Yarn and hook are held in the same way as for ordinary crochet.

### PLAIN TUNISIAN CROCHET

This basic Tunisian crochet stitch pattern can be adapted using common knitting techniques such as intarsia and cabling.

### WORKING PLAIN TUNISIAN STITCH

Tunisian crochet fabric is made on a foundation chain, and each row is worked in two stages. In the first stage, the loop row, a series of loops are made on to the needle, then on the return row the loops are worked off the needle in pairs without turning the work. Plain Tunisian is the simplest technique, but variations can be made by inserting the hook in different positions and changing how the loops are worked.

**1  BEGIN FIRST LOOP ROW:** After making a foundation chain in the usual way, insert the hook under the back loop of the second chain from the hook, wrap the yarn over the hook and draw a loop through the chain so that you have two loops on the hook.

**2**  Insert the hook under the back loop of the third chain from the hook, wrap the yarn over the hook and draw a loop through so that you have three loops on the hook.

**3** Repeat along the row until you have made a loop from each chain and have a row of loops on the hook. Do not turn the work.

**4** BEGIN FIRST RETURN ROW: Wrap the yarn over the hook and draw it through the first loop on the hook. Wrap the yarn over the hook again and draw it through the next two loops on the hook. Continue working from left to right, working off two loops at a time until only one loop remains on the hook.

**5** BEGIN SECOND LOOP ROW: To work the second loop row, skip the first vertical bar and insert the hook from right to left under the next vertical bar. Wrap the yarn over the hook and draw it through to make a loop on the hook so that you have two loops on the hook.

**6** Insert the hook under the next vertical bar, wrap the yarn over the hook and draw a loop through so that you have three loops on the hook. Repeat along the row until you have a row of loops on the hook. Do not turn the work.

**7** BEGIN SECOND RETURN ROW: To work the return row, wrap the yarn over the hook and draw it through the first loop on the hook, then work off the row of loops in the same way as step 4, leaving one loop on the hook at the end of the row. Repeat from step 5 for length required, ending with a return row.

**TUNISIAN CROCHET HOOK**
Like knitting, the width of your Tunisian crochet is determined by the length of the hook.

**PLAIN TUNISIAN CROCHET CHART**
The symbol in each block of this chart indicates that you should work one plain Tunisian crochet stitch.

### FINISHING THE TOP EDGE OF TUNISIAN CROCHET

After working a piece of Tunisian crochet, finish off the top edge with a row of double crochet stitches to neaten and strengthen the edge.

**1** Wrap the yarn over the hook and draw it through the loop on the hook to make a turning chain.

**2** Insert the hook from right to left under the second vertical bar, wrap the yarn over the hook and draw a loop through so that you have two loops on the hook.

**3** Wrap the yarn over the hook again and draw it through both loops on the hook to complete the double crochet stitch.

**4** Work a double crochet stitch under each vertical bar of the row, then fasten off the yarn.

## Tunisian knit stitch

ANY NUMBER OF CHAINS PLUS 1

This variation of plain Tunisian crochet looks like knitted stocking stitch on the right side, but the fabric is thicker and more substantial than stocking stitch. You may find that you need to use a larger hook when working this stitch.

**ROW 1: (LOOP ROW)** Insert hook into 2nd ch from hook, yo, draw lp through, * [insert hook into next ch, yo, draw lp through]; rep from * to end, leaving all lps on hook. Do not turn.

**ROW 1: (RETURN ROW)** Yo, draw through one lp on hook, * [yo, draw through 2 lps on hook]; rep from * to end, leaving last lp on hook.

**ROW 2: (LOOP ROW)** Sk first vertical bar, insert hook from front to back through next vertical bar, yo, draw lp through, * [insert hook from front to back through next vertical bar, yo, draw lp through]; rep from * to end, leaving all lps on hook. Do not turn.

**ROW 2: (RETURN ROW)** Yo, draw through one lp on hook, * [yo, draw through 2 lps on hook]; rep from * to end, leaving last lp on hook.

Rep row 2 for length required, ending with return row.

To finish the top edge, work as shown in the step-by-step sequence on the left, but insert the hook from front to back through each vertical bar.

Fasten off yarn.

# Tunisian mesh stitch

This variation makes a lovely, lacy fabric with good drape, perfect for making a baby blanket or shawl.

**ROW 1: (LOOP ROW)** Insert hook into 3rd ch from hook, yo, draw lp through, ch 1, * [insert hook into next ch, yo, draw lp through, ch 1]; rep from * to end, leaving all lps on hook. Do not turn.

**ROW 1: (RETURN ROW)** Yo, draw through one lp on hook, * [yo, draw through 2 lps on hook]; rep from * to end, leaving last lp on hook.

**ROW 2: (LOOP ROW)** Ch 1, sk first vertical bar, * [insert hook under horizontal bar slightly above and behind next vertical bar, yo, draw lp through, ch 1]; rep from * to end, leaving all lps on hook. Do not turn.

**ROW 2: (RETURN ROW)** Yo, draw through one lp on hook, * [yo, draw through 2 lps on hook]; rep from * to end, leaving last lp on hook.

Rep row 2 for length required, ending with a return row.

To finish the top edge, work as shown in the step-by-step sequence opposite, but insert the hook under the horizontal bar slightly above and behind the next vertical bar. Fasten off yarn.

Tunisian knit stitch

Tunisian mesh stitch

KEY TO ABBREVIATIONS AND SYMBOLS **pages 150–151**

# BROOMSTICK CROCHET

BROOMSTICK CROCHET IS WORKED WITH AN ORDINARY CROCHET HOOK AND A LARGE KNITTING NEEDLE, AND MAKES A SOFT, VERY LACY FABRIC.

## SEE ALSO
• Basic skills and stitches, pages 14–21

The length of the knitting needle determines the width of the crochet fabric, so you may need to make several strips and sew them together to get the desired width. This technique is used to make shawls, scarves, wraps and blankets, and it looks good worked in a smooth woollen yarn or a soft mohair.

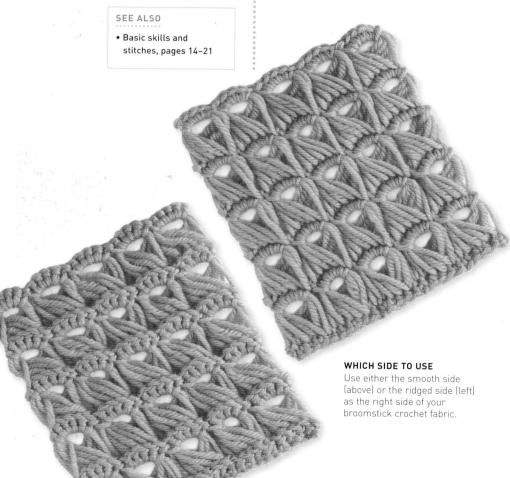

**WHICH SIDE TO USE**
Use either the smooth side (above) or the ridged side (left) as the right side of your broomstick crochet fabric.

## WORKING BROOMSTICK CROCHET

Each row of broomstick crochet is worked in two stages. In the first stage, the loop row, a series of loops is worked and transferred on to the knitting needle. On the return row, all the loops are slipped off the needle, then crocheted together to make groups. For the beginner, it is best to make a two-row foundation as shown below, but the more experienced crocheter may be able to work the first row directly into a foundation chain.

**1** Make a foundation chain to the width required, making sure that you have a multiple of five stitches plus turning chain, then turn and work a row of double crochet into the chain.

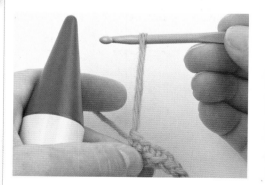

**2** BEGIN LOOP ROW: Hold the knitting needle securely under your left arm, extend the loop already on the crochet hook and slip it over the needle.

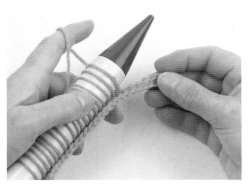

**3** Insert the hook into the second stitch, wrap the yarn over the hook and draw a loop through, then extend the loop and slip it on to the needle.

**4** Draw a loop through each stitch of the foundation row in this way to complete the loop row. Check that the number of loops is a multiple of five.

**5** **BEGIN RETURN ROW:** Slip all the loops off the needle and hold the work in your left hand. Insert the hook from right to left through the first five loops.

**6** Wrap the yarn over the hook, draw a loop through the centre of the five-loop group, and make one chain.

**7** Work five double crochet stitches through the centre of the loops. Continue along the row of loops in this way, grouping five loops together and working five double crochet stitches through the centre of each group of loops to complete the first return row.

**8** To work the next loop row, do not turn the work. Extend the first loop over the needle as before, and repeat the loop row as above. Continue working alternate loop and return rows until the fabric is the required length, ending with a return row.

**Tip**

*You may find that broomstick crochet is rather fiddly to work at first, especially when working the loop rows. Gripping the knitting needle between your knees instead of holding it under your arm can make handling the needle easier.*

# HAIRPIN CROCHET

HAIRPIN CROCHET (ALSO CALLED HAIRPIN LACE AND HAIRPIN BRAID) IS WORKED WITH AN ORDINARY CROCHET HOOK AND A SPECIAL HAIRPIN TOOL. THE TECHNIQUE MAKES STRIPS OF VERY LACY CROCHET THAT ARE OFTEN USED TO DECORATE THE EDGES OF ORDINARY CROCHET.

Hairpin tools are adjustable, so you can make different widths of crochet. The metal pins are held in position by plastic clips or bars at the top and bottom, and the pins can be placed close together to make a narrow strip or moved farther apart to make a wide strip.

A series of loops are made between the two pins using the yarn and the crochet hook until the tool is full of loops. At this point, the loops are taken off the pins, leaving the final few loops on the pins so that work can continue. When the strip reaches the desired length, all the loops are taken off the tool. You can use the hairpin crochet exactly as it comes off the tool, or you can work a row of double crochet stitches along each looped edge if you prefer.

**HAIRPIN CROCHET TOOL**
Hairpin crochet tools are adjustable.

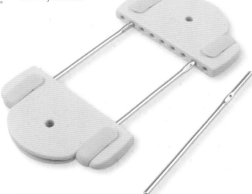

### Tip

*If you find it difficult to keep the work centred between the pins, secure the yarn end to the bottom clip of the tool with a piece of masking tape after you have centred the knot in step 2.*

**HAIRPIN CROCHET STRIP**
Strips of hairpin crochet can be joined together to make a fabric.

## WORKING HAIRPIN LACE

**1** Arrange the pins in the bottom clip of the hairpin tool so that the pins are the required distance apart. Make a slip knot in the yarn and loop it over the left-hand pin.

**2** Ease the knot across so that it lies in the centre between the pins. Take the yarn back around the right-hand pin, tensioning it with your fingers as if you were working ordinary crochet.

3  Insert the crochet hook into the loop on the left-hand pin, wrap the yarn over the hook and draw it through the loop.

4  Wrap the yarn over the hook again and draw it through the loop on the hook to secure the yarn.

5  Holding the hook vertically, turn the hairpin tool 180 degrees clockwise to make a half turn. The yarn is now wound around the right-hand pin and the other side of the clip is facing you.

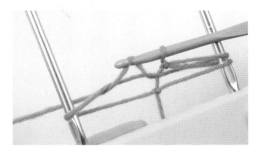

6  Insert the hook under the front loop on the left-hand pin, pick up the yarn at the back of the tool and draw a loop of yarn through so that there are two loops on the hook.

7  Wrap the yarn over the hook and draw it through the two loops on the hook to make a double crochet stitch.

8  Repeat steps 5, 6 and 7 until the hairpin tool is filled with braid, remembering to turn the tool clockwise each time.

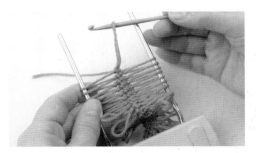

9  When the tool is full, put the top clip on to the pins, remove the lower clip and slide the crochet strip downwards, leaving the last few loops on the pins.

10  Reinsert the lower clip, remove the top clip and continue working the strip as before. When the strip is the required length, pull the yarn end through the last stitch with the hook and slide the strip off the pins.

11  To work an edging, make a slip knot on the hook, insert the hook into the first loop along one edge and work a double crochet stitch. Keeping the loops twisted in the same direction, work a double crochet into each loop along the edge, then fasten off the yarn. Repeat along the second edge.

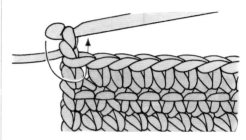

# EDGE FINISHES

AN EDGE FINISH IS A TYPE OF CROCHET EDGING THAT IS WORKED DIRECTLY ON TO THE EDGES OF ANOTHER PIECE OF CROCHET (AS OPPOSED TO BEING WORKED SEPARATELY AND THEN ATTACHED).

**SEE ALSO**
- Basic skills and stitches, pages 14–21
- Edgings, pages 108–109

The basic edge finish is a row of double crochet stitches, and this is often worked as a base before other, more decorative, edgings are worked. Crab stitch edging (also known as reversed double crochet) makes a hard-wearing knotted edge; shell edging adds a pretty, feminine finish to garments; and picot edging makes a delicately toothed edge.

**WORKING A DOUBLE CROCHET EDGING**

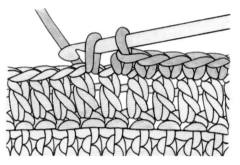

Working from right to left along the row, work a row of double crochet stitches into the edge of the crochet fabric, spacing the stitches evenly along the edge.

**WORKING A CRAB STITCH EDGING**

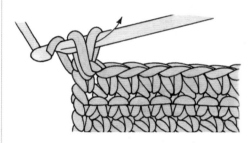

1 Unlike most other crochet techniques, this stitch is worked from left to right along the row. Keeping the yarn at the back of the work, insert the hook from front to back into the next stitch.

2 Wrap the yarn over the hook and draw the loop through to the front so that there are two loops on the hook. Wrap the yarn over the hook again, then draw the yarn through both loops to complete the stitch. Continue in this way along the edge.

Double crochet edging

Crab stitch edging

## WORKING A SHELL EDGING

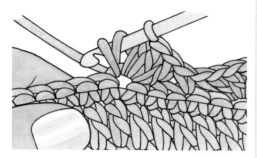

**1** Work a foundation row of double crochet (a multiple of 6 stitches plus 1) into the edge of the crochet fabric, then make one chain and turn. Working from right to left along the row, work one double crochet into the first stitch, * skip the next two stitches and then work five treble crochet stitches into the next stitch to make a shell.

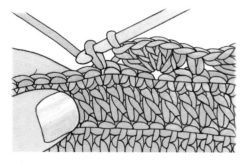

**2** Skip two stitches and work a double crochet into the next stitch. Repeat from * along the edge.

## WORKING A PICOT EDGING

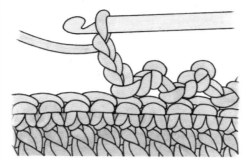 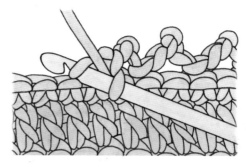

**1** With wrong side facing, work a row of an even number of double crochet stitches along the edge and turn. * To work a picot, make three chains.

**2** Insert the hook into the back of the third chain from the hook and work a slip stitch into it.

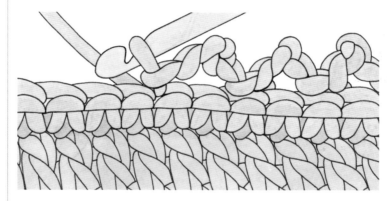

**3** Working from right to left along the row, skip one stitch along the double crochet edge and work a slip stitch into the next double crochet. Repeat from * along the edge.

Shell edging

Picot edging

# BUTTONHOLES AND BUTTON LOOPS

BANDS WITH BUTTONS, BUTTONHOLES AND BUTTON LOOPS ARE BEST WORKED IN DOUBLE CROCHET FOR STRENGTH AND NEATNESS. BUTTON LOOPS ARE A DECORATIVE ALTERNATIVE TO THE ORDINARY BUTTONHOLE, AND ARE ESPECIALLY SUITABLE FOR LACY GARMENTS.

**SEE ALSO**
• Basic skills and stitches, pages 14–21
• Edge finishes, pages 98–99

Make the button band first, mark the positions of the buttons with safety pins and work the buttonhole (or button loop) band to match, making holes or loops opposite the safety pin markers.

**WORKING BUTTONHOLES**

To make a buttonhole band, work a row of evenly spaced double crochet stitches along the garment edge, with the right side of the garment facing you. Work additional rows of double crochet until the band is the required width for positioning the buttonholes (about half of the total width of the button band), ending with a wrong side row.

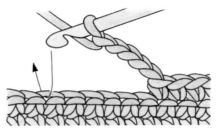

1 Work in double crochet to the position of the buttonhole, skip a few stitches to accommodate the size of the button and work the same number of chains over the skipped stitches.

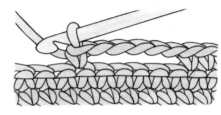

2 Anchor the chain by working a double crochet stitch after the skipped stitches. Continue in this way along the band until all the buttonholes have been worked.

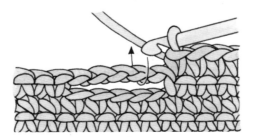

3 On the return (wrong side) row, work a double crochet into each stitch and work the same number of stitches into each chain loop as there are chains.

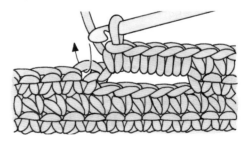

4 Continue along the row in this way, then work additional rows of double crochet until the buttonhole band is the same width as the button band.

## WORKING BUTTON LOOPS

To make a band for button loops, work a row of evenly spaced double crochet stitches along the garment edge, with the right side of the garment facing you. Work additional rows of double crochet until the band is the required width, ending with a wrong side row. Bands for button loops are usually narrower than those with buttonholes.

### CHOOSING BUTTONS

Buttons come in all shapes and sizes, and can add a unique touch to any crochet project. Take care to choose buttons that suit your project – for baby garments, choose small flat buttons; for adult garments or an accessory such as a bag, you can make a feature of large decorative buttons. A button collection found in a second-hand shop can be a great bargain, and just one extraordinary button can even inspire a new project. To sew on buttons, use a sharp needle and matching yarn, or sewing thread in a matching or contrasting colour.

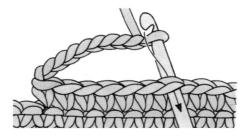

1 Work in double crochet to the position of the loop, then work several more stitches. Work a loop of chains to accommodate the button and turn it towards the right. Slip the hook out of the chain and insert it into the crochet at the point where you want the loop to finish.

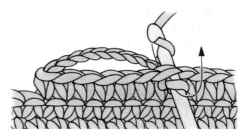

2 Insert the tip of the hook into the last chain, wrap the yarn over the hook and join the loop to the band with a slip stitch.

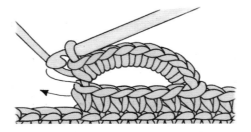

3 To complete the loop, work a series of double crochet stitches into the loop until the chain is completely covered.

4 Insert the hook into the last double crochet worked before making the chain and work a slip stitch. Continue along the row in double crochet until all the loops have been worked.

# CORDS

CROCHET CORDS CAN BE FLAT OR ROUNDED, NARROW OR WIDE. THEY ARE USED TO MAKE HANDLES AND SHOULDER STRAPS FOR BAGS, AND AS TIES TO SECURE A NECKLINE OR THE FRONT OF A GARMENT. NARROW CORD CAN BE SEWN ON TO A PLAIN PIECE OF CROCHET TO DECORATE IT WITH SHAPES SUCH AS SPIRALS, STRIPES OR SWIRLS.

### SEE ALSO

• Tubular crochet, pages 72–73

Single slip stitch cord

Double slip stitch cord

Double crochet cord

Striped double crochet cord

Round cord

When making a crochet cord, you will need to make the foundation chain longer than the finished cord you require, because the chain will contract as you work into it. Make several more centimetres of chain than you think you will need. Using slip stitch is the quickest and easiest way of making a narrow yet substantial cord that is good for making ties and using as decoration. The double slip stitch cord is wider than the single slip stitch version.

### MAKING A SINGLE SLIP STITCH CORD

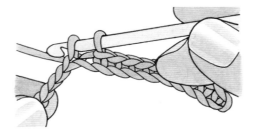

Work a foundation chain to the required length. Change to a size smaller hook, insert it into the second chain from the hook and work a row of slip stitch along the top of the chain. You can alter the effect by working the slip stitch row into the back bumps of the chain rather than into one or both of the top loops.

### MAKING A DOUBLE SLIP STITCH CORD

Work a foundation chain to the required length. Change to a size smaller hook, insert it into the second chain from the hook and work a row of slip stitch along the first side of the chain. At the end of the first side, work one chain, turn and continue along the second side of the chain in the same way.

### MAKING A DOUBLE CROCHET CORD

This makes a flat cord that is wider than a slip stitch cord. You can leave the cord plain or add a contrasting row of crochet down the centre for added interest.

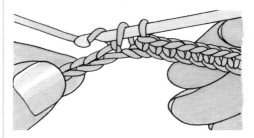

1  Work a foundation chain to the required length. Change to a size smaller hook, insert it into the second chain from the hook and work a row of double crochet along one side of the chain.

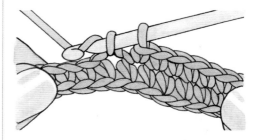

2  At the end of the first side, work one chain, turn and continue along the second side of the chain in the same way.

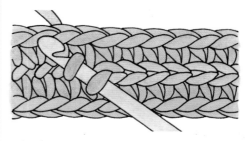

3  Using a contrast yarn, work a row of slip stitch down the centre of the cord. You may need to use a larger hook size for the contrast yarn in order to prevent the stitches from puckering.

## MAKING A ROUND CORD

Unlike the other types of crochet cord, this one is worked around and around in a continuous spiral of double crochet stitch until the cord is the required length. It makes a chunky cord that is good for bag handles and straps.

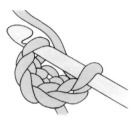

1 Make five chains and join into a ring with a slip stitch. Make one chain and then work a double crochet stitch into the top loop of the next chain.

2 Work one double crochet stitch into the top loop of each chain, then continue working around and around making one double crochet into the top loop of each stitch. As the cord grows, it will twist slightly into a spiral.

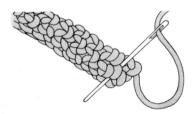

3 When the cord reaches the required length, fasten off the yarn. Thread the yarn end into a yarn or tapestry needle, catch the top loop of each stitch with the needle and draw up the stitches to close the end of the spiral. Weave in the yarn end to finish. Close the beginning of the spiral in the same way.

## CROCHET SPIRALS

Use a crochet spiral to trim a keyring or the tab on a zip. You can make a large cluster of spirals to decorate each corner of a crochet throw as a novel alternative to a tassel. Experiment with different yarn combinations, such as a striped spiral in smooth yarn edged with a row of fluffy mohair or angora yarn.

### MAKING A PLAIN SPIRAL

1 Work a loose foundation chain of 30 stitches. Change to a size smaller hook and work two treble crochet stitches into the fourth chain from the hook. Continue along the chain, working four treble crochet stitches into each chain.

2 As you work, the crochet will begin to twist naturally into a spiral formation. Fasten off the yarn at the end of the row, leaving a yarn end of about 30cm (12in) to attach the spiral.

## MAKING A STRIPED SPIRAL

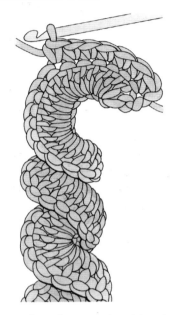

Using one colour of yarn, work a plain spiral. Leave a long end for attaching the finished spiral. Join a contrasting yarn to the outer edge of the top of the spiral and work a row of double crochet stitches along the edge. Fasten off the ends of the contrast yarn.

Plain spiral

Striped spiral

# FLOWERS

FLOWERS ARE QUICK TO MAKE, LOOK GREAT AND CAN ADD THE FINISHING PERSONAL TOUCH TO ALL SORTS OF HOUSEHOLD ITEMS OR GARMENTS. DECORATE GARMENTS AND ACCESSORIES WITH SINGLE FLOWERS, OR WORK SEVERAL USING DIFFERENT COLOURS AND YARNS AND ARRANGE THEM IN A GROUP.

### SEE ALSO
• Basic skills and stitches, pages 14–21

**SMALL FLOWERS**
These flowers have been worked in crochet cotton by adapting the cluster circle pattern (see page 79).

### Tip
*Sew-on embellishments such as flowers provide the perfect opportunity for experimenting with fancy and novelty yarns. Try combining textured and metallic yarns to make really unusual flowers.*

## MAKING A FRILLED FLOWER

**1** Make the base of the first petal by working the required stitches into a foundation ring, then turn the work over so that the wrong side is facing you.

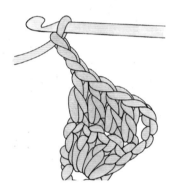

**2** Work the remaining section of the petal into the base, then make three chains and turn the work so that the right side is facing you once more.

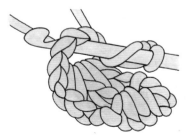

**3** From the right side, take the hook and working yarn behind the petal just worked and then work the first stitch of the new petal into the ring. This will fold the first petal into a three-dimensional shape. Continue working the rest of the round as instructed in the pattern.

## MAKING A LAYERED FLOWER

**1** Work the first round into a foundation ring, making eight central spokes to form the centre of the flower. Work a round of petals into the chain spaces between the spokes. At the end of this round, break off the yarn.

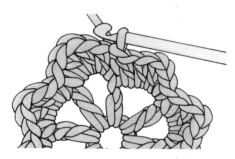

**2** Make a slip knot on the hook with the second colour and, working on the wrong side of the flower, insert the hook under one of the central spokes and slip stitch to join.

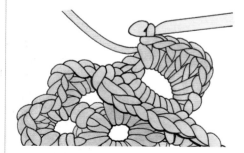

**3** Work the final round of petals from the right side of the flower, folding over the petals you made on the second round to keep them out of the way of the hook.

# Stitch collection

## Frilled flower

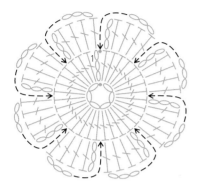

Pretty frilled petals make up this one-round flower. Each petal is completed and then folded over to make the frilled effect. Vary the flower by working it in a hand-painted yarn rather than a solid colour.

**FOUNDATION RING:** Ch 6 and join with sl st to form a ring.

**ROUND 1:** Ch 3 (counts as 1 tr), 3 tr into ring, ch 3, turn; 1 tr into first tr, 1 tr into each of next 2 tr, 1 tr into 3rd of ch 3 (petal made), ch 3, turn; * working across back of petal just made, work 4 tr into ring, ch 3, turn; 1 tr into first tr, 1 tr into each of next 3 tr (petal made), ch 3, turn; rep from * 6 times, join with sl st into 3rd of beg ch 3 of first petal.
Fasten off yarn.

Layered flower

Frilled flower

## Layered flower

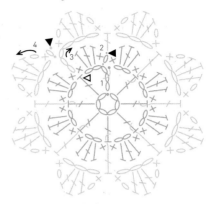

This flower looks pretty when two different types of yarn are used, so try combining a metallic yarn with a mohair yarn. The lower round of petals is worked behind the previous one to produce a three-dimensional effect.

**YARN:** Worked in two colours, A and B.

**FOUNDATION RING:** Using yarn A, ch 6 and join with sl st to form a ring.

**ROUND 1:** Ch 5 (counts as 1 tr, ch 2), [1 tr into ring, ch 2] 7 times, join with sl st into 3rd of ch 5.

**ROUND 2:** Sl st into next ch 2 sp, ch 1, [1 dc, 1 htr, 1 tr, 1 htr, 1 dc] into same sp (petal made), [1 dc, 1 htr, 1 tr, 1 htr, 1 dc] into each ch sp to end, join with sl st into first dc.
Break off yarn A. On the WS, join yarn B to one of the central spokes.

**ROUND 3:** Working on WS, ch 6 (counts as 1 tr, ch 3), [1 tr around next spoke, ch 3] 7 times, join with sl st into 3rd of ch 6.

**ROUND 4:** Ch 1, turn flower to RS, working behind petals of round 2, [1 dc, ch 1, 3 tr, ch 1, 1 dc] into each ch 3 sp to end [8 petals made], join with sl st into first dc.
Fasten off yarn.

**KEY TO ABBREVIATIONS AND SYMBOLS pages 150–151**

# BRAIDS AND INSERTIONS

BRAIDS AND INSERTIONS ARE STRIPS OF CROCHET THAT CAN BE STITCHED TO OTHER PIECES OF CROCHET OR TO WOVEN FABRICS AS AN EMBELLISHMENT.

SEE ALSO
• Basic skills and stitches, pages 14–21

Making your own braids and insertions can be very rewarding. When using a small hook and fine cotton, cotton blend or metallic yarn, the effect is similar to the purchased braids used to decorate home furnishings such as lampshades, cushions and fabric-covered boxes and baskets. Using a matching sewing thread, hand stitch a braid to fabric using tiny stitches down the centre or stitch an insertion along each edge. Provided the glue is compatible with the fibre composition of the yarn or thread, you can use a glue gun to attach braid to a box or basket.

## BRAIDS

Braids are usually narrow, with both edges or at least one edge shaped rather than straight. Some braid patterns may be worked in more than one colour of yarn.

## INSERTIONS

Insertions are similar to braids but they tend to be narrow and have two straight edges. Often used for shaped lingerie (but not corsetry), these decorative lengths of crochet are often hand stitched between two pieces of fabric. Insertions have a practical as well as a decorative purpose. If worked in fine cotton or silk, the elasticity of the inserted crochet strip along a seam line adds some ease to the garment and makes the two pieces of fabric easier to join. Braid patterns can easily be adapted to become insertions by working lengths of chain between the shaped peaks of the braid edge and then perhaps working a row of double crochet stitches.

## WORKING BRAIDS

1 Many braids are worked widthways on a small number of stitches. Keep turning the braid and repeating the pattern row until it is the required length, then fasten off the yarn.

2 Fancy braid patterns worked in two or more colours usually have a foundation made in one colour and a trim in a contrasting colour. Work the first row of the contrasting trim along the top of the foundation, along the opposite side to the foundation chain.

3 Break off the contrast yarn and rejoin it on the other side of the foundation, then work this side to match the one already worked.

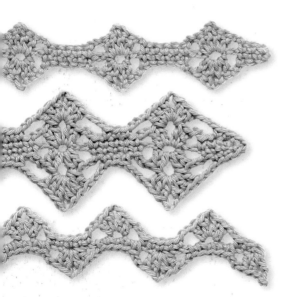

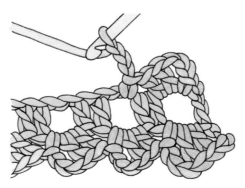

### INSPIRATION FOR BRAIDS

These three braids are adaptations of the shell edging pattern (see page 109). To make the top braid, work the first row of the edging pattern along both sides of the foundation chain. For the middle braid, work both rows of the edging pattern along both sides of the foundation chain. To make the bottom braid, work one row of the edging pattern and offset the stitch repeat on the underside of the foundation chain.

# Stitch collection

## Interwoven braid

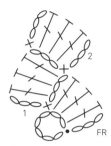

This braid is worked widthways.

**FOUNDATION RING:** Ch 7 and join with sl st to form a ring.

**FOUNDATION ROW:** Ch 3, 3 tr into ring, ch 3, 1 dc into ring, turn.

**ROW 1:** Ch 3, 3 tr into ch 3 sp, ch 3, 1 dc into same ch 3 sp, turn.

Rep row 1 for length required.

## Two-colour braid

> **MULTIPLE OF 3 CHAINS**

This braid is worked lengthways.

**YARN:** Worked in two colours, A and B. Using yarn A, make the required length of foundation chain.

**FOUNDATION ROW:** 1 tr into 6th ch from hook, 1 tr into next ch, * ch 1, sk next ch, 1 tr into each of next 2 chs; rep from * to last 2 chs, ch 1, sk next ch, 1 tr into last ch. Break off yarn A and join yarn B to penultimate ch of beg skipped ch.

**ROW 1:** Ch 1, 1 dc into first ch sp, ch 3, 2 tr into same ch sp, * [1 dc, ch 3, 2 tr] into next ch 1 sp; rep from * to last tr, 1 dc into last tr.

Break off yarn B and rejoin yarn B to opposite side of braid with sl st into foundation ch below first tr.

**ROW 2:** Ch 1, 1 dc into first ch sp, ch 3, 2 tr into same ch sp, * [1 dc, ch 3, 2 tr] into next ch 1 sp; rep from * ending last rep with 1 dc into 2nd ch of last ch sp. Fasten off yarn.

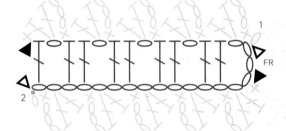

**KEY TO ABBREVIATIONS AND SYMBOLS  pages 150–151**

# EDGINGS

EDGINGS ARE USED TO TRIM THE EDGES OF OTHER PIECES OF CROCHET OR WOVEN FABRICS. UNLIKE EDGE FINISHES THAT ARE WORKED DIRECTLY ON TO THE CROCHET FABRIC, THE EDGINGS DESCRIBED HERE ARE WORKED SEPARATELY AND THEN ATTACHED.

**SEE ALSO**
• Basic skills and stitches, pages 14–21
• Edge finishes, pages 98–99

Edgings usually have one straight and one shaped edge. Deep edgings are also known as borders. Edgings can be worked in short rows across the width of the crochet piece or in long rows across the length. When working edgings in long rows, it is a good idea to make a longer chain than you think you will need and unravel the unused chains after the edging is finished.

## CORNERS

There is a simple trick to remember for working edgings around corners. Count a corner stitch as either three or five stitches and work the required next three or five stitches of the repeat into the corner stitch. The number of stitches that should be worked into the corner stitch can vary, so it is always advisable to try out an edging on a swatch of the fabric to which it will eventually be applied.

To plan what part of the edging repeat will be worked into the corner stitches, work a swatch of the edging in the yarn to be used, lay it along the edge to be embellished and use pins to mark out the repeats around the corner as well as the start and finish positions of the first and last repeats.

## ADAPTING EDGE FINISHES

This chain loop edge finish has been worked directly on to the project, but it could have been worked along a foundation row of double crochet stitches as a separate edging and then stitched to the crochet fabric.

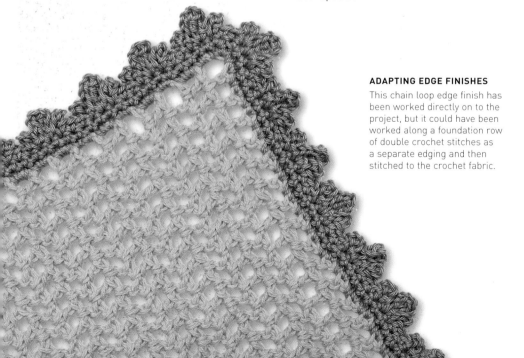

## USING AN APPROXIMATE FOUNDATION CHAIN

When working long edgings that are to be hand stitched to a fabric, it is often useful to make an approximate foundation chain, then work a row of the pattern and stretch or ease the edging to the nearest repeat.

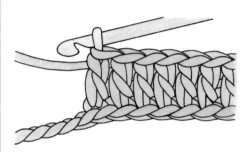

**1** Make the foundation chain and work the appropriate number of repeats of your edging pattern. At this point, turn and continue the pattern, leaving any surplus chains unworked.

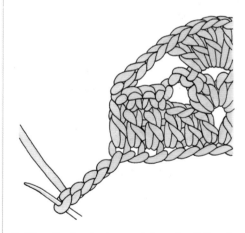

**2** When the border is complete, snip off the slip knot at the end of the unworked chains. Using a yarn or tapestry needle, carefully unravel the chains until you reach the edge of the work, then weave in the yarn end on the wrong side.

# Stitch collection

## Shell edging

| MULTIPLE OF 10 CHAINS PLUS 3 |

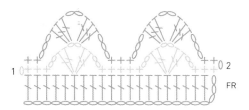

This edging is worked lengthways.

**FOUNDATION ROW: (RS)** 1 tr into 4th ch from hook, 1 tr into each ch to end.

**ROW 1:** Ch 1, 1 dc into each of first 3 tr, * ch 2, sk next 2 tr, [2 tr, ch 2] twice into next tr, sk next 2 tr, 1 dc into each of next 5 tr; rep from * to end omitting 2 dc at end of last rep and working last dc into top of beg skipped ch 3, turn.

**ROW 2:** Ch 1, 1 dc into each of first 2 dc, * ch 3, sk next ch 2 sp, [3 tr, ch 2, 3 tr] into next ch 2 sp, ch 3, sk next dc, 1 dc into each of next 3 dc; rep from * to end omitting 1 dc at end of last rep.
Fasten off yarn.

## Deep mesh edging

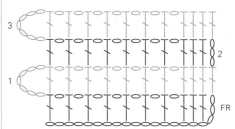

This edging is worked widthways.

**FOUNDATION CHAIN:** Ch 20.

**FOUNDATION ROW: (RS)** 1 tr into 4th ch from hook, 1 tr into each of next 2 chs, * ch 1, sk next ch, 1 tr into next ch; rep from * to end, turn.

**ROW 1:** Ch 7, 1 tr into first tr, [ch 1, 1 tr into next tr] 7 times, 1 tr into each of next 2 tr, 1 tr into 3rd of beg skipped ch 3, turn.

**ROW 2:** Ch 3 (counts as 1 tr), 1 tr into each of next 3 tr, * ch 1, 1 tr into next tr; rep from * to end, turn.

**ROW 3:** Ch 7, 1 tr into first tr, [ch 1, 1 tr into next tr] 7 times, 1 tr into each of next 2 tr, 1 tr into 3rd of ch 3, turn.

Rep rows 2 and 3 for desired length, ending with a row 3.

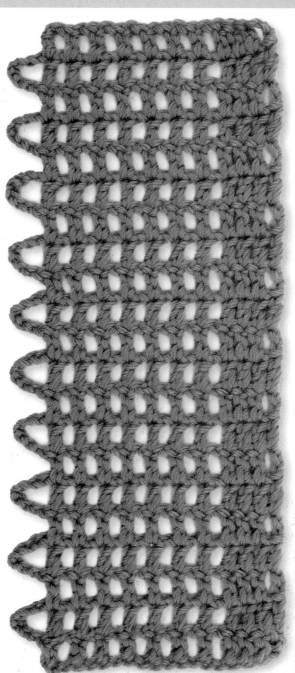

# FRINGES AND TASSELS

AS A CHANGE FROM THE USUAL YARN FRINGE OF THE TYPE FOUND ON SCARVES, TRY MAKING ONE OF THESE CROCHET FRINGES OR TASSELS. NEARLY EVERY FRINGE PATTERN CAN BE ADAPTED TO MAKE TO A TASSEL.

**SEE ALSO**

..........

- Basic skills and stitches, pages 14–21
- Edgings, pages 108–109

A chain fringe or tassel is made from loops of crochet chain, while a corkscrew fringe or tassel is made from strips of double crochet worked so that they curl around and around.

## WORKING A CROCHET CHAIN FRINGE

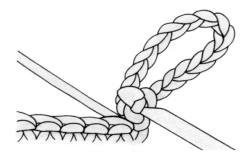

On the fringe row, make 15 chains and join the end of the chain with a slip stitch into the same place as the previous crochet stitch.

## WORKING A CORKSCREW FRINGE

To make the corkscrew shapes, make 15 chains and turn. Work two double crochet stitches into the second chain from the hook and into each remaining chain.

## CORKSCREW TASSEL

To make this corkscrew tassel, work rows 1 and 2 of the chain loop tassel opposite, and then work row 2 to the required depth. Finish by working the fringe row, but replace the chain loop with a chain approximately twice the required length and work three treble crochet stitches into each chain.

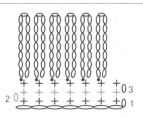

## Chain fringe

ANY NUMBER OF CHAINS

This fringe is worked lengthways.

**FOUNDATION CHAIN:** Make the required length of foundation chain.

**ROW 1:** 1 dc into 2nd ch from hook, 1 dc into each ch to end, turn.

**ROW 2:** Ch 1, 1 dc into each dc to end, turn.

**ROW 3:** Ch 1, 1 dc into first dc, * 1 dc into next dc, ch 15, sl st into same place as dc just worked; rep from * to end.

Fasten off yarn.

# Corkscrew fringe

ANY NUMBER OF CHAINS

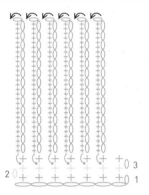

This fringe is worked lengthways.

**FOUNDATION CHAIN:** Make the required length of foundation chain.

**ROW 1:** 1 dc into 2nd ch from hook, 1 dc into each ch to end, turn.

**ROW 2:** Ch 1, 1 dc into each dc to end, turn.

**ROW 3:** Ch 1, 1 dc into first dc, * 1 dc into next dc, ch 15, turn; working back along the chain, sk first ch, 2 dc into each rem ch, sl st into same place as dc before the ch 15; rep from * to end.

Fasten off yarn.

# Chain loop tassel

**FOUNDATION CHAIN:** Leaving a long tail, ch 19.

**ROW 1:** 1 dc into 2nd ch from hook, 1 dc into each ch to end, turn.

**ROW 2:** Ch 1, sk first dc, 1 dc into each dc to end, 1 dc into ch 1, turn.

**ROW 3:** Ch 2, sk first dc, * htr4tog into next dc, ch 1, 1 htr into next dc; rep from * ending with 1 htr into ch 1, turn.

**ROW 4:** Ch 1, sk [first htr and ch 1] * 1 dc into htr4tog, sk next htr, 1 dc into ch sp; rep from * ending with 1 dc into top of ch 2, turn.

**FRINGE ROW:** Ch 1, [1 dc, ch 36, 1 sl st] into each dc ending with [1 dc, ch 36, 1 sl st] into ch 1.

Fasten off yarn, leaving a long tail. Tightly roll up the rows of dc and use the starting tail to stitch firmly across the top of the tassel head through all the layers, ending with a stitch in the centre. Use the finishing tail to stitch in and out around the base of the roll and draw tight. Secure with a back stitch, then join the side edge of the roll and bring the tail out at the centre top. Use the two tails to secure the tassel where required.

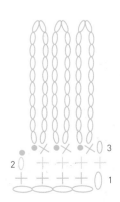

# SURFACE CROCHET

SURFACE CROCHET IS EXACTLY AS THE NAME SUGGESTS: CROCHET WORKED ON TOP OF A CROCHET BACKGROUND. YOU CAN WORK ON PLAIN DOUBLE CROCHET FABRIC, BUT THE LINES OF SURFACE SLIP STITCH LOOK MUCH MORE EFFECTIVE WORKED ON A MESH BACKGROUND.

**SEE ALSO**
• Openwork and lace stitches, pages 52–55

**ADDING COLOUR**
Try mixing metallic and smooth yarns.

Choose a smooth yarn to make the mesh background, then add rows of contrasting colours and textures to the surface using this simple, but effective, technique.

**WORKING SURFACE CROCHET**

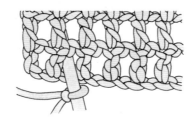

1 Work a mesh background. Make a slip knot in the contrasting yarn and slip it on to the hook. Insert the hook through a hole along the lower edge of the mesh.

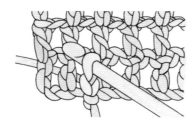

2 Holding the contrast yarn behind the mesh, draw a loop of yarn through the mesh and through the loop on the hook to make a slip stitch. Continue in this way, working up the mesh and making one slip stitch in each hole.

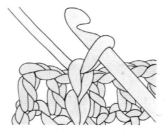

3 At the top of the row, break off the yarn and pull it through the last stitch to secure.

## Stitch collection

### Openwork mesh

MULTIPLE OF 2 CHAINS PLUS 4

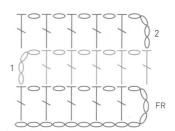

To make the mesh background, work a piece of fabric in the openwork mesh pattern (see page 53). Work vertical rows of surface crochet to make solid stripes across the background. This mesh has fairly large holes, so it is a good idea to use a heavier weight of yarn to work the surface crochet than the one used for the background.

**Tip**
*As well as the two mesh background stitches shown here, you can use other crochet stitches as a background for this technique, including double and half treble crochet, but remember not to work the background stitches too tightly.*

# Small mesh

MULTIPLE OF 2 CHAINS

This background fabric has much smaller holes than the larger openwork mesh example. You can work surface crochet in rows on this fabric, but the smaller mesh means that you can experiment and work all sorts of random patterns like those shown here.

**FOUNDATION ROW: (RS)** 1 dc into 2nd ch from hook, * ch 1, sk next ch, 1 dc into next ch; rep from * to end, turn.

**ROW 1:** Ch 1, 1 dc into first dc, * ch 1, 1 dc into next dc; rep from * to end, turn. Rep row 1 for length required.

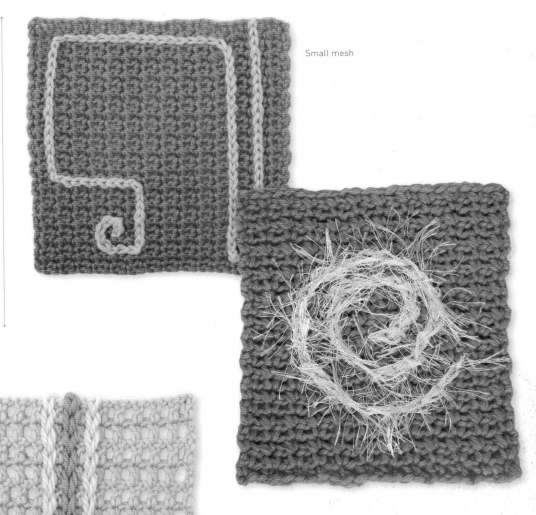

Small mesh

**ADDING TEXTURE**
Try working surface crochet with a contrasting yarn texture in a freestyle design.

Openwork mesh

# APPLYING BEADS

BEADS CAN BE APPLIED TO CROCHET AT THE SAME TIME AS THE STITCHES ARE BEING WORKED. THEY LOOK MOST EFFECTIVE AGAINST A DOUBLE CROCHET BACKGROUND, AND ADD TOUCHES OF COLOUR AS WELL AS GLITZ AND SPARKLE.

**SEE ALSO**
• Applying sequins, pages 116–117

**BEADS**
Choose beads to match your yarn.

Before starting to crochet, thread all of the beads on to the ball of yarn. If you are using several balls, the pattern will tell you how many beads to thread on to each ball. When working with several bead colours in a particular sequence, you need to thread them on to the yarn in reverse order, so that the pattern will be correct as you crochet.

**BEADING WITH DOUBLE CROCHET**

1 Work to the position of the first bead on a wrong side row. Slide the bead down the yarn until it rests snugly against the right side of the work.

2 Keeping the bead in position, insert the hook into the next stitch and draw the yarn through so that there are two loops on the hook.

3 Wrap the yarn over the hook again and draw it through to complete the stitch. Continue adding beads in this way across the row, following the pattern instructions.

## Stitch collection

### All-over beads

| MULTIPLE OF 4 CHAINS PLUS 4 |

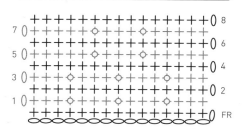

Beads added to every wrong side row make a heavily beaded fabric that would be perfect for making an evening bag. You could also work several rows of this pattern in a narrow band around the hem of a sweater. This stitch pattern uses several colours of beads threaded randomly on to the yarn. Thread all of the beads on to the yarn before starting to crochet.

**NOTE:** B = beaded double crochet stitch.
**FOUNDATION ROW: (RS)** 1 dc into 2nd ch from hook, 1 dc into each ch to end, turn.
**ROW 1: (WS BEAD ROW)** Ch 1, 1 dc into each of first 3 dc, * B, 1 dc into each of next 3 dc; rep from * to last 4 dc, B, 1 dc into each of next 3 dc, turn.
**ROW 2:** Ch 1, 1 dc into each dc to end, turn.
**ROWS 3–4:** Rep rows 1 and 2.
**ROW 5: (WS BEAD ROW)** Ch 1, 1 dc into each of next 5 dc, * B, 1 dc into each of next 3 dc; rep from * to last 6 dc, B, 1 dc into each of next 5 dc, turn.
**ROW 6:** Ch 1, 1 dc into each dc to end, turn.
**ROWS 7–8:** Rep rows 5 and 6.
Rep rows 1–8 for length required, ending with a RS row.

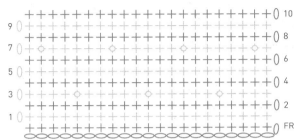

# Alternate beads

**MULTIPLE OF 6 CHAINS PLUS 4**

All-over beads

Alternate beads

Beads of one colour are arranged alternately to make this elegant beaded pattern. Use matt beads, like those shown, or choose from metallic and glitter types to add more sparkle. Thread all of the beads on to the yarn before starting to crochet.

**NOTE:** B = beaded double crochet stitch.

**FOUNDATION ROW: (RS)** 1 dc into 2nd ch from hook, 1 dc into each ch to end, turn.

**ROWS 1–2:** Ch 1, 1 dc into each dc to end, turn.

**ROW 3: (WS BEAD ROW)** Ch 1, 1 dc into each of next 4 dc, * B, 1 dc into each of next 5 dc; rep from * to last 5 dc, B, 1 dc into each of next 4 dc, turn.

**ROWS 4–6:** Rep row 1.

**ROW 7: (WS BEAD ROW)** Ch 1, 1 dc into first dc, * B, 1 dc into each of next 5 dc; rep from * to last 2 dc, B, 1 dc into last dc, turn.

**ROWS 8–10:** Rep row 1.

Rep rows 3–10 for length required, ending with a row 5.

## Tip

*When choosing beads, match the size of the holes in the beads to the thickness of the yarn. Small beads are best on fine yarns, and larger beads on chunky yarns.*

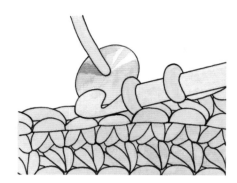

# APPLYING SEQUINS

SEQUINS CAN BE APPLIED TO A BACKGROUND OF DOUBLE CROCHET IN A SIMILAR WAY TO BEADS. ROUND SEQUINS, EITHER FLAT OR CUP-SHAPED, ARE THE BEST ONES TO USE.

**SEE ALSO**
• Applying beads, pages 114–115

When crocheting with cup-shaped sequins, make sure that you thread them on to the yarn so that the convex side (the bottom of the 'cup') of each sequin faces the same way towards the ball of yarn. When crocheted, the 'cup' should face away from the crochet fabric. This displays the sequin to best advantage and also prevents it from damaging the crochet. As a general rule, thread sequins on to the yarn in the same way as beads.

**ALTERNATE SEQUINS**
This crochet sample is made using the alternate beads pattern (see page 119) but with sequins instead of beads.

**ADDING SEQUINS TO DOUBLE CROCHET**

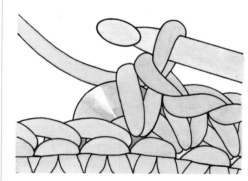

1 Work to the position of the first sequin on a wrong side row. Work the first stage of the double crochet, leaving two loops on the hook. Slide the sequin down the yarn until it rests snugly against the right side of the work. If you are using cup-shaped sequins, remember that the convex side (the bottom of the 'cup') should be next to the fabric.

2 Keeping the sequin in position, wrap the yarn over the hook and draw it through to complete the stitch. Continue adding sequins in this way across the row, following the pattern instructions.

# Stitch collection

## Sequin stripes

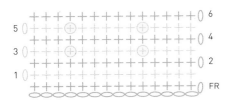

Sequins often look best when used sparingly to accentuate a design. Here, flat round sequins in one colour are arranged in neat vertical rows so that the sequins touch. You can use a contrasting sequin colour or match them to the background fabric for a more subtle effect. Thread all of the sequins on to the yarn before starting to crochet.

**NOTE:** S = sequined double crochet stitch.

**FOUNDATION ROW: (RS)** 1 dc into 2nd ch from hook, 1 dc into each ch to end, turn.

**ROWS 1–2:** Ch 1, 1 dc into each dc to end, turn.

**ROW 3: (WS SEQUIN ROW)** Ch 1, 1 dc into each of next 3 dc, * S, 1 dc into each of next 5 dc; rep from * to last 5 dc, S, 1 dc into each of next 4 dc, turn.

**ROW 4:** Ch 1, 1 dc into each dc to end, turn. Rep rows 3 and 4 for length required, ending with a row 4.

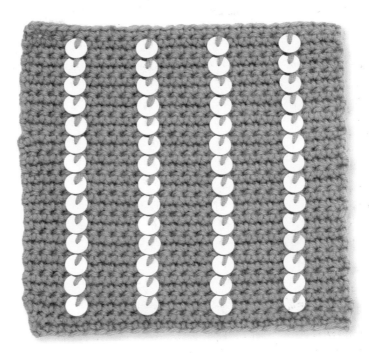

### Tip

*Knitting sequins have larger holes than ordinary ones, and they are often sold threaded on to a loop of strong thread. To use the sequins, cut the loop, knot one end of the thread on to the yarn and carefully slide the sequins over the knot and on to the yarn.*

KEY TO ABBREVIATIONS AND SYMBOLS **pages 150–151**

# CHAPTER THREE

· · · · · · · · · · · · · · · · · · · · · · · · · · · · · · · ·

## Projects

This chapter shows you how to make a variety of projects using the skills you have mastered in the previous two chapters. Whether you want to make a small crochet accessory such as a pretty scarf or flower-trimmed bag, or feel ready to try something a little more complicated, there is something here for everyone.

# BUTTONHOLE BAG

BRIGHTLY COLOURED FLOWERS AND
LEAVES TRIM A PLAIN BUTTONHOLE BAG
THAT IS LARGE ENOUGH TO HOLD PURSE,
KEYS, PHONE AND OTHER ESSENTIALS. THE
BAG PATTERN ALSO LOOKS GOOD WITHOUT
THE ADDED TRIMMINGS, AND IT CAN BE
WORKED IN ONE COLOUR OR IN STRIPES.

## YOU WILL NEED

• 4 balls of double knitting yarn with approx.
  120m (131yds) per 50g ball in a neutral colour
• Oddments of same yarn in red, yellow
  and green
• 4mm (size F), 6mm (J) and 6.5mm (K)
  crochet hooks, or sizes needed to
  achieve tension
• Yarn or tapestry needle

### EMBELLISHMENT

Decorating with sew-on
motifs allows you to
add as little or as much
embellishment to the
bag as you like.

## TENSION

14 stitches and 17 rows to 10cm (4in)
measured over double crochet worked using
6mm (size J) crochet hook and two strands
of main yarn held together.

## FINISHED SIZE

25cm (10in) high and 27cm (10½in) wide.

## FRONT PANEL

Using 6.5mm (size K) hook and holding
two strands of main yarn together, ch 37.
Change to 6mm (size J) hook.
**FOUNDATION ROW: (RS)** 1 dc into 2nd ch from
hook, 1 dc into each ch to end, turn.
**ROW 1:** Ch 1, 1 dc into each dc to end, turn.
(36 dc)
Rep last row 30 times more, ending with a
RS row.

## MAKING THE BUTTONHOLE

**ROW 1: (WS)** Ch 1, 1 dc into each of next 12 dc,
ch 12, sk next 12 dc, 1 dc into each of next
12 dc, turn.
**ROW 2:** Ch 1, 1 dc into each of next 12 dc, 1 dc
into each of next 12 chs, sk next 12 dc, 1 dc into
each of next 12 dc, turn. (36 dc)

## MAKING THE HANDLE

**ROW 1: (WS)** Ch 1, 1 dc into each dc to end, turn.
Rep last row three times more, ending with a
RS row.
Fasten off yarn.

## BACK PANEL

Work as for front panel.

## FLOWERS AND LEAVES

Using 4mm (size F) hook and a single strand
of contrast yarn, make three red and three
yellow frilled flowers (see page 105).
Using 4mm (size F) hook and green yarn,
make two short lengths of double crochet
cord (see page 102).

## FINISHING

Weave in the yarn ends (see page 25), then
press the pieces lightly on the wrong side
(see pages 28–29). Pin flowers and leaves to
front panel, making sure that flowers overlap
ends of leaves. Secure flowers with a few
stitches worked in matching yarn, taking the
stitches over the chains behind each flower
petal. Stitch leaves in place down the centre
of each leaf. Place front and back panels
right sides together and pin around the edges.
Using matching yarn, join side and base seams
(see pages 30–31), then turn bag right side out.

# INTARSIA POTHOLDER

COMBINE ODDMENTS OF DOUBLE KNITTING
YARN WITH ONE BALL OF MAIN COLOUR
TO MAKE THIS CHEERFUL INTARSIA
POTHOLDER. THE BACK PIECE IS WORKED
IN DOUBLE CROCHET USING THE MAIN
COLOUR, BUT YOU COULD WORK TWO
PATTERNED PIECES IF YOU PREFER.

## YOU WILL NEED

- 1 ball of double knitting yarn with
  approx.120m (131yds) per 50g ball in
  main colour (A)
- Oddments of same yarn in four toning
  colours (B, C, D and E)
- 4mm (size F) and 4.5mm (G) crochet hooks,
  or sizes needed to achieve tension
- Yarn or tapestry needle

## TENSION

17 stitches and 21 rows to 10cm (4in)
measured over double crochet worked using
4mm (size F) crochet hook.

## FINISHED SIZE

Approximately 19cm (7in) square, including
edge finish but excluding hanging loop.

## FRONT PANEL

Using 4.5mm (size G) hook and yarn A, ch 31.
Change to 4mm (size F) hook. Following
guidelines for working intarsia (see pages
70–71), work the pattern from the chart
(see right), reading upwards from the bottom.
Start at the right-hand edge and read right
side (odd-numbered) rows from right to left
and wrong side (even-numbered) rows from
left to right. When the chart has been
completed, fasten off yarn.

**STASH BUSTER**
This is the ideal project
for using up some of the
oddments of yarn that
you have in your stash.

## BACK PANEL

Using 4.5mm (size G) hook and yarn A, ch 31.
Change to 4mm (size F) hook.
**FOUNDATION ROW: (RS)** 1 dc into 2nd ch from
hook, 1 dc into each ch to end, turn. (30 dc)
**ROW 1:** Ch 1, 1 dc into each dc to end, turn.
Rep last row 32 times more, ending with a
WS row.
Fasten off yarn.

## FINISHING

Weave in the yarn ends (see page 25), then
block each panel to same size (see pages
28–29). Place panels wrong sides together
and pin around the edges. With front piece
facing, join yarn A to one corner of potholder.
**ROUND 1: (RS)** Ch 1, 1 dc into same place, work
evenly spaced dc all around edge of potholder
working 3 dc into each corner, join with sl st
into first dc.

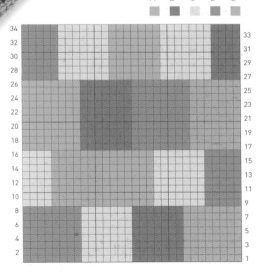

A  B  C  D  E

**ROUND 2:** Make hanging loop (ch 9, insert hook
into last st of previous round and work sl st),
ch 1, 15 dc into loop, 1 dc into each dc around
edge of potholder working 3 dc into centre
stitch of 3 dc group at each corner, join with
sl st into first dc of loop.
Fasten off yarn and weave in yarn ends.

# BABY AFGHAN

AN AFGHAN FOR A NEW BABY IS ALWAYS
A POPULAR GIFT. THIS DESIGN IS FAIRLY
SMALL, BUT YOU CAN EASILY MAKE IT
LARGER SIMPLY BY ADDING MORE MOTIFS
BEFORE YOU WORK THE EDGE FINISH.
IF YOU DO THIS, REMEMBER THAT YOU
WILL NEED TO BUY MORE YARN THAN
THE AMOUNT SUGGESTED HERE.

## YOU WILL NEED
- 5 balls of double knitting yarn with approx.
  120m (131yds) per 50g ball in 3 coordinating
  colours: 1 ball of pale green, 2 balls of white,
  2 balls of pale yellow
- 3.5mm (size E) and 4mm (F) crochet hooks,
  or sizes needed to achieve tension
- Yarn or tapestry needle

## TENSION
After blocking, each motif measures
14cm (5in) square.

## FINISHED SIZE
48cm (18in) wide and 72cm (28in) long,
including edge finish.

## MOTIFS
Using 4mm (size F) hook, follow the pattern
for the Croydon square (see page 82).
### MOTIF A (MAKE 8)
Use white as yarn A, pale green as yarn B
and pale yellow as yarn C.
### MOTIF B (MAKE 7)
Use pale yellow as yarn A, pale green as
yarn B and white as yarn C.

## MAKING UP THE AFGHAN
Weave in the yarn ends (see page 25), then
block each motif to same size (see pages
28–29). Arrange motifs as shown in diagram
below and stitch together using matching yarn
(see pages 80–81).

### ADJUSTING THE SIZE
The baby afghan is worked
as separate square motifs
that are stitched together, so
it can easily be made larger.

## EDGE FINISH

Using 3.5mm (size E) hook, join pale yellow yarn to any dc along edge of afghan.

**ROUND 1:** Ch 3, 1 tr into each dc around afghan working 5 tr into centre stitch of 3 dc group at each corner, join with sl st into 3rd of ch 3. Break off pale yellow yarn and join white yarn in same place.

**ROUND 2:** Ch 3, 1 tr into each tr working 5 tr into centre stitch of 5 tr group at each corner, join with sl st into 3rd of ch 3. Break off white yarn and join pale green yarn in same place.

**ROUND 3:** Ch 1, 1 dc into same place, 1 dc into each tr working 3 dc into centre stitch of 5 tr group at each corner, join with sl st into first dc. Fasten off yarn.

## FINISHING

Press edge finish lightly on wrong side with warm iron or block the afghan again.

## USING A DIFFERENT MOTIF

For a baby afghan, there are a few practical issues to consider. First, choose a yarn that is both washable and does not have long, loose fibres. In addition, select a yarn that will break if it is pulled sharply. This does not mean that the afghan will not be hard wearing, but if a small child decides to twist the blanket with his or her fingers, those fingers are less likely to become trapped. Another measure to safeguard against trapped fingers is to choose a design with large holes rather than one with long chains that are not worked over or into on subsequent rounds.

A multicoloured blanket can be more forgiving between washes. A colourful blanket will also appeal more to the baby, and it provides an excellent opportunity for using up oddments of yarn.

## ALTERNATIVE MOTIF

You can choose a different square motif to make the afghan if you prefer. This circle in a square motif (see page 83) would look good worked in a single colour or in several colours.

## BLANKET SIZE

It is a good idea to make a baby blanket that is just big enough for a cot or buggy.

# HEXAGON CUSHION

MAKING A CUSHION COVER FROM MOTIFS IS A GREAT WAY TO SHOW OFF YOUR CROCHET SKILLS. IN THIS PATTERN, 24 HEXAGONS WORKED IN A NEUTRAL PALETTE ARE JOINED TOGETHER TO MAKE A RECTANGULAR COVER. YOU CAN USE A COORDINATING COLOUR SCHEME LIKE THAT FEATURED HERE, OR WORK EACH HEXAGON IN A DIFFERENT COLOUR USING ODDMENTS OF YARN FROM YOUR STASH.

### HEXAGON MOTIFS

You could replace the wheel hexagon motif used here with the classic or granny hexagon (see pages 87 and 89), but work each one in a single colour rather than in three colours.

### YOU WILL NEED

- Shetland double knitting yarn with approx. 122m (134yds) per 50g ball in 7 coordinating colours: 1 ball each of mustard (A), rust (B), cream (C) and lemon (G); 2 balls each of gold (D), brown (E) and nutmeg (F)
- 4mm (size F) crochet hook, or size needed to achieve tension
- Yarn or tapestry needle
- 40 x 50cm (16 x 20in) cushion pad

### TENSION

After blocking, each motif measures 13cm (5in) from side to side and 14.5cm (5¾in) from point to point.

### FINISHED SIZE

Fits a 40 x 50cm (16 x 20in) cushion pad.

### MOTIFS

Using the wheel hexagon pattern (see page 88), work three motifs in each of yarns A, B, C and G, and four motifs in each of yarns D, E and F.

### FINISHING

Weave in the yarn ends (see page 25), then block each motif to same size (see pages 28–29). Arrange motifs as shown in diagram below, then stitch together using matching yarn (see pages 30–31). When the motifs have been joined, fold the crochet to the back following the dotted lines on the diagram and join the edges of the remaining motifs. Leave the motif edges numbered 1, 2, 3 and 4 on the diagram unstitched to make the opening on the back of the cover. Turn cover right side out and insert cushion pad. Matching the edges of the motifs along the opening, pin and stitch carefully together.

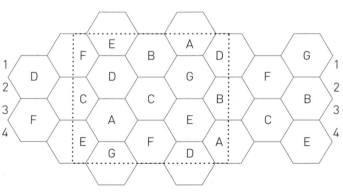

·············· Fold line

**COLOUR INSPIRATION**
The colour palette for this cushion was inspired by the autumn landscape.

**WARM COLOURS**
The colour of this scarf will reflect flattering warm pink on to the skin.

# WINTER SCARF

A SCARF MAKES THE PERFECT PROJECT FOR A BEGINNER TO CROCHET. THERE IS NO SHAPING, THE WORK IS NARROW ENOUGH TO GROW QUICKLY AND YOU CAN CHOOSE FROM MANY OF THE PATTERNS FEATURED IN THE STITCH COLLECTIONS THROUGHOUT THIS BOOK. THE SCARF SHOWN HERE IS WORKED IN A FAN LACE PATTERN USING A PURE WOOL YARN.

## YOU WILL NEED
• 2 balls of double knitting yarn with approx. 120m (131yds) per 50g ball
• 4mm (size F) and 4.5mm (G) crochet hooks, or sizes needed to achieve tension
• Yarn or tapestry needle

## TENSION
After blocking, one complete pattern repeat measures 6cm (2in) wide and 3cm (1in) deep.

## FINISHED SIZE
After blocking, approximately 18cm (7in) wide and 117cm (46in) long.

## FAN LACE PATTERN
The stitch pattern for fan lace (see page 55) requires a multiple of 12 chains plus 3. The scarf shown here was worked on a foundation chain of 39 = (12 x 3) + 3.
Using 4.5mm (size G) hook, ch 39.
Change to 4mm (size F) hook and work in pattern for approximately 117cm (46in), ending with a row 4.

## FINISHING
Weave in the yarn ends (see page 25), then block the scarf (see pages 28–29).

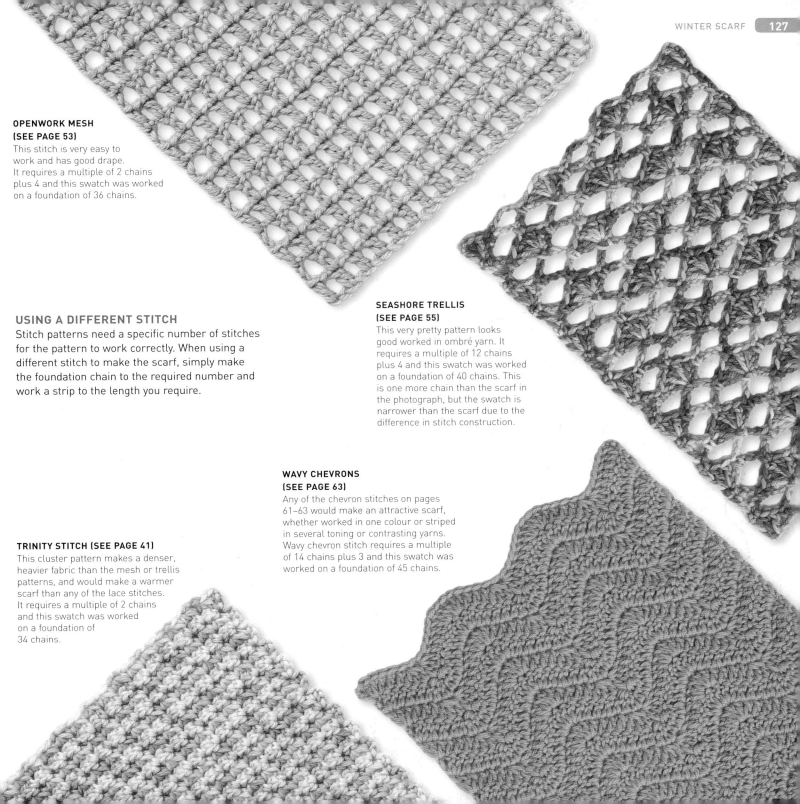

## OPENWORK MESH (SEE PAGE 53)

This stitch is very easy to work and has good drape. It requires a multiple of 2 chains plus 4 and this swatch was worked on a foundation of 36 chains.

## USING A DIFFERENT STITCH

Stitch patterns need a specific number of stitches for the pattern to work correctly. When using a different stitch to make the scarf, simply make the foundation chain to the required number and work a strip to the length you require.

## SEASHORE TRELLIS (SEE PAGE 55)

This very pretty pattern looks good worked in ombré yarn. It requires a multiple of 12 chains plus 4 and this swatch was worked on a foundation of 40 chains. This is one more chain than the scarf in the photograph, but the swatch is narrower than the scarf due to the difference in stitch construction.

## WAVY CHEVRONS (SEE PAGE 63)

Any of the chevron stitches on pages 61–63 would make an attractive scarf, whether worked in one colour or striped in several toning or contrasting yarns. Wavy chevron stitch requires a multiple of 14 chains plus 3 and this swatch was worked on a foundation of 45 chains.

## TRINITY STITCH (SEE PAGE 41)

This cluster pattern makes a denser, heavier fabric than the mesh or trellis patterns, and would make a warmer scarf than any of the lace stitches. It requires a multiple of 2 chains and this swatch was worked on a foundation of 34 chains.

# FILET CROCHET WRAP

FILET CROCHET CREATES A DELIGHTFUL LACY ACCESSORY. WORKED IN ROWS ACROSS THE WIDTH OF THE WRAP, EACH END IS DECORATED WITH A PRETTY BORDER PATTERN. THE MAIN PART OF THE WRAP IS IN FILET MESH, DOTTED HERE AND THERE WITH TINY FOUR-BLOCK MOTIFS.

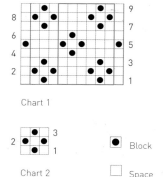

Chart 1

Chart 2

● Block

☐ Space

## YOU WILL NEED
• 8 balls of double knitting yarn with approx. 120m (131yds) per 50g ball
• 4mm (size F) and 4.5mm (G) crochet hooks, or sizes needed to achieve tension
• Yarn or tapestry needle

## TENSION
Approx. eight spaces to 10cm (4in) measured widthways and lengthways over filet mesh worked using 4mm (size F) hook.

## FINISHED SIZE
Approximately 58cm (23in) wide and 170cm (67in) long.

## FILET PATTERN
Using 4.5mm (size G) hook, ch 146. Change to 4mm (size F) hook and, following the guidelines for working filet crochet on pages 56–58, work two rows of spaces. Begin working the border pattern from chart 1 (above), repeating the section of the chart inside the red lines six times more. Work upwards from the bottom of the chart, starting at the right-hand edge and reading right side (odd-numbered) rows from right to left and wrong side (even-numbered) rows from left to right. At the end of the border pattern, work in filet mesh, dotting several repeats of the tiny motif from chart 2 (left) at random across the mesh. Continue until work measures approximately 157cm (62in) long, ending with a WS row. Work the border chart once more, then finish by working two rows of spaces to match the opposite end.

## FINISHING
Weave in the yarn ends (see page 25), then block the wrap or press lightly on the wrong side (see pages 28–29).

## USING A DIFFERENT FILET CROCHET DESIGN
Designing the perfect wrap can mean making it the perfect size, using your favourite colour, treating yourself to a special hank of yarn or using images in your design that have a special meaning to you. The filet crochet technique can be used to work any design charted on a square grid in a single colour. Many multicoloured designs can be converted to a single colour. As well as traditional filet crochet table mat and curtain motifs, cross-stitch designs and knitting patterns are also good sources of inspiration. Filet crochet looks good worked in almost any fibre, and can be quickly embellished with beads, surface crochet or with fibre strands woven through the mesh. Quick to work, filet crochet is a very versatile crochet technique.

**FILET CROCHET WORKED IN CHUNKY YARN**
The use of a chunky yarn gives a modern twist to traditional filet crochet designs.

**EVENING WEAR**
Filet crochet creates a
lacy fabric, perfect for
evening wear.

# STRIPED BAG

USE ODDMENTS OF YARN FROM YOUR STASH TO MAKE THIS PRETTY DRAWSTRING BAG. THE BAG SHOWN HERE WAS MADE USING A VARIETY OF DOUBLE KNITTING YARNS, INCLUDING SHINY RIBBON, METALLIC CHAINETTE, NOVELTY YARN AND SMOOTH WOOL. YOU CAN CHANGE YARN AT THE END OF EVERY ROUND, OR WORK SEVERAL ROUNDS IN THE SAME YARN – THE CHOICE IS UP TO YOU.

## YOU WILL NEED

- Double knitting yarns in varying colours and textures – as a guide, to work one round of treble crochet at the bag's widest point, you will need about 3.2m (3yds) of yarn
- 4mm (size F) and 4.5mm (G) crochet hooks
- Yarn or tapestry needle

## TENSION

Working to an exact tension is not necessary when making this project.

## FINISHED SIZE

Approximately 33cm (13in) deep from top to bottom, 52cm (20in) circumference around widest point and 33cm (13in) circumference around opening at top.

**THE PERFECT KNITTING BAG**
Natural fibres do not become charged with static electricity or attract dust. A yarn made from a fibre that does not shed would be perfect for making a storage bag for your crochet and knitting work.

## BAG SECTION

The bag is worked from the centre of the base. Using 4mm (size F) hook, work rounds 1–4 of the treble crochet circle motif (see page 77). Continue as follows, changing colours as desired.

**ROUND 5:** Work as round 4, but work 3 tr between the increases. (80 sts)

**ROUND 6:** Ch 3, 1 tr into each of next 2 tr, * 2 tr into next tr, 1 tr into each of next 4 tr; rep from * to last 2 tr, 2 tr into next tr, 1 tr into last tr, join with sl st into 3rd of ch 3. (96 sts)

**ROUND 7:** Ch 1, 1 dc into each tr to end, join with sl st into first dc.

**ROUNDS 8–10:** Ch 1, 1 dc into each dc to end, join with sl st into first dc.

**ROUND 11:** Ch 3, sk first dc, 1 tr into each dc to end, join with sl st into 3rd of ch 3.

**ROUND 12:** Ch 3, sk first tr, 1 tr into each tr to end, join with sl st into 3rd of ch 3.
Continue in the same way without increasing, working either a dc or tr round as follows:

**ROUNDS 13, 15, 16, 17, 18, 22 & 23:** Work a round of tr.

**ROUNDS 14, 19, 20 & 21:** Work a round of dc.

**ROUND 24:** Ch 3, 1 tr into each of next 2 tr, *tr2tog, 1 tr into each of next 4 tr; rep from * to last 3 sts, tr2tog, 1 tr into last tr; join with sl st into 3rd of ch 3. (80 sts)

**ROUNDS 25–27:** Work a round of tr.

**ROUND 28:** Ch 3, 1 tr into next tr, *tr2tog, 1 tr into each of next 3 tr; rep from * to last 3 sts, tr2tog, 1 tr into last tr, join with sl st into 3rd of ch 3. (64 sts)

**ROUNDS 29–32:** Work a round of tr.

**ROUND 33:** Ch 3, 1 tr into each of next 3 tr, * ch 2, sk next 2 tr, 1 tr into each of next 6 tr; rep from * to last 4 sts, ch 2, sk next 2 tr, 1 tr into each of last 2 tr, join with sl st into 3rd of ch 3.

**ROUND 34:** Ch 1, 1 dc into first tr, * 1 dc into each of next 2 chs, 1 dc into each of next 6 tr; rep from * to last ch 2 sp, 1 dc into each of next 2 chs, 1 dc into each of next 2 tr, join with sl st into first dc.

**ROUNDS 35–40:** Work a round of dc.
**ROUND 41:** Ch 1, sl st into each st to end.
Fasten off yarn.

## DRAWSTRINGS (MAKE 2)

Using 4.5mm (size G) hook and a smooth yarn,
ch 125 and work a length of double crochet
cord (see page 102).

## FINISHING

Weave in the yarn ends (see page 25). If
necessary, press lightly on the wrong side
(see pages 28–29). Thread the two drawstrings
through the holes in the top of the bag, pulling
the ends free at opposite sides of the bag.
Stitch across the short ends of each
drawstring, then weave in the yarn ends.

**CHOOSING YARN**
Be imaginative with your
choice of yarns when
creating this bag to make
a really unique piece.

# CHAPTER FOUR

· · · · · · · · · · · · · · · · · · · ·

# Gallery

Drawn from a variety of sources around the world, this chapter features a wide range of crochet garments, accessories and other items designed to inspire and challenge you with new ideas. Dip into a bounty of colour, shape, pattern and texture and investigate some of the possibilities offered by the wonderful craft of crochet.

◄ **HAPPY CUSHIONS**
Ilaria Chiaratti

Variations on the basic granny square (see page 84) are worked in acrylic and wool yarn in a rainbow of colours on unifying white backgrounds for a bright, modern reworking of a well-known traditional design.

# CROCHET IN THE HOME

CROCHET IS A VERSATILE TECHNIQUE FOR MAKING HOME ACCESSORIES, PARTICULARLY THOSE ON A LARGE SCALE SUCH AS AFGHANS, BLANKETS AND THROWS, WHICH CAN EASILY BE MADE IN ONE PIECE. CIRCULAR, SQUARE AND HEXAGONAL MOTIFS COMBINE WELL TO MAKE CUSHION COVERS AND THROWS THAT WILL ADD INTEREST TO ANY HOME DECOR.

**◀ LAYERED CROCHET CUSHION**
Rowan Yarns

A layered circle, worked in the round, is expanded to cushion size by working with a large hook and chunky yarn. The harmonious shades of green and blue emphasise the different textures of the various rounds of stitches, and the cushion is finished with a central bright button.

**▼ LAMP AND BUNTING**
Ilaria Chiaratti

Contrasting bright colours in acrylic/wool yarn are used on a white background for the lampshade, the careful choice of colours giving the granny square (see page 84) a new look. More granny squares are used to make the bunting.

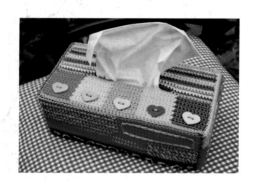

**▲ TISSUE BOX COVER**
Karin Mijsen

Cotton yarn, worked in double crochet, makes a firm fabric that will keep its shape. Contrasting panels of multicoloured stripes (see pages 34–35) and intarsia blocks (see pages 70–71) form the box shape, which is then decorated with surface crochet details (see pages 112–113) and a row of bright buttons.

**▲ LACY BOLSTER**
Rowan Yarns

Chunky yarn and lacy stitches give an up-to-date look to this bolster. The lacy circles on the ends of the bolster allow the patterned lining to show through, accentuated by the central fabric-covered button.

**▲ STOOL COVERS**
Ingrid Jansen

These simple stools are made from recycled painted wood, and topped with crochet slipcovers in hard-wearing chunky wool/acrylic/cotton yarn. The contrasting textures of crochet and wood are enhanced by the soft neutral colours.

**▲ CHILD'S BEDSPREAD**
Ingrid Jansen

Each of the 36 square blocks (see pages 80–84) that form this bedspread is worked with a different colour for the lacy circular flower at the centre, then completed with a white border. The narrow edging in pink, black and white is a simple but effective finishing touch.

# GARMENTS

CROCHET CAN BE USED TO CREATE A WIDE VARIETY OF GARMENTS, RANGING FROM DELICATE LACY ITEMS FOR EVENING WEAR TO A TRADITIONAL WARM BUT STYLISH SWEATER FOR EVERYDAY USE. CROCHET STITCHES CAN BE WORKED TO A SET PATTERN OR THEY CAN BE EMPLOYED IN A MORE ADVENTUROUS WAY TO MAKE ONE-OF-A-KIND FREEFORM WEARABLES.

### ▸ LINED BLUE SKIRT
Rowan Yarns

Openwork floral motifs worked in chunky yarn are designed to show the slim-fitting patterned fabric lining that helps the skirt to keep its shape. The ribbed waistband is knitted directly on to the crochet fabric for a slim fit at the waist.

### ▾ WHITE LACE DRESS
Luanna Perez-Garreaud

Worked in crisp, white cotton yarn, this dress features panels of mesh stitches alternated with panels of lacy circles and trellis patterns (see pages 52–55), and is edged with layers of lacy scallops.

◄ **JACKET AND STRIPED SKIRT**
Kazekobo (Yoko Hatta)

This orange mohair buttoned jacket,
worked in an all-over lace pattern,
has elbow-length sleeves, a neat collar
and tie cords trimmed with tassels.
The jacket teams perfectly with the
slim-fit wool skirt, which is striped in
coordinating colours and finished with
an interesting tie detail at the waist.

▲ **IVORY COTTON DRESS**
Kazekobo (Yoko Hatta)

A simple openwork sheath dress, worked
in fine ivory cotton, is decorated with
elaborate layered flowers (see pages
104–105), leaves and bunches of grapes
in relief, in the manner of traditional
Irish crochet lace. This timeless design
is bordered with ruffled scallop edgings
and lined with ivory silk fabric.

◄ **MATCHING TOP AND HAT**

Anna Sui, Spring 2011 Collection

The top is created from soft, fuzzy flower motifs joined with crochet chain, teamed with panels of chevron stitch (see pages 60–63) for the yoke and hem. The same flowers are used for the hat, with a scallop border. The clever selection of subtle colours coordinates perfectly with the printed fabric skirt.

▲ **SWEATER DRESS**

Milly by Michelle Smith, Spring 2011 Collection

Part-circles, blocks and stripes in simple crochet stitches are worked in neutral shades, using black to emphasise the bold geometry of this sweater dress. A touch of gold lurex in the yarn combination adds glamour to the impact.

# SCARVES

HIGHLY FASHIONABLE AND POPULAR, CROCHET SCARVES CAN TAKE MANY FORMS, FROM A LACY EVENING ACCESSORY TO A SNUG WINTER WARMER. EXPLORE THE MANY POSSIBLE METHODS OF CONSTRUCTION, FROM USING FREEFORM CROCHET PIECES TO WORKING A LACY STITCH ALL OVER, AND ADDING FRINGES AND TEXTURES.

### ▲ ▶ PANDA AND REINDEER SCARVES
Jennifer Turco

Basic stitches are worked in the round and cleverly shaped, enabling the designer to give these beasts their individual personalities. The small details, such as toy eyes, embroidered claws and divided hooves, add the important finishing touches. Made in merino wool, these scarves are both cosy and great fun to wear.

▾ **SPRIAL ROPE SCARF**
De*Nada Designs

This scarf has a most unusual construction – a wide loop worked in treble crochet holds a collection of big, bold spirals (see page 103) and tasselled braids of different lengths. The use of a single colour throughout emphasises the contrasting textures.

▲ **MOTIF SCARF**
Rowan Yarns

Large-scale flower motifs of several different designs, worked in the round, form this bold and beautiful scarf. The chunky yarn and soft, pale colour show off the details of the stitches.

**▲ CREAMY CAPPUCCINO COWL**
Maarja Torga

Worked lengthways in subtle shades of
coffee and cream wools, the main section
of this cowl is worked in rows of plain
stitches, and then edged with elaborate
scallops to form a spiral of frothy textures.

**◄ DRUID DANCE COWL**
Maarja Torga

Heavily textured, multi-shaded chunky
wool in a basic stitch is used for the
main part of this cowl. Coordinating
shades of green are used for the
three-dimensional rose trims in finer,
smooth yarns.

**▲ ROSE RUFFLE SCARF**
Maarja Torga

Worked lengthways in treble crochet, this
wool scarf begins at the inner edge, with
the number of stitches then increased all
along the length several times. The outer
edge is therefore four or five times
longer, forming a deep, luxurious ruffle.

# HEAD, NOSE, HANDS AND TOES

CROCHET IS IDEAL FOR MAKING COSY AND PRACTICAL WINTER HATS AND MITTENS, BUT WHY STOP THERE? A FRILLED EDGE, BOBBLES, TASSELS OR CORDS CAN TRANSFORM YOUR CREATIONS INTO FUN AND FASHIONABLE ACCESSORIES. EXPLORE THE POSSIBILITIES OFFERED BY NOVELTY YARNS, SUCH AS EYELASH, CHENILLE, BOUCLE AND MOHAIR, TO ADD TEXTURAL INTEREST TO YOUR CROCHET.

## ▲ BEARD BEANIE
### Celina Lane

As seen on the ski slopes of Switzerland and at the latest trendy parties, the beard beanie is worked in the round in homespun Aran-weight yarn. The knobbly texture is created with increased and decreased stitches, stacked closely together by working into both the front and back loops of stitches.

## ▶ PIXIE HAT
### Ira Rott

Worked in the round from the point downwards, the designer uses Aran-weight yarn and a firm textured stitch to create the unusual shape of this hat. The quirky flower trim (see pages 104–105) is made from toning oddments of various yarns.

## ▲ MONSTER EARFLAP HAT
### Alessandra Hayden

A child's earflap hat in merino wool takes on a new personality with the addition of bright contrasting scales, multicoloured braided ties and comical features made from appliqué felt.

### ◀ USHANKA
Lajla Nuhic

The top section of this cosy hat is worked in a blend of mohair and wool, with the lower section and the ties in hand-dyed cotton chenille. The spiral decoration is added in surface crochet (see pages 112–113), firming up the pixie point to help the hat stay in shape.

### ▼ ICE LOLLY AND CUPCAKE BOOTEES
Brigitte Read

Novelty bootees make a great gift for a new baby. The ice lolly bootees are worked in simple stripes of treble crochet, with a little cord in double crochet (see pages 102–103) for the stick. The cupcake bootees have a scalloped border on the multicoloured frosting, and are finished with a cherry and a little stalk.

### ▲ LONG FINGERLESS GLOVES
Rowan Yarns

These unusual gloves feature a two-row openwork pattern, worked in a repeating sequence of three colours. The use of chunky yarn enlarges the scale of the stitches, making an intriguing multicoloured texture.

### ▶ JELLY BABY BOOTEES
Brigitte Read

These little guys are worked throughout in double crochet, with added bobbles (see pages 44–45) for the eyes and noses, and slip stitch for the smiles.

# BAGS AND ACCESSORIES

CROCHET IS THE PERFECT MEDIUM FOR MAKING BAGS AND TOTES BECAUSE IT CREATES A STRONG, SUBSTANTIAL FABRIC THAT WILL KEEP ITS SHAPE WELL IN WEAR. WORKED IN THE ROUND OR IN SEPARATE PIECES, A CROCHET BAG PROVIDES THE PERFECT OPPORTUNITY FOR MAKING SMALL-SCALE EXPERIMENTS WITH DIFFERENT YARNS, COLOURS AND TEXTURES.

**▼ MOBILE PHONE AND IPOD POUCHES**
Loretta Grayson

The careful choice of colours makes these little pouches special. Both are worked in merino wool, with one in chevron stripes (see pages 60–63), shading from dark to light blue, and the other in plain stripes (see pages 34–35), shading from bright turquoise through to acid green. Both are finished with chain loops and vintage buttons.

**▲ FLORAL TOTE BAG**
Neyya

Floral blocks worked in the round are joined to make this pretty bag and lined with plain blue fabric. The top of the bag and the double crochet handles are finished with a picot edging (see page 99).

**▲ CAT BAG**
Carol Ventura

Worked in the round using double crochet, this neat bag is worked in a multicoloured crochet technique known as tapestry crochet, which originated in Guatemala and areas of South America.

**◀ WATER BOTTLE COSIES**
Loretta Grayson

Worked in firm cotton yarn, brightly coloured stripes of double crochet chevrons (see pages 60–63) are cleverly finished at the neck of the bottle with a drawstring through the points of the chevrons.

**▶ BASKETWEAVE SHOPPER**
Alexandra Feo

Basketweave blocks (see page 67) in strong, bright colours are edged with white double crochet and seamed together to make this useful shopper. For sturdiness, the top edge and handles are worked in double crochet.

# WHIMSY

WHATEVER YOUR FANCY, CROCHET IS THE PERFECT FLEXIBLE MEDIUM FOR EXPERIMENTING WITH CRAZY IDEAS. ALL OF THE DESIGNS INCLUDED HERE USE ONLY SIMPLE, BASIC STITCHES, WHICH ARE EASY TO SHAPE AND MANIPULATE, ALLOWING THE DESIGNERS TO CONCENTRATE ON THE FORM OF EACH PIECE. BE INSPIRED!

### ▲ BOW TIE
Theodor Sundh

Double crochet rectangles make up this cheerful bow tie, guaranteed to add the finishing touch to any party outfit. One in every colour, please!

### ◄ DAISY WATCH
Luise Roberts

Inspired by childhood daisy chains, the watch strap is worked in fine green crochet cotton with daisies applied on top. Each flower is worked from the centre outwards in yellow cotton, with petals formed from white cotton chains slip stitched back along their length to the centre.

### ▲ BINKY RABBIT
Dennis Hansbury and Denika Robbins

Binky is a stuffed toy in the Japanese 'Amigurumi' style, worked throughout in double crochet for its firmness and ease of shaping. The non-matching eyes and embroidered nose are carefully placed to give Binky the deadpan expression characteristic of the style.

### ◄ CIRCLE BRACELET
Karin Mijsen

This fun bracelet in jelly bean colours is formed from five interlocking circles worked in smooth cotton yarns. Each circle is composed of several rings covered in double crochet, linked by lengths of chains.

## ▲ PUG-NACIOUS!

Julie and Bernadette / Sweethoots

One basic hat, three crazy styles – the cactus hat (left) has flyaway ears in double crochet and spikes made from tufts of white eyelash yarn; the fruit hat (upper right) is trimmed with leaves and three-dimensional stuffed fruit; the heart hat (lower right) features stand-up heart ears (worked in the round) and matching red edgings.

## ▶ MINIATURE CROCHET

Maria Kamenska

Fine cotton yarns and small hooks are used to work these cute pieces in basic stitches. The miniature size is enhanced by the attention given to the tiniest of details, such as the sandal straps and the rose trim on the hat. Both the miniature crochet pieces and the hook are shown at actual size.

# CARE OF CROCHET

FOLLOWING A FEW SIMPLE GUIDELINES WHILE YOU ARE WORKING WILL HELP YOU TO KEEP YOUR PIECES OF CROCHET LOOKING FRESH AND CLEAN DURING THE MAKING PROCESS. ONCE A PROJECT IS COMPLETED, IT IS IMPORTANT ALWAYS TO FOLLOW THE YARN MANUFACTURER'S LAUNDERING INSTRUCTIONS AND TO STORE CROCHETED PIECES CAREFULLY AND APPROPRIATELY.

## WORKING GUIDELINES

Always wash your hands thoroughly before starting to crochet, and avoid using hand cream because the oils in the cream may transfer to the yarn. When crocheting with light-coloured yarns, try to avoid wearing dark-coloured garments that shed 'bits' while you are working – angora and mohair sweaters are the worst because they shed tiny hairs that get trapped in the crochet. Getting cat and dog hairs on your crochet is also best avoided because they are difficult to remove.

When you have finished making a crochet project, store a small amount of leftover yarn from each project carefully, just in case you need to make repairs in the future. You can wind a length of yarn around a piece of cardboard, making a note of the yarn type and colour as well as details of the project. It is also a good idea to attach one of the ball bands from the yarn because this will remind you of the yarn composition, and any special pressing and laundering instructions. File the cards neatly in a dustproof box, and store in a cool, dry place.

## LOOKING AFTER CROCHET

Follow the laundering and pressing instructions on the ball band for the particular yarn you have used (for more information on ball bands, see page 22). If the yarn is machine-washable, put the item into a zipped mesh laundry bag to prevent stretching and snagging during the wash cycle. If you do not have a mesh bag, you can use an old, clean white pillowcase instead; simply secure the open end with an elastic ponytail band or work a row of running stitches across the opening to close the pillowcase. If you have household items such as tablecloths or tray cloths trimmed with crochet, treat spills and stains as soon as they occur and repair any damage to the crochet fabric before laundering the item.

For crochet pieces made from yarns that are not machine-washable, wash carefully by hand in hand-hot water with a mild, detergent-free cleaning agent. Most specialist wool or fabric shampoos are ideal, but check that the one you choose does not contain optical brighteners, which will cause yarn colours to fade. Rinse the piece thoroughly in several changes of water at the same temperature as the washing water to avoid felting. Carefully squeeze out as much surplus water as you can, without wringing, then roll the damp item in a towel and press to remove more moisture. Gently ease the item into shape and dry flat, out of direct sunlight. Follow the instructions on the ball band for pressing once the item is dry.

## STORING CROCHET

The main enemies of crochet fabrics – apart from dust and dirt – are direct sunlight, which can cause yarn colours to fade and fibres to weaken; excess heat, which makes yarn dry and brittle; damp, which rots fibres; and moths, which can seriously damage woollen yarns. Avoid storing yarns or finished crochet items for any length of time in polythene bags

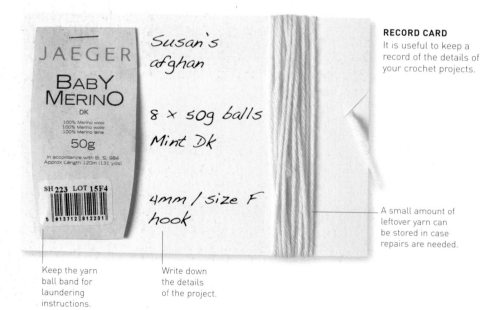

**RECORD CARD**
It is useful to keep a record of the details of your crochet projects.

A small amount of leftover yarn can be stored in case repairs are needed.

Keep the yarn ball band for laundering instructions.

Write down the details of the project.

*(handwritten on card:)* Susan's afghan — 8 × 50g balls — Mint DK — 4mm / size F hook

*(ball band:)* JAEGER BABY MERINO DK — 100% Merino wool — 100% Merino wolle — 100% Merino laine — 50g — In accordance with B.S. 984 — Approx Length 120m (131 yds) — SH 223 LOT 15F4

## CARE INSTRUCTIONS

Check the yarn ball band for washing and pressing instructions. Below are the standard laundering symbols used on ball bands.

| HAND WASHING | MACHINE WASHING | BLEACHING | PRESSING | DRY CLEANING |
|---|---|---|---|---|
|  Do not wash by hand or machine |  86°F 30° Machine washable in warm water at stated temperature |  Bleaching not permitted |  Do not press |  Do not dry clean |
|  Hand washable in warm water at stated temperature |  86°F 30° Machine washable in warm water at stated temperature, cool rinse and short spin |  CL Bleaching permitted (with chlorine) |  Press with a cool iron |  A May be dry cleaned with all solutions |
| |  104°F 40° Machine washable in warm water at stated temperature, short spin | |  Press with a warm iron |  P May be dry cleaned with perchlorethylene or fluorocarbon or petroleum-based solvents |
| | | |  Press with a hot iron |  F May be dry cleaned with fluorocarbon or petroleum-based solvents only |

because polythene attracts dirt and dust that will transfer readily to your work. Polythene also prevents yarns containing natural fibres such as cotton and linen from breathing, which can result in mildew attacks and eventually weaken or rot the fibres. Instead, store small items by wrapping them in white, acid-free tissue paper or an old cotton pillowcase. For large, heavy items such as winter-weight jackets and sweaters, which might drop and stretch out of shape if stored on coat hangers, fold them loosely between layers of white tissue paper, making sure that each fold is padded with tissue. Store all of the items in a drawer, cupboard or other dark, dry, moth-free place and check them regularly, refolding larger items. It is also a good idea to make small fabric bags filled with dried lavender flowers and tuck them into the drawer or cupboard with your crochet because the smell deters moths.

**STORING PROJECTS**
When storing crochet for a long time, wrap it in white, acid-free tissue paper.

# ABBREVIATIONS AND SYMBOLS

THESE ARE THE ABBREVIATIONS AND SYMBOLS USED IN THIS BOOK. THERE IS NO WORLDWIDE STANDARD, SO IN OTHER PUBLICATIONS YOU MAY FIND DIFFERENT ABBREVIATIONS AND SYMBOLS.

## STANDARD CROCHET ABBREVIATIONS

| | |
|---|---|
| alt | alternate |
| beg | beginning |
| ch(s) | chain(s) |
| CL | cluster |
| cont | continue |
| dc | double crochet |
| dtr | double treble crochet |
| foll | following |
| htr | half treble crochet |
| lp(s) | loop(s) |
| patt | pattern |
| rem | remaining |
| rep | repeat |
| RS | right side |
| sk | skip |
| sl st | slip stitch |
| sp(s) | space(s) |
| st(s) | stitch(es) |
| tog | together |
| tr | treble crochet |
| WS | wrong side |
| yo | yarn over |

## STITCH SYMBOLS

| | |
|---|---|
| Beaded double crochet | |
| Bobble | |
| Chain | |
| Cluster | |
| Double crochet | |
| Double crochet into back loop | |
| Double crochet into front loop | |
| Double treble crochet | |
| Half treble crochet | |
| Loop stitch | |
| Plain Tunisian stitch | |
| Popcorn | |
| Puff stitch | |
| Raised treble crochet worked around back post | |
| Raised treble crochet worked around front post | |
| Sequined double crochet | |
| Shell | |
| Slip stitch | |
| Spike stitch | |
| Treble crochet | |
| Treble crochet into back loop | |
| Treble crochet into front loop | |
| Tunisian knit stitch | |
| Tunisian mesh stitch | |

## ADDITIONAL CHART SYMBOLS

| | |
|---|---|
| Change colour | ▲ ▽ |
| Direction of working | → |
| Do not turn | ↱↲ |
| Fasten off | ◀ |
| Foundation row | FR |
| Join in new colour | ◁ |

## ENGLISH/AMERICAN TERMINOLOGY

The patterns in this book use English terminology. Patterns published using American terminology can be very confusing because some American terms differ from the English system, as shown below:

| English | American |
|---|---|
| double crochet (dc) | single crochet (sc) |
| extended double crochet (exdc) | extended single crochet (exsc) |
| half treble crochet (htr) | half double crochet (hdc) |
| treble crochet (tr) | double crochet (dc) |
| double treble crochet (dtr) | treble crochet (tr) |
| triple treble crochet (trtr or ttr) | double treble crochet (dtr) |

## ARRANGEMENTS OF SYMBOLS

| Description | Symbol | Explanation |
|---|---|---|
| Symbols joined at top | | A group of symbols may be joined at the top, indicating that these stitches should be worked together as a cluster. |
| Symbols joined at base | | Symbols joined at the base should all be worked into the same stitch below. |
| Symbols joined at top and bottom | | Sometimes a group of stitches is joined at both top and bottom, making a popcorn, bobble or puff. |
| Symbols on a curve | | Sometimes symbols are drawn along a curve, depending on the construction of the stitch pattern. |
| Distorted symbols | | Some symbols may be lengthened, curved or spiked to indicate where the hook is inserted below, as for spike stitches. |

## CATEGORIES OF YARN, TENSION RANGES AND RECOMMENDED HOOK SIZES

Below are the most commonly used tensions and needle or hook sizes for specific yarn categories.

| Yarn weight category | Super fine | Fine | Light | Medium | Bulky | Super bulky |
|---|---|---|---|---|---|---|
| Type of yarns in category | 3ply, sock, fingering, baby | 4ply, sport, baby | DK, light worsted | Aran, worsted, afghan | Chunky, craft, rug | Super chunky, roving |
| Crochet tension ranges in double crochet to 10cm (4in) | 21–32 sts | 16–20 sts | 12–17 sts | 11–14 sts | 8–11 sts | 5–9 sts |
| Recommended hook in metric size range | 2.25–3.5mm | 3.5–4.5mm | 4.5–5.5mm | 5.5–6.5mm | 6.5–9mm | 9mm and larger |
| Recommended hook in US size range | B–1 to E–4 | E–4 to 7 | 7 to I–9 | I–9 to K–10½ | K–10½ to M–13 | M–13 and larger |

**CROCHET HOOKS**
Crochet hooks are available in a wide range of sizes, shapes and materials.

Super fine   Medium   Bulky

Fine   Light   Super bulky

**YARN WEIGHTS**
It is not always possible to guess a yarn weight from simply looking at a strand of yarn.

# GLOSSARY

**BALL BAND**
The paper strip or paper tag on a ball or skein of yarn. A ball band gives information about weight, shade number, dye lot number and fibre content of the yarn. It may also show care instructions and other details, including length and suggested tension and hook size.

**BLOCKING**
Setting a piece of crochet by stretching and pinning it out on a flat surface before steaming or treating with cold water.

**BOBBLE**
Several stitches worked in the same place and joined together at the top to make a decorative raised bump. Bobbles are often worked on a background of shorter stitches.

**BORDER**
A decorative strip of crochet, usually deep with one straight and one shaped edge, that is used for trimming pieces of crochet or fabric.

**BRAID**
A narrow, decorative strip of crochet similar in appearance to a purchased furnishing braid.

**BROOMSTICK CROCHET**
A type of crochet that is worked with both a crochet hook and a 'broomstick' such as a large knitting needle.

**CHAIN SPACE**
Space formed by working lengths of chain stitches between other stitches. Also known as chain loops or chain arches.

**CLUSTER**
Several incomplete stitches worked together so that they join at the top.

**DECREASE**
Removing one or more stitches to reduce the number of working stitches.

**DYE LOT**
The batch of dye used for a specific ball of yarn. Shades can vary between batches, so use yarn from the same dye lot to make an item.

**EDGE FINISH**
A decorative crochet edging worked directly on to the edge of a piece of crochet.

**EDGING**
A decorative trim applied to the edges of a crochet or woven fabric. Crochet edgings can either be worked separately and then attached (such as a border), or they can be worked directly on to the crochet fabric (an edge finish).

**FAN**
Several stitches worked into the same chain or stitch to create a fan or shell shape.

**FIBRE**
Natural or synthetic substances spun together to make yarn.

**FILET CROCHET**
A type of crochet based on a regular mesh grid, with certain holes filled by extra stitches to form a pattern. Filet crochet is usually worked from a chart rather than written instructions.

**FOUNDATION CHAIN**
A length of chain stitches that forms the base for a piece of crochet.

**FOUNDATION ROW**
In a stitch pattern, the first row worked into the foundation chain. The foundation row is not repeated as part of the pattern.

**HEADING**
Extra rows of plain crochet worked on the long straight edge of an edging or border to add strength and durability.

**INCREASE**
Adding one or more stitches to increase the number of working stitches.

**INSERTION**
A narrow, decorative strip of crochet, similar to braid, that is sewn between two pieces of fabric.

**INTARSIA**
Intarsia produces a design featuring areas of different colours that are each worked with a separate small ball of yarn. Intarsia patterns are worked in two or more colours from a coloured chart on a grid. Each coloured square on the chart represents one stitch.

**JACQUARD**
Jacquard patterns appear similar to intarsia, but the yarns are carried along the row rather than being used separately. This produces a slightly denser fabric if worked with the same hook size as that used for the same pattern worked in intarsia. A jacquard pattern is shown as a coloured chart on a grid. Each coloured square on the chart represents one stitch.

**LACE**
A stitch pattern forming an openwork design similar in appearance to lace fabric.

**MESH**
An open stitch pattern forming a regular geometric grid.

**MOTIF**
A shaped piece of crochet, often worked in rounds. Several motifs can be joined together rather like fabric patchwork to make a larger piece. Also known as a medallion or block.

**PATTERN**
A set of instructions showing exactly how to make a garment or other crochet item.

**PATTERN REPEAT**
The specific number of rows or rounds that are needed to complete one stitch pattern.

**PICOT**
A decorative chain space often closed into a ring with a slip stitch. The number of chains in a picot can vary.

**PLY**
A single strand of yarn made by twisting fibres together. Most yarn is made from two or more plies twisted together to make different yarn weights, although some woollen yarns are made from a single thick ply.

**PUFF**
Several half treble crochet stitches worked in the same place, and joined together at the top to make a raised stitch.

**RIGHT SIDE**
The front of crochet fabric. This side is usually visible on a finished item, although some stitch patterns may be reversible.

**ROUND**
A row of crochet worked in the round; the end of one round is joined to the beginning of the same round. Rounds of crochet can form flat motifs or tubular shapes.

**ROW**
A line of stitches worked from side to side to make a flat piece of crochet.

**SEAM**
The join made where two pieces of crochet are stitched or crocheted together.

**SEWING NEEDLE**
A needle with a sharp point used for applying a crochet braid, edging or border to a piece of fabric.

**SPIKE**
A decorative stitch worked by inserting the hook from front to back of the work, one or more rows below the normal position, and/or to the right or left of the working stitch.

**STARTING CHAIN**
A specific number of chain stitches worked at the beginning of a round to bring the hook up to the correct height for the next stitch that is being worked.

**STITCH PATTERN**
A sequence or combination of crochet stitches that is repeated over and over again to create a piece of crochet fabric.

**SURFACE CROCHET**
Rows of decorative crochet worked on top of a crochet background.

**SYMBOL CHART**
A chart that describes a crochet pattern visually, using symbols to indicate the different stitches and exactly where and how they should be placed in relation to one another.

**TAPESTRY NEEDLE**
A large, blunt-ended embroidery needle used for sewing pieces of crochet together.

**TENSION**
The looseness or tightness of a crochet fabric expressed as a specific number of stitches and rows in a given area, usually 10cm (4in) square, with a suggested hook size.

**TRIM**
A length of crochet worked separately and sewn on to a main piece, or on to plain fabric, as a decoration.

**TUNISIAN CROCHET**
A type of crochet worked with a special long hook. Tunisian crochet is worked back and forth in rows without turning the work.

**TURNING CHAIN**
A specific number of chain stitches worked at the beginning of a row to bring the hook up to the correct height for the next stitch that is being worked.

**WRONG SIDE**
The reverse side of crochet fabric. This side is not usually visible on a finished item.

**YARN NEEDLE**
A blunt-ended needle with a large eye used for sewing pieces of crochet together.

# SUPPLIERS

**ENGLAND**

**NORTH EAST**
The Wool Shop
13 Castlegate
Berwick-upon-Tweed TD15 1JS
01289 306 104

Ring a Rosie
272–274 Whitley Road
Whitley Bay NE26 2TG
0191 252 8874
www.ringarosie.co.uk

Just for Ewe
Fountain Cottage
Bellingham
Hexham NE48 2DE
01434 221 270

**NORTH WEST**
Woolly, Madly, Deeply
9 Kirk Flatt
Great Urswick
Ulverston LA12 0TB
01229 480 488
www.woollymadlydeeply.com

& Sew What
247 Eaves Lane
Chorley PR6 0AG
01257 267 438
www.sewwhat.gb.com

Victoria Grant
Waterways
High Street
Uppermill
Oldham OL3 6HT
01457 870 756

**John Lewis**
Liverpool One
70 South John Street
Liverpool L1 1BJ
0151 709 7070
www.johnlewis.com

**Stash Fine Yarns**
Unit 48, Evans Business Centre
Minerva Avenue
Chester CH1 4QL
01244 389 310
www.celticove.com

**YORKSHIRE**
**Bobbins**
Wesley Hall
Church Street
Whitby YO22 4DE
01947 600 585
www.bobbins.co.uk

**Spinning Jenny**
Bark Hill
Flasby
Skipton BD23 3QD
01756 749 200
www.spinningjenny.co.uk

**The Wool Shop**
Whingate Junction
Tong Road
Leeds LS12 4NQ
0113 263 8383
www.thewoolshopleeds.co.uk

**Attica Yarns**
Unit 2, Brier Hey Business Park
Hebden Bridge HX7 5PF
01422 884 885
www.attica-yarns.co.uk

**WEST MIDLANDS**
**knit2together**
111 High Street
Wolstanton
Newcastle-under-Lyme ST5 8BB
01782 862 332

**Warwick Wools**
17 Market Place
Warwick CV34 4SA
01926 492 853
www.warwickwools.co.uk

**EAST MIDLANDS**
**Patchwork Direct**
Wesleyan House
Darley Dale DE4 2HX
01629 734 100
www.patchworkdirect.com

**Strand Wools**
20 The Strand
Derby DE1 1BE
01332 365 910
www.strandwools.co.uk

**Quorn Country Crafts**
18 Churchgate
Loughborough LE11 1UD
01509 211 604
www.quorncountrycrafts.com

**Bee Inspired**
Market Street
Kettering NN16 0AH
01536 514 646
www.beeinspired.co.uk

**The Knitting Parlour**
12 Graham Road
Great Malvern WR14 2HN
01684 892 079
www.theknittingparlour.co.uk

**EAST ANGLIA**
**Sew Creative**
Wroxham Barns
Tunstead Road
Hoveton
Wroxham NR12 8QU
01603 781 665
www.sewcreativequilts.co.uk

**Norfolk Yarn**
288 Aylsham Road
Hellesdon
Norwich NR3 2RG
01603 417 001
www.norfolkyarn.co.uk

**Sew Creative**
97–99 King Street
Cambridge CB1 1LD
01223 350 691
www.sewcreative.co.uk

**SOUTH EAST**
**The Wool Shop**
18 High Street
Olney MK46 4BB
01234 910 547
www.the-wool-shop.com

**Portmeadow Designs**
104 Walton Street
Oxford OX2 6EB
01865 311 008

**Black Hills Yarn**
69 Hart Street
Henley-on-Thames RG9 2AU
01491 412 590
www.blackhills-yarn.com

**Loop**
15 Camden Passage
London N1 8EA
020 7288 1160
www.loopknitting.com

**Gades**
10–12 Clarence Street
Southend-on-Sea SS1 1BD
01702 435 730

**Myfanwy Hart**
Winifred Cottage
17 Elms Road
Fleet GU15 3EG
01252 617 667
www.myfanwyhart.co.uk

**Pandora**
196 High Street
Guildford GU1 3HZ
01483 572 558
www.pandoracrafts.co.uk

**Battle Wool Shop**
2 Mount Street
Battle TN33 0EG
01424 775 073

**Purl**
16 Upper Hamilton Road
Brighton BN1 5DF
01273 248 642
www.purl-brighton.co.uk

**Shoreham Knitting & Needlecraft**
19 East Street
Shoreham-by-Sea BN43 5ZE
01273 456 570
www.englishyarns.co.uk

**SOUTH WEST**
**Heavenly Yarns**
137 Fore Street
Exeter EX4 3AN
01392 215 131
www.heavenlyyarns.co.uk

**Spin a Yarn**
26 Fore Street
Bovey Tracey TQ13 9AD
01626 836 203
www.spinayarndevon.co.uk

**The Wool Gallery**
51 Queen Street
Newton Abbot TQ12 2AU
07899 987 718
www.thewoolgallery.co.uk

## WALES

**Copperfield Crafts**
Four Mile Bridge Road
Valley
Anglesey LL65 3HV
01407 740 982
www.copperfield-crafts.co.uk

**Clare Wools**
13 Great Darkgate Street
Aberystwyth SY23 1DE
01970 617 786
www.clarewools.co.uk

**The Cotton Angel**
2 Church Street
Monmouth NP25 3BY
01600 713 548
www.thecottonangel.com

**Knit and Sew**
21–22 Park Street
Swansea SA1 3DJ
0845 094 0835
www.knitandsew.co.uk

## SCOTLAND

### ISLES

**Victoria Gibson**
Greig's Pier, Esplanade
Lerwick
Shetland ZE1 0LL
01595 692 816
www.gibsons.org.uk

**Hume Sweet Hume**
Pierowall Village
Westray
Orkney KW17 2BZ
01856 677 259
www.humesweethume.com

**Orkney Angora**
Sanday
Orkney KW17 2AZ
01857 600 421
www.orkneyangora.co.uk

**Elizabeth Lovick**
17 Burnside
Flotta
Orkney KW16 3NP
01856 701 962
www.northernlace.co.uk

**Ragamuffin**
Armadale Pier
Sleat
Skye IV45 8RS
01471 844 217
www.ragamuffinonline.co.uk

### MAINLAND

**Patterns of Light**
Kishorn
Strathcarron
Wester Ross IV54 8XA
01520 733 363
www.patterns-of-light.com

**Cormack's and Crawford's**
56–57 High Street
Dingwall
Ross-shire IV15 9HL
01349 562 234

**Krafty Knits**
134 High Street
Forres
Morayshire IV36 1 NP
01343 543 333

**The Wool Shed**
Ryehill
Oyne
Aberdeenshire AB52 6QS
01464 851 539
www.thewoolshed.co.uk

**Twist Fibre Craft Studio**
88 High Street
Newburgh
Cupar
Fife KY14 6AQ
01337 842 843
www.twistfibrecraft.co.uk

**Di Gilpin**
The Bothy, 16 Cupar Road
Largoward
Fife KY9 1HX
01334 840 431
www.digilpin.com

**K1 Yarns Knitting Boutique**
89 West Bow
Edinburgh EH1 2JP
0131 226 7472
www.k1yarns.com

**Ragamuffin**
The Canongate
Royal Mile
Edinburgh EH8 8AA
0131 557 6007
www.ragamuffinonline.co.uk

**Outback Yarns**
130–132 King Street
Castle Douglas
Kirkcudbrightshire DG7 1LU
01556 504 900
www.outbackyarns.co.uk

## NORTHERN IRELAND

**Jean's Woolshop**
26 Cregagh Road
Belfast
County Antrim BT6 9EQ
028 90456 388
www.jeanswoolshop.co.uk

## AUSTRALIA

**Australian Country Spinners**
Level 7, 409 St Kilda Road
Melbourne VIC 3004
03 9380 3888
www.auspinners.com.au

**Morris & Sons**
Level 1, 234 Collins Street
Melbourne VIC 3000
03 9654 0888
www.morrisandsons.com.au

**Calico House**
397 Brunswick Street
Melbourne VIC 3065
03 9417 6111
www.calicohouse.com.au

**Sunspun**
185 Canterbury Road
Canterbury VIC 3126
03 9830 1609
www.sunspun.com.au

**Wool Baa**
124 Bridport Street
Albert Park VIC 3206
03 9690 6633
www.woolbaa.com.au

**Woolshed**
Shop 7B, Manuka Court
Bougainville Street
Manuka
Canberra ACT 2603
02 6295 0061
www.woolshed.com.au

**Black Sheep Wool 'n' Wares**
118A Bradley Street
Guyra NSW 2365
02 6779 1196
www.blacksheepwool.com.au

**Morris & Sons**
50 York Street
Sydney NSW 2000
02 9299 8588
www.morrisandsons.com.au

**Threads and More**
7/637 Sherwood Road
Sherwood QLD 4075
07 3379 6699
www.threadsandmore.com.au

**The Wool Shack**
PO Box 743, Inglewood
Perth WA 6932
08 9371 8864
www.thewoolshack.com

**Yarns Galore**
3/38 Ardross Street
Applecross WA 6153
08 9315 3070
www.yarnsgalore.com.au

## NEW ZEALAND

### NORTH ISLAND

**Alterknitives by Mail**
PO Box 47961
Ponsonby
Auckland 1011
09 376 0337

**Crafty Knitwits**
101 Kitchener Road
Milford
North Shore City
Auckland 0630
09 486 2724
www.craftyknitwits.co.nz

**Busy Needles**
73B Victoria Street
Cambridge
Waikato 3434
07 827 5000

**Skeinz**
5 Husheer Place
Onekawa
Napier 4110
06 843 3174
www.skeinz.com

**Joy of Yarn**
Scarlet Oak Cottage
143 Main Street
Greytown
South Wairarapa 5712
06 304 9805
www.joyofyarn.co.nz

**Knit World Mail Order**
PO Box 30645
Lower Hutt 5040
04 586 4530
www.knitworld.co.nz

**Knit World**
Shop 210b, Left Bank
Cuba Mall
Wellington 6011
04 385 1918
www.knitworld.co.nz

### SOUTH ISLAND

**Knit World**
189 Peterborough Street
Christchurch 8013
03 379 2300
www.knitworld.co.nz

**The Main Skein Wool Shop**
Bush Inn Centre
364 Riccarton Rd
Upper Riccarton
Christchurch 8041
03 348 6899
www.themainskein.co.nz

**Touch Yarns**
PO Box 213
Alexandra 9340
03 449 3204
www.touchyarns.com

**Treliske Organic Wools**
2RD Roxburgh
Central Otago 9500
03 446 6828
www.treliskeorganic.com

**Knit World**
139 Stuart Street
Dunedin 9016
03 477 0400
www.knitworld.co.nz

## ADDITIONAL WEB RESOURCES

The Craft Yarn Council: www.craftyarncouncil.com
The Crochet Guild of America: www.crochet.org

SELECTED SUPPLIERS
www.buy-mail.co.uk
www.cascadeyarns.com
www.coatscrafts.co.uk
www.colourway.co.uk
www.coolwoolz.co.uk
www.crystalpalaceyarns.com
www.designeryarns.uk.com
www.diamondyarns.com
www.ethknits.co.uk
www.e-yarn.com
www.hantex.co.uk
www.hook-n-needle.com
www.kangaroo.uk.com
www.karpstyles.ca
www.knitrowan.com
  (features worldwide list of stockists of Rowan yarns)
www.knittersdream.com
www.knittingfever.com
www.knitwellwools.co.uk
www.lacis.com
www.maggiescrochet.com
www.mcadirect.com
www.patternworks.com
www.patonsyarns.com
www.personalthreads.com
www.ravelry.com
www.sakonnetpurls.com
www.shetlandwoolbrokers.co.uk
www.sirdar.co.uk
www.spiningayarn.co.uk
www.theknittinggarden.com
www.upcountry.co.uk
www.yarncompany.com
www.yarnexpressions.com
www.yarnmarket.com

# INDEX

Page numbers in *italic* refer to pattern instructions in the stitch collections

## A

abbreviations 150
Afghan, Baby (project) 122–123
all-over:
    beads *114*, 115
    bobbles *44*, 45
alternate:
    beads *115*
    bobbles *45*
    sequins 116
    shells *42*, 43
    spikes *65*
angled clusters *40*, 41
astrakhan stitch 50, *51*

## B

Baby Afghan (project) 122–123
back stitch seam 30
bags and accessories:
    Buttonhole Bag (project) 120
    gallery 144–145
    Striped Bag (project) 130–131
ball bands/tags 22, 148, 153
banded loop stitch *51*
basic skills and stitches 14–21
    chain stitch 15
    counting chains 16
    double crochet stitch 18
    double treble crochet stitch 21
    foundation chains 16
    half treble crochet stitch 19
    holding the hook 14
    holding the yarn 14
    slip knot 14
    slip stitch 15
    starting chains 17
    treble crochet stitch 20
    turning chains 17
basketweave *67*
Basketweave Shopper 144, 145

beads:
    all-over *114*, 115
    alternate *115*
    applying 114
Beard Beanie 142
Binky Rabbit 146
blocking 28–29, 153
    board 28, 29
bobbles 44, *44–45*, 153
bootees (gallery) 143
border 108, 153
Bow Tie 146
braids 106, *107*, 153
broomstick crochet 94–95, 153
button loops 101
Buttonhole Bag (project) 120
buttonholes 100
buttons, choosing 101

## C

care of crochet 148–149
Cat Bag 144
cat, sitting *59*
chain fringe 110
chain loop tassel *111*
chain space 153
chain stitch 15
    counting 16
    seams 30, 31
    turning/starting chains 17, 154
    *see also* foundation chain
charts:
    reading 26–27
    symbols 150–151
checquerboard *58*
chevron:
    edging 60
    patterns 60, *61*, 62, *62–63*, 127
Chiaratti, Ilaria:
    Happy Cushions 132, 133
    Lamp and Bunting 134
Child's Bedspread 135
Circle Bracelet 146
circle in a square *83*, 123
circle with spokes *76*

circular motifs 74–75, *76–79*
    joining 75
classic hexagon *87*
cluster circle *79*
    crochet cotton 79
clusters 40, *40–41*, 153
colour block charts 27
cords:
    double crochet 102
    double slip stitch 102
    round 103
    single slip stitch 102
    spiral 103
corkscrew:
    fringe 110, *111*
    tassel 110
crab stitch edging 98
Creamy Cappuccino Cowl 141
Croydon square *82*, 122
Cushion, Hexagon (project) 124–125
cylinders 72–73

## D

Daisy Watch 146
decreases 38, 39, 153
deep mesh edging *109*
De*Nada Designs:
    Spiral Rope Scarf 140
double crochet chevrons *61*
double crochet stitch 17, 18
    adding sequins to 116
    beading with 114
    cords 102
    edging 98
    joining a new yarn in 24
    seams 31
double treble crochet stitch 17, 21
Druid Dance Cowl 141
dye lot 153

## E

edge finishes 153
    crab stitch 98
    double crochet 98
    picot 99
    shell 99
edges, neat 36, 38

edgings 108, 153
    chevron 60
    deep mesh *109*
    ric rac 60
    shell *109*
equipment 10–11

## F

fan 153
fan lace *55*, 126
fancy openwork *54*
fastening off 25
    in rounds 75
faux ribbing *37*
Feo, Alexandra:
    Basketweave Shopper 144, 145
fibre 12–13, 153
filet crochet 56–58, *58–59*, 153
    charts 27, 56
Filet Crochet Wrap (project) 128–129
Floral Tote Bag 144
flowers:
    frilled 104, *105*
    layered 104, *105*
    tiny *59*
foundation chain 16, 153
    working into 16
foundation row 153
frilled flower *105*
fringes 110, *110–111*

## G

gallery:
    bags and accessories 144–145
    home 132, 133, 134–135
    garments 136–138
    hats and accessories 142–143
    scarves 139–141
    whimsy 146–147
garments (gallery) 136–138
generous shells 43
gloves (gallery) 143
granny hexagon *89*
granny square *84*
Grayson, Loretta:
    Mobile Phone and iPod Pouches 144
    Water Bottle Cosies 144

**H**

hairpin crochet 96–97
half treble crochet stitch 17, 19
Hansbury, Dennis:
  Binky Rabbit 146
Happy Cushions 132, 133
hats (gallery) 138, 142, 143, 147
Hayden, Alessandra:
  Monster Earflap Hat 142
heading 153
heart motif 56
Hexagon Cushion (project) 124–125
hexagon motifs 85–86, 87–89, 124
  joining 85, 86
home, crochet in the (gallery) 132, 133, 134–135
hooks 10–11
  holding 14
  recommended sizes 152

**I**

Ice Lolly and Cupcake Bootees 143
increases 38, 39, 153
insertions 106, 153
intarsia patterns 70–71, 71, 153
  charts 27, 70
Intarsia Potholder (project) 121
interwoven braid 107
Ivory Cotton Dress 137

**J**

Jacket and Striped Skirt 137
jacquard patterns 68, 69, 153
  charts 27, 68
Jansen, Ingrid 32
  Child's Bedspread 135
  Stool Covers 135
Jelly Baby Bootees 143
jewellery (gallery) 146
joining:
  edges 30
  yarns 24
Julie and Bernadette /
  Sweethoots: Pug-nacious! 147

**K**

Kamenska, Maria:
  Miniature Crochet 147
Kazekobo (Yoko Hatta):
  Ivory Cotton Dress 137
  Jacket and Striped Skirt 137

**L**

lace 153
lace stitches 52, 55, 126
Lacy Bolster 134
lacy popcorns 46, 47
Lamp and Bunting 134
Lane, Celina:
  Beard Beanie 142
Layered Crochet Cushion 134
layered flower 105
Lined Blue Skirt 136
Long Fingerless Gloves 143
looking after crochet 148–149
loop stitches 50, 51

**M**

magic stripes 35
Matching Top and Hat 138
mesh 52, 153
  deep mesh edging 109
  openwork mesh 53, 127
  small mesh 113
  Tunisian mesh stitch 93
  with surface crochet 112, 113
Mijsen, Karin 2–3
  Circle Bracelet 146
  Tissue Box Cover 134
Milly by Michelle Smith:
  Sweater Dress 138
Miniature Crochet 147
Mobile Phone and iPod Pouches 144
Monster Earflap Hat 142
motif 153
Motif Scarf 140

**N**

natural fibres 12, 28–29
needles 11, 154
Neyya: Floral Tote Bag 144
Nuhic, Lajla: Ushanka 143

**O**

openwork 52, 53–55, 127
  with surface crochet 112, 113

**P**

Panda and Reindeer Scarves 139
pattern 153
  reading 26–27
  repeat 153
Perez-Garreaud, Luanna:
  White Lace Dress 136
picot 153
picot edging 99
pinning out 28, 29
pins 11
Pixie Hat 142
plain trellis 15, 53
ply 154
popcorns 46, 46–47
Potholder, Intarsia (project) 121
pressing 28
projects:
  Baby Afghan 122–123
  Buttonhole Bag 120
  Filet Crochet Wrap 128–129
  Hexagon Cushion 124–125
  Intarsia Potholder 121
  Striped Bag 130–131
  Winter Scarf 126–127
puff stitch:
  stripes 48, 49
  waves 49
puff stitches 48, 48–49, 154
Pug-nacious! 147

**Q**

quilter's wadding 28

**R**

raised:
  columns 66, 67
  stitches 66, 66–67
random stripes 35
Read, Brigitte:
  Ice Lolly and Cupcake Bootees 143
  Jelly Baby Bootees 143
record card 148
repeating stripes 35

ric rac edging 60
ridge stitches 36, 37
right side 154
ring of stitches 74
ring, yarn 75
Robbins, Denika:
  Binky Rabbit 146
Roberts, Luise:
  Daisy Watch 146
Rose Ruffle Scarf 141
Rott, Ira: Pixie Hat 142
round cord 103
rounds 154
  working in 74–75
row 154
Rowan Yarns:
  Lacy Bolster 134
  Layered Crochet Cushion 134
  Lined Blue Skirt 136
  Long Fingerless Gloves 143
  Motif Scarf 140

**S**

scarves:
  gallery 139–141
  Winter Scarf (project) 126–127
scissors 11
seams 30–31, 154
seashore trellis 54, 55, 127
sequin stripes 117
sequins:
  alternate 116
  applying 116
sewing needle 154
shaping 38–39
shell edging 99, 109
shell stitches 42, 42–43
simple ridges 37
sitting cat 59
slip knot 14
slip stitch 15
  cords 102
  joining a new yarn using 24
  seams 31
small mesh 113
spike stitches 64, 64–65, 154
spiked stripes 64, 65
Spiral Rope Scarf 140
spirals 103

square motifs 80–81, *82–84*
    joining 80–81
starting chain 17, 154
stitch pattern 154
Stool Covers 135
storing crochet 148–149
stripe patterns 34, *35*
Striped Bag (project) 130–131
stripes, sequin *117*
Sui, Anna:
    Matching Top and Hat 138
sunburst circle *78*
Sundh, Theodor: Bow Tie 146
suppliers 154–157
surface crochet 112, *112–113*, 154
Sweater Dress 138
symbol charts 27, 154
symbols 150–151
synthetic yarns 13, 28–29

T
tape measure 11
tapestry needle 11, 154
tassels:
    chain loop *111*
    corkscrew 110
tension 10, 22–23, 154
    adjusting 23
    comparing 23
    making and measuring
        sample 22–23
    ranges 152
terminology, UK/US 151
threads 12, 13
tiny flowers *59*
Tissue Box Cover 134
Torga, Maarja:
    Creamy Cappuccino Cowl 141
    Druid Dance Cowl 141
    Rose Ruffle Scarf 141
toys (gallery) 146
treble crochet chevrons *62*, 63
treble crochet circle *77*
    striped variation 77
treble crochet stitch 17, 20
    joining a new yarn in 24
trellis 15, 52
    plain *53*
    seashore 54, *55*, 127

trim 154
trinity stitch *41*, 127
tubular crochet 72–73
Tunisian crochet 90–92, *92–93*, 154
Turco, Jennifer:
    Panda and Reindeer
        Scarves 139
turning chain 17, 154
two-colour braid *107*

U
Ushanka 143

V
Ventura, Carol:
    Cat Bag 144

W
Water Bottle Cosies 144
wave pattern 62
wavy chevrons 62, *63*, 127
weaving in yarn ends 25
wheel hexagon *88*, 124
whimsy (gallery) 146–147
White Lace Dress 136
wide ridges *37*
Winter Scarf (project) 126–127
woven seam 30
Wrap, Filet Crochet (project)
        128–129
wrong side 154

Y
yarn needles 11, 154
yarn ring 75
yarns 12–13
    ball bands/tags 22, 148, 153
    blocking 28–29
    categories 152
    changing colours 34, 68
    fastening off 25, 75
    holding 14
    joining 24
    pressing 28
    weaving in ends 25

# CREDITS

Quarto would like to thank the following designers for kindly supplying images reproduced in this book. Designers are acknowledged beside their work featured in the gallery.

- Ilaria Chiaratti: www.idainteriorlifestyle.blogspot.com
- Rowan Yarns: www.knitrowan.com, 01484 681 881
- De*Nada Designs: www.denadadesign.com
- Alexandra Feo (pattern and photography): www.madamecraft.com
- Loretta Grayson: www.rettg.blogspot.com
- Dennis Hansbury and Denika Robbins
- Alessandra Hayden: www.justbehappycrochet.com
- Ingrid Jansen: www.woodwoolstool.com (Ingrid's work is also featured on page 32)
- Julie and Bernadette / Sweethoots: www.sweethoots.etsy.com
- Maria Kamenska: www.MariaKonstantin.etsy.com
- Kazekobo (Yoko Hatta): www.kazekobo.net
- Celina Lane: www.SimplyCollectible.etsy.com
- Karin Mijsen: www.karinaandehaak.blogspot.com (Karin's work is also featured on pages 2–3)
- Lajla Nuhic: www.lajla.ca
- Luanna Perez-Gareaud
- Brigitte Read from Roman Sock: www.littlegreen.typepad.com
- Ira Rott: www.irarott.com
- Theodor Sundh: www.crochetbloke.blogspot.co.uk
- Maarja Torga: www.WhisperTwister.etsy.com
- Jennifer Turco: www.beeskneesknitting.com
- Carol Ventura: www.tapestrycrochet.com

Quarto would also like to acknowledge the following:
- Pages 4 & 138: Nata Pupo / Shutterstock.com (www.annasui.com & www.millyny.com)
- Page 144: Neyya / istockphoto.com

Thanks also to the models, Isabelle Crawford and Kryssy Moss, and to Betty Barnden for writing the gallery captions.

All other photographs and illustrations are the copyright of Quarto Publishing plc. While every effort has been made to credit contributors, Quarto would like to apologise should there have been any omissions or errors – and would be pleased to make the appropriate correction for future editions of the book.